The READ THROUGH THE BIBLE IN A YEAR PLANNER

2023 EDITION

BARBOUR
PUBLISHING

Print 978-1-63609-303-1

Cover Design: Greg Jackson, Thinkpen Design

Published by Barbour Publishing, Inc., 1810 Barbour Drive, Uhrichsville, Ohio 44683, www.barbourbooks.com

Our mission is to inspire the world with the life-changing message of the Bible.

Printed in China.

Many people would like to read through the Bible in a year—but we know, from personal experience, that can be a real challenge. That's why we created *The Read through the Bible in a Year Planner*—to give you the encouragement you need as you begin this life-changing journey. This planner offers both inspiration and practical space for organizing every day of your 2023.

In addition to daily scripture readings for every day of the year—an Old Testament, New Testament, and either Psalms or Proverbs passage—this planner also features 365 challenging and encouraging devotional thoughts, each highlighting a particular Bible verse from that day's scripture selection.

Each day's reading should take 15 to 30 minutes to complete. If you stay with it, you'll soon be able to say, "I read through the Bible in a year!"—and you'll undoubtedly find your life changed by the great promises of God's Word.

The Publisher

Today's Bible Reading:

GENESIS 1–2; MATTHEW 1; PSALM 1

And God saw every thing that he had made, and, behold, it was very good. And the evening and the morning were the sixth day.
GENESIS 1:31

In this first reading of the year, we get a glimpse into the beautiful story that is woven throughout scripture. Genesis 1 speaks of the perfect world that God created. Psalm 1 is written in a fallen world that is marred by sin where we must actively avoid wickedness and seek purity. Matthew 1 is the beginning of God redeeming His people by sending His Son as one of us. Christ's very lineage is strewn with the aroma of redemption. His ancestors include such redeemed sinners as the harlot Rahab, the incestuous Judah and Tamar, the pagan Ruth, and the adulterous David and Bathsheba. God makes it no secret that His business is to redeem sinners and to show His power through the unlikely and the weak.

TOP 3 PRIORITIES:

- [ ] ....
- [ ] ....
- [ ] ....

SCHEDULE/TO-DO LIST:

- [ ] ....
- [ ] ....
- [ ] ....
- [ ] ....

REFLECTIONS ON TODAY'S BIBLE READING

8 glasses a day: ⬜ ⬜ ⬜ ⬜ ⬜ ⬜ ⬜ ⬜

REMEMBER

January

S	M	T	W	T	F	S
1	2	3	4	5	6	7
8	9	10	11	12	13	14
15	16	17	18	19	20	21
22	23	24	25	26	27	28
29	30	31				

Today's Bible Reading:

GENESIS 3–4; MATTHEW 2; PSALM 2

Yet have I set my king upon my holy hill of Zion. I will declare the decree: the Lord hath said unto me, Thou art my Son; this day have I begotten thee. Ask of me, and I shall give thee the heathen for thine inheritance, and the uttermost parts of the earth for thy possession.
PSALM 2:6–8

Genesis 3 presents a grim outlook on the future of humanity. But even in the midst of this chaos, God assures the serpent that one will come to wage war against him. Then in Psalm 2 an anointed King is proclaimed as ruler over all the earth. And finally in Matthew, we catch a glimpse of this King. Though He was still a young child, the magi recognized Him as the King who was anointed to reign over the nations. A beautiful story of redemption begins to unfold.

REFLECTIONS ON TODAY'S BIBLE READING

8 glasses a day:

REMEMBER

TOP 3 PRIORITIES:

- [ ] ....
- [ ] ....
- [ ] ....

SCHEDULE/TO-DO LIST:

- [ ] ....
- [ ] ....
- [ ] ....
- [ ] ....

February

S	M	T	W	T	F	S
			1	2	3	4
5	6	7	8	9	10	11
12	13	14	15	16	17	18
19	20	21	22	23	24	25
26	27	28				

Today's Bible Reading:

GENESIS 5–7; MATTHEW 3; PSALM 3

And saying, Repent ye: for the kingdom of heaven is at hand.
MATTHEW 3:2

The holiness of God is vividly and frighteningly displayed in the account of the Flood. Tragically, God in His holiness could not look on the degradation and sin being practiced by those He had created. The God we serve today is just as holy and just as incensed by sin, but mercifully, we have been saved from His just wrath through the sacrifice of Christ. Repent of your sins, and rest in the knowledge of your forgiveness through Christ.

TOP 3 PRIORITIES:

- ☐ ....
- ☐ ....
- ☐ ....

SCHEDULE/TO-DO LIST:

- ☐ ....
- ☐ ....
- ☐ ....
- ☐ ....

REFLECTIONS ON TODAY'S BIBLE READING

8 glasses a day: ☐ ☐ ☐ ☐ ☐ ☐ ☐ ☐

January

S	M	T	W	T	F	S
1	2	3	4	5	6	7
8	9	10	11	12	13	14
15	16	17	18	19	20	21
22	23	24	25	26	27	28
29	30	31				

REMEMBER

Today's Bible Reading:

GENESIS 8–10; MATTHEW 4; PSALM 4

*I will both lay me down in peace, and sleep:
for thou, Lord, only makest me dwell in safety.*
PSALM 4:8

No amount of money, prestige, or security measures can make you truly safe. It is only in Christ that you can find genuine rest knowing that you are cared for and loved by the ruler of the universe. Your heavenly Father has secured your future—an eternity with Him. So sleep peacefully, knowing that nothing can touch you outside of His will. God is faithful to His Word and dearly loves His children.

REFLECTIONS ON TODAY'S BIBLE READING

8 glasses a day:

TOP 3 PRIORITIES:

SCHEDULE/TO-DO LIST:

REMEMBER

February

S	M	T	W	T	F	S
			1	2	3	4
5	6	7	8	9	10	11
12	13	14	15	16	17	18
19	20	21	22	23	24	25
26	27	28				

Thursday
JANUARY 5

Today's Bible Reading:

GENESIS 11–13; MATTHEW 5:1–20; PSALM 5

*My voice shalt thou hear in the morning, O Lord; in the morning
will I direct my prayer unto thee, and will look up.*
PSALM 5:3

Just like David, pray with confidence that God will hear you, and then eagerly watch for His answer. Start your day off in conversation with your Father. To actively enter into His presence in the morning will make you more aware of Him the rest of the day. Pray for the small things and the big things, knowing that not only will God listen to you, but He will also act on your behalf.

TOP 3 PRIORITIES:

- [ ] ....
- [ ] ....
- [ ] ....

SCHEDULE/TO-DO LIST:

- [ ] ....
- [ ] ....
- [ ] ....
- [ ] ....

REFLECTIONS ON TODAY'S BIBLE READING

8 glasses a day: ☐ ☐ ☐ ☐ ☐ ☐ ☐ ☐

REMEMBER

January

S	M	T	W	T	F	S
1	2	3	4	5	6	7
8	9	10	11	12	13	14
15	16	17	18	19	20	21
22	23	24	25	26	27	28
29	30	31				

Today's Bible Reading:

GENESIS 14–16; MATTHEW 5:21–48; PSALM 6

And he brought him forth abroad, and said, Look now toward heaven, and tell the stars, if thou be able to number them: and he said unto him, So shall thy seed be. And he believed in the Lord; and he counted it to him for righteousness.
GENESIS 15:5–6

Do you have faith like Abraham, who believed God that his descendants would be as numerous as the stars of heaven when at the time he had no children? His wife was past the age of childbearing, and they certainly would have been past the point of hoping for such a miracle. He had no earthly evidence that would have made him think that he could have innumerable descendants. But his faith in God caused him to disregard earthly circumstances in favor of heavenly promises.

REFLECTIONS ON TODAY'S BIBLE READING

8 glasses a day:

TOP 3 PRIORITIES:

- [ ]
- [ ]
- [ ]

SCHEDULE/TO-DO LIST:

- [ ]
- [ ]
- [ ]
- [ ]

REMEMBER

February

S	M	T	W	T	F	S
			1	2	3	4
5	6	7	8	9	10	11
12	13	14	15	16	17	18
19	20	21	22	23	24	25
26	27	28				

Saturday
JANUARY 7

Today's Bible Reading:

GENESIS 17–18; MATTHEW 6:1–18; PSALM 7

The Lord said unto Abraham. . . . Is any thing too hard for the
Lord? At the time appointed I will return unto thee, according
to the time of life, and Sarah shall have a son.
GENESIS 18:12–14

How often do you fail to take God's promises seriously? Maybe you feel you're not worthy. Maybe deep down you just don't think that God cares enough to keep His promises to you. Or maybe your doubt lies in a lack of faith in His power—that perhaps He can't actually do what He says. Fortunately, our lack of faith does not affect God's faithfulness. God will always keep His promises, whether or not we initially believe it. He will prove Himself to you as He did to Sarah.

TOP 3 PRIORITIES:

- [ ] ....
- [ ] ....
- [ ] ....

SCHEDULE/TO-DO LIST:

- [ ] ....
- [ ] ....
- [ ] ....
- [ ] ....

REFLECTIONS ON TODAY'S BIBLE READING

8 glasses a day: ▢ ▢ ▢ ▢ ▢ ▢ ▢ ▢

REMEMBER

January

S	M	T	W	T	F	S
1	2	3	4	5	6	7
8	9	10	11	12	13	14
15	16	17	18	19	20	21
22	23	24	25	26	27	28
29	30	31				

Today's Bible Reading:

GENESIS 19–20; MATTHEW 6:19–34; PSALM 8

When I consider thy heavens, the work of thy fingers, the moon and the stars, which thou hast ordained; what is man, that thou art mindful of him? and the son of man, that thou visitest him?
PSALM 8:3–4

How would it affect your life if you truly understood how important you are to God? God perfectly cares for everything He has created, including sparrows and wildflowers (Matthew 6:26–30). As His child and image bearer, you are much more important to Him than flowers and birds. He, the Creator of every star in the sky, is mindful of you! You can trust that you have and will have all that you need under His protection.

REFLECTIONS ON TODAY'S BIBLE READING

8 glasses a day: ▢ ▢ ▢ ▢ ▢ ▢ ▢ ▢

REMEMBER

TOP 3 PRIORITIES:

☐ ....
☐ ....
☐ ....

SCHEDULE/TO-DO LIST:

☐ ....
☐ ....
☐ ....
☐ ....

February

S	M	T	W	T	F	S
			1	2	3	4
5	6	7	8	9	10	11
12	13	14	15	16	17	18
19	20	21	22	23	24	25
26	27	28				

Today's Bible Reading:

GENESIS 21–23; MATTHEW 7:1–11; PSALM 9:1–8

*And Abraham said, My son, God will provide himself a lamb for
a burnt offering: so they went both of them together.*
GENESIS 22:8

God spared Isaac, Abraham's son, and blessed Abraham for having the faith to trust God even in the most confusing and heartbreaking of circumstances. God did not spare His own Son and yet blessed us based on no merit of our own. God did indeed provide the sacrificial Lamb. We have every reason to trust God as Abraham did. He's more than proven Himself.

TOP 3 PRIORITIES:

- ☐ ....
- ☐ ....
- ☐ ....

SCHEDULE/TO-DO LIST:

- ☐ ....
- ☐ ....
- ☐ ....
- ☐ ....

REFLECTIONS ON TODAY'S BIBLE READING

8 glasses a day: ☐ ☐ ☐ ☐ ☐ ☐ ☐ ☐

January

S	M	T	W	T	F	S
1	2	3	4	5	6	7
8	9	10	11	12	13	14
15	16	17	18	19	20	21
22	23	24	25	26	27	28
29	30	31				

REMEMBER

Today's Bible Reading:

GENESIS 24; MATTHEW 7:12–29; PSALM 9:9–20

And they that know thy name will put their trust in thee:
for thou, Lord, hast not forsaken them that seek thee.
Psalm 9:10

Take time to think back over the faithfulness of God in your life. Remember those times when even in the midst of your doubt or fear He showed Himself to you in powerful and visible ways. If you truly know the character and person of God, you will unequivocally, without hesitation put your trust in Him because you know without a shadow of a doubt that He has never and will never forsake you.

REFLECTIONS ON TODAY'S BIBLE READING

8 glasses a day:

REMEMBER

TOP 3 PRIORITIES:

SCHEDULE/TO-DO LIST:

February

S	M	T	W	T	F	S
			1	2	3	4
5	6	7	8	9	10	11
12	13	14	15	16	17	18
19	20	21	22	23	24	25
26	27	28				

Today's Bible Reading:

GENESIS 25–26; MATTHEW 8:1–17; PSALM 10:1–11

And, behold, there came a leper and worshipped him, saying,
Lord, if thou wilt, thou canst make me clean.
MATTHEW 8:2

May we have the same attitude as the leper–coming to God with nothing left to give, bowing before Him in full reliance that He is powerful enough to give us strength and make us well. This leper understood that the healing of his infirmity relied completely on the grace of God. Knowing that God *could* heal him, he didn't demand Him to, beg Him to, or even argue with Him about why He should. Instead, he worshipped Christ by humbly acknowledging His power both to heal and to decide whether to heal. Sometimes we doubt God's power simply because He chooses not to display it in the way we wish He would. If only we would approach every prayer with the same humble and worshipful stance as the leper.

TOP 3 PRIORITIES:

- ☐ ....
- ☐ ....
- ☐ ....

SCHEDULE/TO-DO LIST:

- ☐ ....
- ☐ ....
- ☐ ....
- ☐ ....

REFLECTIONS ON TODAY'S BIBLE READING

8 glasses a day: ☐ ☐ ☐ ☐ ☐ ☐ ☐ ☐

January

S	M	T	W	T	F	S
1	2	3	4	5	6	7
8	9	10	11	12	13	14
15	16	17	18	19	20	21
22	23	24	25	26	27	28
29	30	31				

REMEMBER

Today's Bible Reading:

GENESIS 27:1–28:9; MATTHEW 8:18–34; PSALM 10:12–18

*To judge the fatherless and the oppressed, that the
man of the earth may no more oppress.*
PSALM 10:18

When the darkness and insidious evil of the world seem so powerful, it is imperative that you remember that the one who calmed the wind and the waves is still the ruler of this earth. He will one day vanquish evil for all eternity. He will judge the earth so that man may no longer oppress His image bearers. He will make all things right. You must hold fast to this truth so you won't lose hope.

REFLECTIONS ON TODAY'S BIBLE READING

8 glasses a day:

TOP 3 PRIORITIES:

- [ ] ....
- [ ] ....
- [ ] ....

SCHEDULE/TO-DO LIST:

- [ ] ....
- [ ] ....
- [ ] ....
- [ ]

REMEMBER

February

S	M	T	W	T	F	S
			1	2	3	4
5	6	7	8	9	10	11
12	13	14	15	16	17	18
19	20	21	22	23	24	25
26	27	28				

Friday
JANUARY 13

Today's Bible Reading:

GENESIS 28:10–29:35; MATTHEW 9; PSALM 11

But Jesus turned him about, and when he saw her, he said,
Daughter, be of good comfort; thy faith hath made thee whole.
And the woman was made whole from that hour.
MATTHEW 9:22

Scripture is laden with stories of the compassion of God. Just in today's reading we see that He loves the unloved (Leah), He sees those who feel invisible (the woman with the hemorrhage), He invites the outcasts in (the sinners and tax collectors), and He heals the sick and needy (the synagogue official's daughter and the blind men). You serve a compassionate and loving God who does not overlook any of His children. He cares deeply for you.

TOP 3 PRIORITIES:

- ☐ ....
- ☐ ....
- ☐ ....

SCHEDULE/TO-DO LIST:

- ☐ ....
- ☐ ....
- ☐ ....
- ☐ ....

REFLECTIONS ON TODAY'S BIBLE READING

8 glasses a day: ▯ ▯ ▯ ▯ ▯ ▯ ▯ ▯

REMEMBER

January

S	M	T	W	T	F	S
1	2	3	4	5	6	7
8	9	10	11	12	13	14
15	16	17	18	19	20	21
22	23	24	25	26	27	28
29	30	31				

Today's Bible Reading:

GENESIS 30:1–31:21; MATTHEW 10:1–15; PSALM 12

For the oppression of the poor, for the sighing of the needy, now will I arise, saith the LORD; I will set him in safety from him that puffeth at him.
PSALM 12:5

The Lord sees your struggles and hears your groaning. Your prayers do not fall on deaf ears. God will act in His own perfect timing. God will arise to vindicate the injustices done on His people. If you are oppressed or treated unjustly, recognize that no matter what people may say about you, you are vindicated and justified by the ultimate judge. Doesn't your standing before Him matter infinitely more than your status here on earth?

REFLECTIONS ON TODAY'S BIBLE READING

8 glasses a day:

TOP 3 PRIORITIES:

- [ ] ....
- [ ] ....
- [ ] ....

SCHEDULE/TO-DO LIST:

- [ ] ....
- [ ] ....
- [ ] ....
- [ ] ....

REMEMBER

February

S	M	T	W	T	F	S
			1	2	3	4
5	6	7	8	9	10	11
12	13	14	15	16	17	18
19	20	21	22	23	24	25
26	27	28				

Today's Bible Reading:

GENESIS 31:22–32:21; MATTHEW 10:16–36; PSALM 13

But I have trusted in thy mercy; my heart shall rejoice in thy salvation.
I will sing unto the LORD, because he hath dealt bountifully with me.
PSALM 13:5–6

Although Jacob's prayer in Genesis 32 was probably inspired more by fear than faith, we can emulate him in that he called to mind God's promises. When you're faced with a fearful situation, remember the promises that God has made to you and pray them back to Him. Although He certainly doesn't need to be reminded of the promises He has made, it will bless you to be reminded of them.

TOP 3 PRIORITIES:

- ☐ ....
- ☐ ....
- ☐ ....

SCHEDULE/TO-DO LIST:

- ☐ ....
- ☐ ....
- ☐ ....
- ☐ ....

REFLECTIONS ON TODAY'S BIBLE READING

8 glasses a day: ☐ ☐ ☐ ☐ ☐ ☐ ☐ ☐

January

S	M	T	W	T	F	S
1	2	3	4	5	6	7
8	9	10	11	12	13	14
15	16	17	18	19	20	21
22	23	24	25	26	27	28
29	30	31				

REMEMBER

Martin Luther King Jr. Day

Today's Bible Reading:

GENESIS 32:22–34:31; MATTHEW 10:37–11:6; PSALM 14

*And Jacob called the name of the place Peniel: for I have
seen God face to face, and my life is preserved.*
GENESIS 32:30

It is essential that you remember the times in your life when God has shown Himself to you in special or significant ways. Unlike Jacob, you probably don't have a permanent limp to constantly remind you of your encounter with God. But nevertheless, it is important to remember and celebrate God's faithfulness so that in times of trial, when it can be easy to doubt God, you have something concrete to look back on to remind you of how He always cares for you.

REFLECTIONS ON TODAY'S BIBLE READING

8 glasses a day:

TOP 3 PRIORITIES:

- ☐ ....
- ☐ ....
- ☐ ....

SCHEDULE/TO-DO LIST:

- ☐ ....
- ☐ ....
- ☐ ....
- ☐

REMEMBER

February

S	M	T	W	T	F	S
			1	2	3	4
5	6	7	8	9	10	11
12	13	14	15	16	17	18
19	20	21	22	23	24	25
26	27	28				

Today's Bible Reading:

GENESIS 35–36; MATTHEW 11:7-24; PSALM 15

Lord, who shall abide in thy tabernacle? who shall dwell in thy holy hill? . . . He that doeth these things shall never be moved.
PSALM 15:1, 5

Psalm 15 gives a list of attributes of one who would be worthy to dwell with God. It concludes in asserting that the one who does these things will never be shaken. This is not to say that struggles and heartbreaks will not reach the righteous. But when you dwell with God, the struggles of this world will be insignificant compared to the beauty and glory of your God. Someone that is anchored to an immovable Rock is hard to shake.

TOP 3 PRIORITIES:

- ☐ ....
- ☐ ....
- ☐ ....

SCHEDULE/TO-DO LIST:

- ☐ ....
- ☐ ....
- ☐ ....
- ☐ ....

REFLECTIONS ON TODAY'S BIBLE READING

8 glasses a day: ☐ ☐ ☐ ☐ ☐ ☐ ☐ ☐

January

S	M	T	W	T	F	S
1	2	3	4	5	6	7
8	9	10	11	12	13	14
15	16	17	18	19	20	21
22	23	24	25	26	27	28
29	30	31				

REMEMBER

Today's Bible Reading:

GENESIS 37–38; MATTHEW 11:25–30; PSALM 16

Thou wilt shew me the path of life: in thy presence is fulness of joy; at thy right hand there are pleasures for evermore.
PSALM 16:11

God will show you the path of life. Put Him before you in every decision of your life. If the decision seems too daunting, simply ask Him to reveal the next right step. Make your most urgent desire be to serve Him. You will find that He will guide, protect, and preserve you. The more closely you bind yourself to Him, the more clearly you will experience the fullness of joy available in His presence. He desires to give you pleasures forevermore.

REFLECTIONS ON TODAY'S BIBLE READING

TOP 3 PRIORITIES:

- [ ] ......
- [ ] ......
- [ ] ......

SCHEDULE/TO-DO LIST:

- [ ] ......
- [ ] ......
- [ ] ......
- [ ] ......

8 glasses a day:

REMEMBER

February

S	M	T	W	T	F	S
			1	2	3	4
5	6	7	8	9	10	11
12	13	14	15	16	17	18
19	20	21	22	23	24	25
26	27	28				

Today's Bible Reading:

GENESIS 39–40; MATTHEW 12:1–29; PSALM 17

Keep me as the apple of the eye, hide me under the shadow of thy wings.
PSALM 17:8

You instinctively protect your eyes from harm. When startled, you blink. If something comes flying suddenly in your direction, you immediately shield your face. The apple of your eye is valuable; therefore you protect it. God's children are like the apple of His eye–something precious that He has taken great pains to protect. He will never fail or cease to protect you. Rest securely in the shadow of His wings.

TOP 3 PRIORITIES:

- ☐ ....
- ☐ ....
- ☐ ....

SCHEDULE/TO-DO LIST:

- ☐ ....
- ☐ ....
- ☐ ....
- ☐ ....

REFLECTIONS ON TODAY'S BIBLE READING

8 glasses a day: ▭ ▭ ▭ ▭ ▭ ▭ ▭ ▭

REMEMBER

January

S	M	T	W	T	F	S
1	2	3	4	5	6	7
8	9	10	11	12	13	14
15	16	17	18	19	20	21
22	23	24	25	26	27	28
29	30	31				

Today's Bible Reading:

GENESIS 41; MATTHEW 12:30–50; PSALM 18:1-15

And Joseph answered Pharaoh, saying, It is not in me:
God shall give Pharaoh an answer of peace.
GENESIS 41:16

When you are honored and glorified on earth, use it as an opportunity to turn the eyes of those praising you to God. May everything that you do on earth be to His glory, for then you will be fulfilling your purpose in this life. True humility is recognizing that your achievements are owed to God and to what others have done to get you where you are. So direct the praise to God and to others–that's where it belongs.

REFLECTIONS ON TODAY'S BIBLE READING

8 glasses a day:

TOP 3 PRIORITIES:

- [ ] ....
- [ ] ....
- [ ] ....

SCHEDULE/TO-DO LIST:

- [ ] ....
- [ ] ....
- [ ] ....
- [ ] ....

REMEMBER

February

S	M	T	W	T	F	S
			1	2	3	4
5	6	7	8	9	10	11
12	13	14	15	16	17	18
19	20	21	22	23	24	25
26	27	28				

Today's Bible Reading:

GENESIS 42–43; MATTHEW 13:1–9; PSALM 18:16–29

*For thou wilt light my candle: the LORD
my God will enlighten my darkness.*
PSALM 18:28

God knows your future, for He planned it out before you were even born. So ask the one who already knows your path to light your candle and enlighten your darkness. He will give you enough illumination to guide your feet to the next step you should take.

TOP 3 PRIORITIES:

- [ ] ....
- [ ] ....
- [ ] ....

SCHEDULE/TO-DO LIST:

- [ ] ....
- [ ] ....
- [ ] ....
- [ ] ....

REFLECTIONS ON TODAY'S BIBLE READING

8 glasses a day: ☐ ☐ ☐ ☐ ☐ ☐ ☐ ☐

January

S	M	T	W	T	F	S
1	2	3	4	5	6	7
8	9	10	11	12	13	14
15	16	17	18	19	20	21
22	23	24	25	26	27	28
29	30	31				

REMEMBER

Today's Bible Reading:

GENESIS 44–45; MATTHEW 13:10–23; PSALM 18:30–50

*Now therefore, I pray thee, let thy servant abide instead of the lad
a bondman to my lord; and let the lad go up with his brethren.*
GENESIS 44:33

Never assume that someone is unable to be transformed by God's grace. Based upon the remarkably cruel way they treated Joseph, it would be easy to think that his brothers were past saving. And yet, in Judah (one of the brothers who was part of the horrific plan to kill Joseph) we see a dim and imperfect but unmistakable picture of Christ—he was willing to sacrifice his own life for the sake of his younger brother. God can work in any life.

REFLECTIONS ON TODAY'S BIBLE READING

8 glasses a day:

TOP 3 PRIORITIES:

- [ ]
- [ ]
- [ ]

SCHEDULE/TO-DO LIST:

- [ ]
- [ ]
- [ ]
- [ ]

REMEMBER

February

S	M	T	W	T	F	S
			1	2	3	4
5	6	7	8	9	10	11
12	13	14	15	16	17	18
19	20	21	22	23	24	25
26	27	28				

Today's Bible Reading:

GENESIS 46:1–47:26; MATTHEW 13:24–43; PSALM 19

*More to be desired are they than gold, yea, than much fine gold:
sweeter also than honey and the honeycomb. Moreover by them is
thy servant warned: and in keeping of them there is great reward.*
PSALM 19:10–11

God's Word is perfect, sure, clean, pure, true, and righteous. It enlightens eyes, makes the simple wise, converts souls, brings joy, and is entirely trustworthy because it endures forever. The words of God are far more valuable than gold. It makes sense, then, that great reward is to be found in following His commandments. With such treasure at your fingertips, why would you not immerse yourself in His Word every day?

TOP 3 PRIORITIES:

- [ ] ....
- [ ] ....
- [ ] ....

SCHEDULE/TO-DO LIST:

- [ ] ....
- [ ] ....
- [ ] ....
- [ ] ....

REFLECTIONS ON TODAY'S BIBLE READING

8 glasses a day:

January

S	M	T	W	T	F	S
1	2	3	4	5	6	7
8	9	10	11	12	13	14
15	16	17	18	19	20	21
22	23	24	25	26	27	28
29	30	31				

REMEMBER

Tuesday
JANUARY 24

Today's Bible Reading:

GENESIS 47:27–49:28; MATTHEW 13:44–58; PSALM 20

Now know I that the LORD saveth his anointed; he will hear him from his holy heaven with the saving strength of his right hand.
PSALM 20:6

Psalm 20 is a beautiful psalm to pray over your life. David's petitions are saturated with the power and knowledge of victory. As someone who has the blessing of living after Christ has conquered death and evil, you can pray with even more confidence in God's victory. You can boast in the name of God for He will save and He will keep you from stumbling. Set up your banners in His name, proclaiming to the world that you are His and that it is His power at work in you.

REFLECTIONS ON TODAY'S BIBLE READING

8 glasses a day:

REMEMBER

TOP 3 PRIORITIES:

SCHEDULE/TO-DO LIST:

February

S	M	T	W	T	F	S
			1	2	3	4
5	6	7	8	9	10	11
12	13	14	15	16	17	18
19	20	21	22	23	24	25
26	27	28

Wednesday
JANUARY 25

Today's Bible Reading:

GENESIS 49:29–EXODUS 1; MATTHEW 14; PSALM 21

*But the more they afflicted them,
the more they multiplied and grew.*
Exodus 1:12

As demonstrated in the account of the Hebrews in Egypt, God will often use suffering to increase His people. The very means that man uses as an attempt to snuff out God's children God uses to make them stronger. So when the suffering inflicted on God's people feels overwhelming, rejoice–knowing that through it God will work mightily, thwarting the arrogant plans of man.

TOP 3 PRIORITIES:

SCHEDULE/TO-DO LIST:

REFLECTIONS ON TODAY'S BIBLE READING

8 glasses a day:

January

S	M	T	W	T	F	S
1	2	3	4	5	6	7
8	9	10	11	12	13	14
15	16	17	18	19	20	21
22	23	24	25	26	27	28
29	30	31				

REMEMBER

Today's Bible Reading:

EXODUS 2–3; MATTHEW 15:1-28; PSALM 22:1-21

And God said unto Moses, I Am That I Am: and he said, Thus shalt thou say unto the children of Israel, I Am hath sent me unto you.
Exodus 3:14

The beautiful, unbreakable thread of God's sovereignty is woven all throughout history. In today's reading, God used an evil Pharaoh, a brutal nationwide infanticide, a "chance" encounter of an Egyptian princess, and a murderer and coward named Moses to accomplish His purposes. Never imagine that a personal besetting sin, weakness, or difficult circumstance is out of God's will or too difficult for Him to use for His glory.

REFLECTIONS ON TODAY'S BIBLE READING

8 glasses a day:

TOP 3 PRIORITIES:

SCHEDULE/TO-DO LIST:

REMEMBER

February

S	M	T	W	T	F	S
			1	2	3	4
5	6	7	8	9	10	11
12	13	14	15	16	17	18
19	20	21	22	23	24	25
26	27	28				

Today's Bible Reading:

EXODUS 4:1–5:21; MATTHEW 15:29–16:12; PSALM 22:22–31

Do ye not yet understand, neither remember the five loaves of the five thousand, and how many baskets ye took up? Neither the seven loaves of the four thousand, and how many baskets ye took up?
MATTHEW 16:9–10

How easily we forget God's power and His goodness. In his fear of speaking to the people, Moses failed to remember that it was God who made him and who could easily help him speak. In the pressure of feeding a crowd, the disciples quickly forgot the miracle that Jesus had already performed to feed thousands. What have you forgotten about God? What anxieties have taken root in your heart simply because you have failed to remember that God is powerful and that He loves you and will fulfill His will for your life?

TOP 3 PRIORITIES:

- [ ] ....
- [ ] ....
- [ ] ....

SCHEDULE/TO-DO LIST:

- [ ] ....
- [ ] ....
- [ ] ....
- [ ] ....

REFLECTIONS ON TODAY'S BIBLE READING

8 glasses a day:

REMEMBER

January

S	M	T	W	T	F	S
1	2	3	4	5	6	7
8	9	10	11	12	13	14
15	16	17	18	19	20	21
22	23	24	25	26	27	28
29	30	31				

Today's Bible Reading:

EXODUS 5:22–7:24; MATTHEW 16:13–28; PSALM 23

And I say also unto thee, That thou art Peter, and upon this rock I will build my church; and the gates of hell shall not prevail against it.
MATTHEW 16:18

Psalm 23 is such a familiar psalm, yet it is so profound and packed with remarkably comforting and empowering truths. Don't overlook the beauty of this little psalm. Similarly, in Matthew 16, don't discount the power of Jesus' promise "I will build my church"–a remarkably simple phrase that speaks of the power, victory, and sovereign plan of God. No earthly or spiritual power can stand in the way of the inevitable progress of Christ's Gospel. Take courage and find peace in this truth.

REFLECTIONS ON TODAY'S BIBLE READING

8 glasses a day:

TOP 3 PRIORITIES:

- [ ] ....
- [ ] ....
- [ ] ....

SCHEDULE/TO-DO LIST:

- [ ] ....
- [ ] ....
- [ ] ....
- [ ] ....

REMEMBER

February

S	M	T	W	T	F	S
			1	2	3	4
5	6	7	8	9	10	11
12	13	14	15	16	17	18
19	20	21	22	23	24	25
26	27	28				

Today's Bible Reading:

EXODUS 7:25–9:35; MATTHEW 17:1–9; PSALM 24

The earth is the LORD's, and the fulness thereof;
the world, and they that dwell therein.
PSALM 24:1

God made the world and everything in it. He still sustains and controls the earth and all its inhabitants. He proved His power over His creation in the multiple plagues He brought down on Egypt. This same God with the same amount of power still reigns today. He is to be feared. But, as one of His children, His power ought to give you comfort and courage because there is nothing in your life that He does not have control over.

TOP 3 PRIORITIES:

☐ ....
☐ ....
☐ ....

SCHEDULE/TO-DO LIST:

☐ ....
☐ ....
☐ ....
☐ ....

REFLECTIONS ON TODAY'S BIBLE READING

8 glasses a day: ▢ ▢ ▢ ▢ ▢ ▢ ▢ ▢

January

S	M	T	W	T	F	S
1	2	3	4	5	6	7
8	9	10	11	12	13	14
15	16	17	18	19	20	21
22	23	24	25	26	27	28
29	30	31				

REMEMBER

Today's Bible Reading:

EXODUS 10–11; MATTHEW 17:10–27; PSALM 25

And the LORD said unto Moses, Go in unto Pharaoh: for I have hardened his heart, and the heart of his servants, that I might shew these my signs before him: and that thou mayest tell in the ears of thy son, and of thy son's son, what things I have wrought in Egypt, and my signs which I have done among them; that ye may know how that I am the LORD.
EXODUS 10:1–2

The process of getting the Israelites out of Egypt was a painful one. God continued to harden Pharaoh's heart, which in turn caused him to oppress the Israelites more and more. In the midst of it all, it would have been difficult not to question what possible purpose God could have for putting His people through this. And yet, we can look back on it now and see that God's purposes were to free His people, to show His power and glory to a heathen nation, and to start His people on a journey to a beautiful land they could call their own. Worship in the midst of confusing and frightening circumstances, relying on God to use your suffering for His glory and for your good.

REFLECTIONS ON TODAY'S BIBLE READING

TOP 3 PRIORITIES:

- [ ]
- [ ]
- [ ]

SCHEDULE/TO-DO LIST:

- [ ]
- [ ]
- [ ]
- [ ]

8 glasses a day:

REMEMBER

February

S	M	T	W	T	F	S
			1	2	3	4
5	6	7	8	9	10	11
12	13	14	15	16	17	18
19	20	21	22	23	24	25
26	27	28				

Today's Bible Reading:

EXODUS 12; MATTHEW 18:1–20; PSALM 26

Judge me, O Lord; for I have walked in mine integrity:
I have trusted also in the Lord; therefore I shall not slide.
PSALM 26:1

Are you as confident in your integrity as David was in his? Could you ask God to judge you with a clear conscience? This kind of confidence in your own innocence may seem impossible—and on your own, it is. But the blood of the Passover Lamb covers you so that you, too, can have confidence in the day of judgment.

TOP 3 PRIORITIES:

- [ ] ....
- [ ] ....
- [ ] ....

SCHEDULE/TO-DO LIST:

- [ ] ....
- [ ] ....
- [ ] ....
- [ ] ....

REFLECTIONS ON TODAY'S BIBLE READING

8 glasses a day: ☐ ☐ ☐ ☐ ☐ ☐ ☐ ☐

January

S	M	T	W	T	F	S
1	2	3	4	5	6	7
8	9	10	11	12	13	14
15	16	17	18	19	20	21
22	23	24	25	26	27	28
29	30	31				

REMEMBER

Today's Bible Reading:

EXODUS 13–14; MATTHEW 18:21–35; PSALM 27

And Moses said unto the people, Fear ye not, stand still, and see the salvation of the Lord, which he will shew to you to day: for the Egyptians whom ye have seen to day, ye shall see them again no more for ever.
EXODUS 14:13

Moses was confident that God would act on behalf of His people. He told the people to watch carefully because he knew that they would see their God's salvation that day. His faith in God's promise to deliver His people from Egypt was so secure that not even six hundred chariots of Egypt could shake his confidence. And God did not let him down. You serve the same promise-keeping, all-powerful God today. May your faith be as strong as the faith of Moses so that you, too, can stand firm, assured of God's salvation even in the face of overwhelming odds.

REFLECTIONS ON TODAY'S BIBLE READING

8 glasses a day:

TOP 3 PRIORITIES:

SCHEDULE/TO-DO LIST:

REMEMBER

February

S	M	T	W	T	F	S
			1	2	3	4
5	6	7	8	9	10	11
12	13	14	15	16	17	18
19	20	21	22	23	24	25
26	27	28				

Thursday
FEBRUARY 2

Today's Bible Reading:

EXODUS 15–16; MATTHEW 19:1–15; PSALM 28

*The Lord is my strength and my shield; my heart trusted in him, and I am helped:
therefore my heart greatly rejoiceth; and with my song will I praise him.*
PSALM 28:7

Psalm 28 provides us with a trustworthy equation: trust in God and you will be helped. Sometimes our prescription of the help we want God to provide is different from the help He does provide. But even though it may not feel like it in the moment, what God prescribes for you is infinitely better than anything you could imagine. Take a moment to recall times in your life when this has proven to be true. Then praise Him for His grace and faithfulness to you.

TOP 3 PRIORITIES:

-
-
-

SCHEDULE/TO-DO LIST:

-
-
-
-

REFLECTIONS ON TODAY'S BIBLE READING

8 glasses a day:

February

S	M	T	W	T	F	S
			1	2	3	4
5	6	7	8	9	10	11
12	13	14	15	16	17	18
19	20	21	22	23	24	25
26	27	28				

REMEMBER

Today's Bible Reading:

EXODUS 17–19; MATTHEW 19:16–30; PSALM 29

Jesus said unto him, If thou wilt be perfect, go and sell that thou hast, and give to the poor, and thou shalt have treasure in heaven: and come and follow me.
MATTHEW 19:21

Is there anything in your life that you would refuse to give up for the sake of Christ and His kingdom? The lack of ability to surrender possessions and earthly treasure to God is an indication that you have not fully known your God or the matchless riches that He offers to those who seek after Him. Jesus asks you to be willing to give up earthly comforts because He knows that what He can give is far better than anything this world can offer. It's only in letting go of earthly treasure that you can grab hold of Him.

REFLECTIONS ON TODAY'S BIBLE READING

8 glasses a day:

TOP 3 PRIORITIES:

- ☐ ....
- ☐ ....
- ☐ ....

SCHEDULE/TO-DO LIST:

- ☐ ....
- ☐ ....
- ☐ ....
- ☐ ....

REMEMBER

March

S	M	T	W	T	F	S
			1	2	3	4
5	6	7	8	9	10	11
12	13	14	15	16	17	18
19	20	21	22	23	24	25
26	27	28	29	30	31	

Today's Bible Reading:

EXODUS 20–21; MATTHEW 20:1–19; PSALM 30

*Is it not lawful for me to do what I will with mine
own? Is thine eye evil, because I am good?*
MATTHEW 20:15

How easily we fall into questioning if God's plan for us is really the best. This doubt is often spurred on when we fall into the dangerous spiral of comparing our lives to the life of someone else. But since God is our Creator and Sustainer, doesn't He have the right to do with us as He pleases? More than that, doesn't He know best what is actually good for us? We must believe wholeheartedly in the goodness of God to protect ourselves from comparing our blessings to the blessings He's given others. There is beautiful freedom in truly accepting that God's treatment of you is perfect.

TOP 3 PRIORITIES:

- ☐ ....
- ☐ ....
- ☐ ....

SCHEDULE/TO-DO LIST:

- ☐ ....
- ☐ ....
- ☐ ....
- ☐ ....

REFLECTIONS ON TODAY'S BIBLE READING

8 glasses a day: ☐ ☐ ☐ ☐ ☐ ☐ ☐ ☐

REMEMBER

February

S	M	T	W	T	F	S
			1	2	3	4
5	6	7	8	9	10	11
12	13	14	15	16	17	18
19	20	21	22	23	24	25
26	27	28				

Today's Bible Reading:

EXODUS 22–23; MATTHEW 20:20–34; PSALM 31:1–8

*Ye shall not afflict any widow, or fatherless child. If thou afflict them
in any wise, and they cry at all unto me, I will surely hear their cry;
and my wrath shall wax hot, and I will kill you with the sword;
and your wives shall be widows, and your children fatherless.*
Exodus 22:22–24

Though the laws of Exodus can sometimes seem tedious, God's character glimmers through in His instructions of how His people ought to live. His love and stalwart defense of the needy is seen in the recompense that He promises for anyone who dares afflict a widow or orphan. To take advantage of the weak and vulnerable is no small offense in God's eyes. God does not overlook those who are so often overlooked in our world—and, therefore, neither should we.

REFLECTIONS ON TODAY'S BIBLE READING

8 glasses a day: ▢ ▢ ▢ ▢ ▢ ▢ ▢ ▢

TOP 3 PRIORITIES:

☐ ....
☐ ....
☐ ....

SCHEDULE/TO-DO LIST:

☐ ....
☐ ....
☐ ....
☐ ....

REMEMBER

March

S	M	T	W	T	F	S
			1	2	3	4
5	6	7	8	9	10	11
12	13	14	15	16	17	18
19	20	21	22	23	24	25
26	27	28	29	30	31	

Today's Bible Reading:

EXODUS 24–25; MATTHEW 21:1–27; PSALM 31:9–18

*My times are in thy hand: deliver me from the hand
of mine enemies, and from them that persecute me.*
PSALM 31:15

How would it change your life if you, like David, could truly grasp that your times are in God's hands? Wouldn't that belief foster an unshakable peace in your heart as it banishes fear from your life? You would know that the trials you go through are ordained by God and will be carefully worked out for your good. Why is it that we so often struggle to live our lives firmly planted in this truth?

TOP 3 PRIORITIES:

- ☐ ....
- ☐ ....
- ☐ ....

SCHEDULE/TO-DO LIST:

- ☐ ....
- ☐ ....
- ☐ ....
- ☐ ....

REFLECTIONS ON TODAY'S BIBLE READING

8 glasses a day: ▢ ▢ ▢ ▢ ▢ ▢ ▢ ▢

February

S	M	T	W	T	F	S
			1	2	3	4
5	6	7	8	9	10	11
12	13	14	15	16	17	18
19	20	21	22	23	24	25
26	27	28				

REMEMBER

Today's Bible Reading:

EXODUS 26–27; MATTHEW 21:28–46; PSALM 31:19–24

*Jesus saith unto them, Verily I say unto you, That the publicans
and the harlots go into the kingdom of God before you.*
MATTHEW 21:31

There is no deference to earthly status in the kingdom of God. All that matters is belief in the Son of God. Take this as an encouragement that no matter what you have done in this life, you are never past saving. And take it as a warning that no amount of good done in this life will get you into heaven apart from a saving knowledge of Christ.

REFLECTIONS ON TODAY'S BIBLE READING

8 glasses a day:

TOP 3 PRIORITIES:

- [ ]
- [ ]
- [ ]

SCHEDULE/TO-DO LIST:

- [ ]
- [ ]
- [ ]
- [ ]

REMEMBER

March

S	M	T	W	T	F	S
			1	2	3	4
5	6	7	8	9	10	11
12	13	14	15	16	17	18
19	20	21	22	23	24	25
26	27	28	29	30	31	

Today's Bible Reading:

EXODUS 28; MATTHEW 22; PSALM 32

*Many sorrows shall be to the wicked: but he that trusteth
in the LORD, mercy shall compass him about.*
PSALM 32:10

Those who trust in God are completely surrounded and encompassed by His mercy. It may be difficult to believe this in times when the hardships of life press so closely that they're almost suffocating. And yet, through all of life's struggles you have a layer of protection that can't be breached. Your life is completely in God's hands, and He will remain forever by your side.

TOP 3 PRIORITIES:

- ☐ ....
- ☐ ....
- ☐ ....

SCHEDULE/TO-DO LIST:

- ☐ ....
- ☐ ....
- ☐ ....
- ☐ ....

REFLECTIONS ON TODAY'S BIBLE READING

8 glasses a day: ▽ ▽ ▽ ▽ ▽ ▽ ▽ ▽

REMEMBER

February

S	M	T	W	T	F	S
			1	2	3	4
5	6	7	8	9	10	11
12	13	14	15	16	17	18
19	20	21	22	23	24	25
26	27	28				

Today's Bible Reading:

EXODUS 29; MATTHEW 23:1–36; PSALM 33:1–12

Rejoice in the Lord, O ye righteous:
for praise is comely for the upright.
Psalm 33:1

Why does God command you to worship Him? Is it because He has some arrogant need to be noticed and praised? Not at all. If you were never to worship Him, it would not affect Him in the least. But it would affect you. Praising God is good, refreshing, and life-giving for you. Don't neglect the wonderful gift of worshipping your God.

REFLECTIONS ON TODAY'S BIBLE READING

8 glasses a day:

TOP 3 PRIORITIES:

- [ ] ....
- [ ] ....
- [ ] ....

SCHEDULE/TO-DO LIST:

- [ ] ....
- [ ] ....
- [ ] ....
- [ ] ....

REMEMBER

March

S	M	T	W	T	F	S
			1	2	3	4
5	6	7	8	9	10	11
12	13	14	15	16	17	18
19	20	21	22	23	24	25
26	27	28	29	30	31	

Today's Bible Reading:

EXODUS 30–31; MATTHEW 23:37–24:28; PSALM 33:13–22

There is no king saved by the multitude of an host: a mighty man is not delivered by much strength. An horse is a vain thing for safety: neither shall he deliver any by his great strength. . . . Our soul waiteth for the LORD: he is our help and our shield.
PSALM 33:16–17, 20

What are you putting your trust in–status, money, health, strength, a good family? Psalm 33 reminds us that security comes from God and God alone. Set your trust on the Rock that will never move or crumble instead of on the shifting sands of the prosperity of this world.

TOP 3 PRIORITIES:

☐ ....
☐ ....
☐ ....

SCHEDULE/TO-DO LIST:

☐ ....
☐ ....
☐ ....
☐ ....

REFLECTIONS ON TODAY'S BIBLE READING

8 glasses a day: ☐ ☐ ☐ ☐ ☐ ☐ ☐ ☐

February

S	M	T	W	T	F	S
			1	2	3	4
5	6	7	8	9	10	11
12	13	14	15	16	17	18
19	20	21	22	23	24	25
26	27	28				

REMEMBER

Today's Bible Reading:

EXODUS 32–33; MATTHEW 24:29–51; PSALM 34:1–7

O magnify the LORD with me, and let us exalt his name together.
PSALM 34:3

Do you spend more time trying to magnify yourself or striving to magnify God? In magnifying and exalting God there is great joy, as it brings you into closer relationship with Him. The more magnified God is in your life, the more perspective you will have regarding how small and insignificant you are. This in turn will inspire you to lean on Him, making you more powerful than you ever would be on your own. Surround yourself with people who are passionate about magnifying God as well.

REFLECTIONS ON TODAY'S BIBLE READING

8 glasses a day: ☐ ☐ ☐ ☐ ☐ ☐ ☐ ☐

TOP 3 PRIORITIES:

☐ ....
☐ ....
☐ ....

SCHEDULE/TO-DO LIST:

☐ ....
☐ ....
☐ ....
☐ ....

REMEMBER

March

S	M	T	W	T	F	S
			1	2	3	4
5	6	7	8	9	10	11
12	13	14	15	16	17	18
19	20	21	22	23	24	25
26	27	28	29	30	31	

Today's Bible Reading:

EXODUS 34:1–35:29; MATTHEW 25:1–13; PSALM 34:8–22

*And when Aaron and all the children of Israel saw Moses, behold,
the skin of his face shone; and they were afraid to come nigh him.*
Exodus 34:30

An encounter with God will inevitably change you. Just as the Israelites noticed that the face of Moses shone after meeting with God, so too when you commit to spending valuable time with God each day, you will be changed in a noticeable and beautiful way. His glory will reflect off you, and His love will work through you.

TOP 3 PRIORITIES:

☐ ....
☐ ....
☐ ....

SCHEDULE/TO-DO LIST:

☐ ....
☐ ....
☐ ....
☐ ....

REFLECTIONS ON TODAY'S BIBLE READING

8 glasses a day: ☐ ☐ ☐ ☐ ☐ ☐ ☐ ☐

REMEMBER

February

S	M	T	W	T	F	S
			1	2	3	4
5	6	7	8	9	10	11
12	13	14	15	16	17	18
19	20	21	22	23	24	25
26	27	28				

Today's Bible Reading:

EXODUS 35:30–37:29; MATTHEW 25:14–30; PSALM 35:1–8

And he hath filled him with the spirit of God, in wisdom, in understanding, and in knowledge, and in all manner of workmanship.
Exodus 35:31

Our talents are God-given. Therefore, don't derive arrogance from them, but instead humbly thank God for the skills He has given you. Conversely, don't allow yourself to belittle the gifts that God has given you. Joyfully and confidently use them for His service.

REFLECTIONS ON TODAY'S BIBLE READING

TOP 3 PRIORITIES:

☐ ....
☐ ....
☐ ....

SCHEDULE/TO-DO LIST:

☐ ....
☐ ....
☐ ....
☐

8 glasses a day: ⬜ ⬜ ⬜ ⬜ ⬜ ⬜ ⬜ ⬜

REMEMBER

March

S	M	T	W	T	F	S
			1	2	3	4
5	6	7	8	9	10	11
12	13	14	15	16	17	18
19	20	21	22	23	24	25
26	27	28	29	30	31	

Today's Bible Reading:

EXODUS 38–39; MATTHEW 25:31–46; PSALM 35:9–17

And the King shall answer and say unto them, Verily I say unto you, Inasmuch as ye have done it unto one of the least of these my brethren, ye have done it unto me.
MATTHEW 25:40

Good deeds are often unnoticed and without thanks in this life. Maybe you even wonder why you still go out of your way to help others. But even if the world doesn't notice, be confident that God notices all the times you reach out to someone in need. God will reward you for your good works. In fact, in doing good for others you will find yourself in a closer relationship with your God, for He says, "Inasmuch as ye have done it unto one of the least of these my brethren, ye have done it unto me."

TOP 3 PRIORITIES:

- ☐ ....
- ☐ ....
- ☐ ....

SCHEDULE/TO-DO LIST:

- ☐ ....
- ☐ ....
- ☐ ....
- ☐ ....

REFLECTIONS ON TODAY'S BIBLE READING

8 glasses a day: ▽ ▽ ▽ ▽ ▽ ▽ ▽ ▽

February

S	M	T	W	T	F	S
				1	2	3	4
5	6	7	8	9	10	11
12	13	14	15	16	17	18
19	20	21	22	23	24	25
26	27	28				

REMEMBER

Today's Bible Reading:

EXODUS 40; MATTHEW 26:1-35; PSALM 35:18-28

And when the cloud was taken up from over the tabernacle, the children of Israel went onward in all their journeys: but if the cloud were not taken up, then they journeyed not till the day that it was taken up.
EXODUS 40:36–37

In the desert, the Israelites in a very tangible way had to rely on God for their next step. If the pillar of cloud or fire moved, they moved. If it stayed in place, they waited. We, too, are on a pilgrimage through this land and must rely on God's guidance for each next step. While we may wish that His presence were as obvious to us as it was to them, we have the greater blessing of having His indwelling Spirit to lead and to guide us. Wait and watch for His movements to guide you into the next phase of your service to Him.

REFLECTIONS ON TODAY'S BIBLE READING

TOP 3 PRIORITIES:

SCHEDULE/TO-DO LIST:

8 glasses a day:

REMEMBER

March

S	M	T	W	T	F	S
			1	2	3	4
5	6	7	8	9	10	11
12	13	14	15	16	17	18
19	20	21	22	23	24	25
26	27	28	29	30	31	

Today's Bible Reading:

LEVITICUS 1–3; MATTHEW 26:36–68; PSALM 36:1–6

But all this was done, that the scriptures of the prophets might be fulfilled. Then all the disciples forsook him, and fled.
MATTHEW 26:56

It is uncomfortable and upsetting to read the account of how all of Jesus' disciples abandoned Him to a violent mob that would treat Him, the Son of God, with a callous and shameful arrogance. And yet, don't we often treat Him in the same way? We fail to speak of Him at the first sign of opposition. We continually go back to the same sin as if to say that His sacrifice was not enough to save us. We move our time with Him to the lowest priority as though anything else in our life would be more important than time with our Savior. Repent of the arrogant ways that you have treated the Son of God.

TOP 3 PRIORITIES:

- [ ] ....
- [ ] ....
- [ ] ....

SCHEDULE/TO-DO LIST:

- [ ] ....
- [ ] ....
- [ ] ....
- [ ] ....

REFLECTIONS ON TODAY'S BIBLE READING

8 glasses a day:

February

S	M	T	W	T	F	S
			1	2	3	4
5	6	7	8	9	10	11
12	13	14	15	16	17	18
19	20	21	22	23	24	25
26	27	28				

REMEMBER

Today's Bible Reading:

LEVITICUS 4:1–5:13; MATTHEW 26:69–27:26; PSALM 36:7–12

And the chief priests took the silver pieces, and said, It is not lawful for to put them into the treasury, because it is the price of blood. And they took counsel, and bought with them the potter's field, to bury strangers in.
MATTHEW 27:6–7

The tainted money that Judas received for betraying Jesus was used to buy a field in which strangers would be buried. It is a testimony to the all-encompassing love of God that He caused even this filthy money to be used for good. The field bought by Jesus' blood was used to give a final resting place to those who otherwise would have had none. God can truly redeem even the most heinous of acts.

REFLECTIONS ON TODAY'S BIBLE READING

TOP 3 PRIORITIES:

☐ ....
☐ ....
☐ ....

SCHEDULE/TO-DO LIST:

☐ ....
☐ ....
☐ ....
☐

8 glasses a day: ☐ ☐ ☐ ☐ ☐ ☐ ☐ ☐

REMEMBER

March

S	M	T	W	T	F	S
			1	2	3	4
5	6	7	8	9	10	11
12	13	14	15	16	17	18
19	20	21	22	23	24	25
26	27	28	29	30	31	

Today's Bible Reading:

LEVITICUS 5:14–7:21; MATTHEW 27:27–50; PSALM 37:1–6

And about the ninth hour Jesus cried with a loud voice,
saying, Eli, Eli, lama sabachthani? that is to say, My
God, my God, why hast thou forsaken me?
MATTHEW 27:46

While on the cross, Christ asked why God had forsaken Him. In answer to that question, God could point to each of His children and say that it is for us that Christ was forsaken on the cross. This kind of love is unfathomable to us, that Christ would endure such pain for a people that would so easily abandon Him and spit in His face. He was forsaken so that we never would be. This is the kind of love that we should never take for granted and that should inspire in us worshipful gratefulness.

TOP 3 PRIORITIES:

- [ ]
- [ ]
- [ ]

SCHEDULE/TO-DO LIST:

- [ ]
- [ ]
- [ ]
- [ ]

REFLECTIONS ON TODAY'S BIBLE READING

8 glasses a day:

February

S	M	T	W	T	F	S
			1	2	3	4
5	6	7	8	9	10	11
12	13	14	15	16	17	18
19	20	21	22	23	24	25
26	27	28				

REMEMBER

Today's Bible Reading:

LEVITICUS 7:22–8:36; MATTHEW 27:51–66; PSALM 37:7–26

The steps of a good man are ordered by the LORD: and he delighteth in his way. Though he fall, he shall not be utterly cast down: for the LORD upholdeth him with his hand.
PSALM 37:23–24

God orders your steps and then delights to see you walking in them. What peace this affords that God knows and lovingly controls all your decisions. And even when you stumble, you will not fall because the almighty God is by your side to catch and uphold you.

REFLECTIONS ON TODAY'S BIBLE READING

8 glasses a day:

TOP 3 PRIORITIES:

SCHEDULE/TO-DO LIST:

REMEMBER

March

S	M	T	W	T	F	S
			1	2	3	4
5	6	7	8	9	10	11
12	13	14	15	16	17	18
19	20	21	22	23	24	25
26	27	28	29	30	31	

Today's Bible Reading:

LEVITICUS 9–10; MATTHEW 28; PSALM 37:27–40

And Jesus came and spake unto them, saying, All power is given unto me in heaven and in earth. Go ye therefore, and teach all nations, baptizing them in the name of the Father, and of the Son, and of the Holy Ghost: teaching them to observe all things whatsoever I have commanded you: and, lo, I am with you always, even unto the end of the world. Amen.
MATTHEW 28:18–20

The reason that God's people are able to go out into the world to make disciples and bring the Gospel to every nation is because all authority has been given to Christ. This knowledge infuses courage into all evangelism. Christ has already won and sits victoriously on His throne and is with us always, even to the end of the world. He has already chosen a people to be His. It is simply our responsibility to faithfully preach His Word. He has already taken care of the hard part.

TOP 3 PRIORITIES:

- [ ] ....
- [ ] ....
- [ ] ....

SCHEDULE/TO-DO LIST:

- [ ] ....
- [ ] ....
- [ ] ....
- [ ] ....

REFLECTIONS ON TODAY'S BIBLE READING

8 glasses a day: ☐ ☐ ☐ ☐ ☐ ☐ ☐ ☐

February

S	M	T	W	T	F	S
			1	2	3	4
5	6	7	8	9	10	11
12	13	14	15	16	17	18
19	20	21	22	23	24	25
26	27	28				

REMEMBER

Today's Bible Reading:

LEVITICUS 11–12; MARK 1:1-28; PSALM 38

For in thee, O Lord, do I hope: thou wilt hear, O Lord my God.
PSALM 38:15

Do you have the same confidence as David wrote about in this psalm that God will hear when you call to Him? Where is your hope? If it is in your own abilities or merit, then you will find yourself disappointed. Securely fasten your hope to God's love and care for you and you will never be let down.

REFLECTIONS ON TODAY'S BIBLE READING

8 glasses a day:

TOP 3 PRIORITIES:

SCHEDULE/TO-DO LIST:

REMEMBER

March

S	M	T	W	T	F	S
			1	2	3	4
5	6	7	8	9	10	11
12	13	14	15	16	17	18
19	20	21	22	23	24	25
26	27	28	29	30	31	

Today's Bible Reading:

LEVITICUS 13; MARK 1:29–39; PSALM 39

*LORD, make me to know mine end, and the measure of my
days, what it is: that I may know how frail I am.*
PSALM 39:4

Pray that God would give you the eternal perspective of how short this life really is. How would it change your life if you knew how it would end? How differently would you live each day if you really understood how few days you had? We are only pilgrims on this earth. Use the short time here to do the greatest good for God's kingdom and for those around you.

TOP 3 PRIORITIES:

- ☐ ....
- ☐ ....
- ☐ ....

SCHEDULE/TO-DO LIST:

- ☐ ....
- ☐ ....
- ☐ ....
- ☐ ....

REFLECTIONS ON TODAY'S BIBLE READING

8 glasses a day: ☐ ☐ ☐ ☐ ☐ ☐ ☐ ☐

February

S	M	T	W	T	F	S
			1	2	3	4
5	6	7	8	9	10	11
12	13	14	15	16	17	18
19	20	21	22	23	24	25
26	27	28				

REMEMBER

Today's Bible Reading:

LEVITICUS 14; MARK 1:40–2:12; PSALM 40:1–8

*And Jesus, moved with compassion, put forth his hand,
and touched him, and saith unto him, I will; be thou clean.*
MARK 1:41

Notice the beautiful juxtaposition in today's reading. The passage in Leviticus laboriously sets out how a leper ought to be treated and the intense work of cleansing that had to happen. The passage in Mark depicts Christ reaching out and touching a leper to instantly make him well. Touching a leper would have been unheard of in the old Law. But Christ came to usher in a new law in which He touches the unclean and invites the outcast in.

REFLECTIONS ON TODAY'S BIBLE READING

8 glasses a day:

TOP 3 PRIORITIES:

SCHEDULE/TO-DO LIST:

REMEMBER

March

S	M	T	W	T	F	S
			1	2	3	4
5	6	7	8	9	10	11
12	13	14	15	16	17	18
19	20	21	22	23	24	25
26	27	28	29	30	31	

Today's Bible Reading:

LEVITICUS 15; MARK 2:13–3:35; PSALM 40:9–17

*And it came to pass, that, as Jesus sat at meat in his house,
many publicans and sinners sat also together with Jesus and
his disciples: for there were many, and they followed him.*
MARK 2:15

What a beautiful God we serve who would rather eat with sinners and outcasts than maintain His social standing in a crowd of hypocrites. If you ever find yourself becoming too concerned about your social image, just remember what kind of Savior you should be emulating.

TOP 3 PRIORITIES:

- ☐ ....
- ☐ ....
- ☐ ....

SCHEDULE/TO-DO LIST:

- ☐ ....
- ☐ ....
- ☐ ....
- ☐ ....

REFLECTIONS ON TODAY'S BIBLE READING

8 glasses a day: ☐ ☐ ☐ ☐ ☐ ☐ ☐ ☐

February

S	M	T	W	T	F	S
			1	2	3	4
5	6	7	8	9	10	11
12	13	14	15	16	17	18
19	20	21	22	23	24	25
26	27	28				

REMEMBER

Today's Bible Reading:

LEVITICUS 16–17; MARK 4:1–20; PSALM 41:1–4

For on that day shall the priest make an atonement for you, to cleanse you, that ye may be clean from all your sins before the Lord.
LEVITICUS 16:30

Once a year the high priest would make atonement for all the people to cleanse them from their sins. But this cleansing would only cover the sins of one year. Now, what beautiful freedom we have that Christ's onetime work on the cross has and will cover all our sins for all time.

REFLECTIONS ON TODAY'S BIBLE READING

8 glasses a day:

TOP 3 PRIORITIES:

- ☐ ....
- ☐ ....
- ☐ ....

SCHEDULE/TO-DO LIST:

- ☐ ....
- ☐ ....
- ☐ ....
- ☐ ....

REMEMBER

March

S	M	T	W	T	F	S
			1	2	3	4
5	6	7	8	9	10	11
12	13	14	15	16	17	18
19	20	21	22	23	24	25
26	27	28	29	30	31	

Today's Bible Reading:

LEVITICUS 18–19; MARK 4:21–41; PSALM 41:5–13

And he arose, and rebuked the wind, and said unto the sea,
Peace, be still. And the wind ceased, and there was a great calm.
MARK 4:39

The same God who controls the winds and the sea lives inside you today. Fear has no place and no power against such a formidable opponent. When it seems like the waves of life are threatening to take you under, remember who it is that reigns as King in your heart. Ask Him to still the fear in your life and grant you peace.

TOP 3 PRIORITIES:

- ☐ ....
- ☐ ....
- ☐ ....

SCHEDULE/TO-DO LIST:

- ☐ ....
- ☐ ....
- ☐ ....
- ☐ ....

REFLECTIONS ON TODAY'S BIBLE READING

8 glasses a day: ▭ ▭ ▭ ▭ ▭ ▭ ▭ ▭

REMEMBER

February

S	M	T	W	T	F	S
			1	2	3	4
5	6	7	8	9	10	11
12	13	14	15	16	17	18
19	20	21	22	23	24	25
26	27	28				

Today's Bible Reading:

LEVITICUS 20; MARK 5; PSALM 42–43

*And he said unto her, Daughter, thy faith hath made thee
whole; go in peace, and be whole of thy plague.*
MARK 5:34

Christ radically changed the life of the woman in Mark 5 in more ways than one. First, He healed her bleeding. But perhaps even more importantly, He called her "daughter." This woman would have been an outcast in her society with little human contact because of her condition. So can you imagine the spiritual and emotional healing she must have felt at the hands of her Savior to have been called His daughter–a term of endearment and belonging? You also are called a child of God and forever belong to Him no matter what happens on this earth.

REFLECTIONS ON TODAY'S BIBLE READING

TOP 3 PRIORITIES:

☐ ....
☐ ....
☐ ....

SCHEDULE/TO-DO LIST:

☐ ....
☐ ....
☐ ....
☐ ....

8 glasses a day: ☐ ☐ ☐ ☐ ☐ ☐ ☐ ☐

REMEMBER

March

S	M	T	W	T	F	S
			1	2	3	4
5	6	7	8	9	10	11
12	13	14	15	16	17	18
19	20	21	22	23	24	25
26	27	28	29	30	31	

Today's Bible Reading:

LEVITICUS 21–22; MARK 6:1–13; PSALM 44

Neither shall ye profane my holy name; but I will be hallowed among the children of Israel: I am the LORD which hallow you, that brought you out of the land of Egypt, to be your God: I am the LORD.
LEVITICUS 22:32–33

Notice the refrain that often punctuates the end of a point of the Law through Leviticus—"I am the Lord." There didn't need to be any other justification for why the Israelites were to follow the laws set forth. There doesn't need to be any other justification for why we ought to follow the commands and guidance of God today. The fact that the one giving the commands is the perfectly holy almighty God is reason enough to follow Him wholeheartedly.

TOP 3 PRIORITIES:

- ☐ ....
- ☐ ....
- ☐ ....

SCHEDULE/TO-DO LIST:

- ☐ ....
- ☐ ....
- ☐ ....
- ☐ ....

REFLECTIONS ON TODAY'S BIBLE READING

8 glasses a day: ☐ ☐ ☐ ☐ ☐ ☐ ☐ ☐

February

S	M	T	W	T	F	S
			1	2	3	4
5	6	7	8	9	10	11
12	13	14	15	16	17	18
19	20	21	22	23	24	25
26	27	28				

REMEMBER

Today's Bible Reading:

LEVITICUS 23–24; MARK 6:14–29; PSALM 45:1–5

*Six days shall work be done: but the seventh day is the sabbath
of rest, an holy convocation; ye shall do no work therein:
it is the sabbath of the LORD in all your dwellings.*
LEVITICUS 23:3

Though the laws in Leviticus may sometimes seem harsh and tedious, God put them in place for the good of His people. God instituted a Sabbath rest because He knew that as humans, it is essential for our well-being to have a day to rest and recuperate. Do you honor this rest that God has given you? Trust God that He knows what is best for you and strive to joyfully keep the Sabbath.

REFLECTIONS ON TODAY'S BIBLE READING

8 glasses a day:

REMEMBER

TOP 3 PRIORITIES:

SCHEDULE/TO-DO LIST:

March

S	M	T	W	T	F	S
			1	2	3	4
5	6	7	8	9	10	11
12	13	14	15	16	17	18
19	20	21	22	23	24	25
26	27	28	29	30	31	

Today's Bible Reading:

LEVITICUS 25; MARK 6:30–56; PSALM 45:6–12

*And he said unto them, Come ye yourselves apart into a
desert place, and rest a while: for there were many coming
and going, and they had no leisure so much as to eat.*
MARK 6:31

If you tend to feel guilty about taking time to rest in a world that demands so much action, take note that Jesus encouraged His disciples to rest from the trying work of evangelism. Seek out time to rest in God and to find rejuvenation in Him. Then go back out into the world refreshed and ready to continue His work.

TOP 3 PRIORITIES:

- ☐ ....
- ☐ ....
- ☐ ....

SCHEDULE/TO-DO LIST:

- ☐ ....
- ☐ ....
- ☐ ....
- ☐ ....

REFLECTIONS ON TODAY'S BIBLE READING

8 glasses a day: ☐ ☐ ☐ ☐ ☐ ☐ ☐ ☐

March

S	M	T	W	T	F	S
			1	2	3	4
5	6	7	8	9	10	11
12	13	14	15	16	17	18
19	20	21	22	23	24	25
26	27	28	29	30	31	

REMEMBER

Today's Bible Reading:

LEVITICUS 26; MARK 7; PSALM 45:13-17

*He answered and said unto them, Well hath Esaias
prophesied of you hypocrites, as it is written, This people
honoureth me with their lips, but their heart is far from me.*
MARK 7:6

May we not be the kind of people that God could say of, "[They] honoureth me with their lips, but their heart is far from me." Instead, ask God that your heart be so filled with love and adoration of Him that it would overflow into praise and service for His kingdom. May our actions prove our words to be true so that we could be faithful witnesses for Christ.

REFLECTIONS ON TODAY'S BIBLE READING

8 glasses a day:

TOP 3 PRIORITIES:

- ☐ ....
- ☐ ....
- ☐ ....

SCHEDULE/TO-DO LIST:

- ☐ ....
- ☐ ....
- ☐ ....
- ☐ ....

REMEMBER

April

S	M	T	W	T	F	S
						1
2	3	4	5	6	7	8
9	10	11	12	13	14	15
16	17	18	19	20	21	22
23	24	25	26	27	28	29
30						

Today's Bible Reading:

LEVITICUS 27; MARK 8; PSALM 46

*Be still, and know that I am God: I will be exalted among
the heathen, I will be exalted in the earth. The Lord of
hosts is with us; the God of Jacob is our refuge. Selah.*
Psalm 46:10–11

Psalm 46 is one of the most comforting psalms to meditate on in times of suffering. Even when the whole world seems to be coming apart at the seams, you have no reason to fear because God is with you and will never forsake you. Take a moment in the chaos of life to be still and dwell on the truths in this psalm. Know that He is God, that He is in complete control, and that He is your ever-present refuge and strength in times of trouble.

TOP 3 PRIORITIES:

☐ ....
☐ ....
☐ ....

SCHEDULE/TO-DO LIST:

☐ ....
☐ ....
☐ ....
☐ ....

REFLECTIONS ON TODAY'S BIBLE READING

8 glasses a day: ☐ ☐ ☐ ☐ ☐ ☐ ☐ ☐

March

S	M	T	W	T	F	S
			1	2	3	4
5	6	7	8	9	10	11
12	13	14	15	16	17	18
19	20	21	22	23	24	25
26	27	28	29	30	31	

REMEMBER

Today's Bible Reading:

NUMBERS 1–2; MARK 9:1–13; PSALM 47

O clap your hands, all ye people;
shout unto God with the voice of triumph.
PSALM 47:1

Along with the people in Psalm 47, you too can "shout unto God with the voice of triumph." Why? Because God has secured victory over the world, sin, and death. It may feel like the battle is still raging here on earth and in your own life. But in heaven the victor, Christ, sits on His throne orchestrating all history under His reign. So shout for joy and rejoice in the victory that you have in Christ.

REFLECTIONS ON TODAY'S BIBLE READING

TOP 3 PRIORITIES:

☐ ....
☐ ....
☐ ....

SCHEDULE/TO-DO LIST:

☐ ....
☐ ....
☐ ....
☐ ....

8 glasses a day: ☐ ☐ ☐ ☐ ☐ ☐ ☐ ☐

REMEMBER

April

S	M	T	W	T	F	S
						1
2	3	4	5	6	7	8
9	10	11	12	13	14	15
16	17	18	19	20	21	22
23	24	25	26	27	28	29
30						

Today's Bible Reading:

NUMBERS 3; MARK 9:14–50; PSALM 48:1–8

*And straightway the father of the child cried out, and said
with tears, Lord, I believe; help thou mine unbelief.*
MARK 9:24

It's often not until we reach rock bottom in our desperation that we truly understand how much we need God. It's in these moments of candid weakness and vulnerability that we can recognize how small we are and how big God is. God also uses these times to show us how little we really know of Him. Notice how in Mark 9 Jesus doesn't heal the man's son right away. Instead, He waits until the man is entirely sure of his total need of Christ. He even needs help to believe. Don't be ashamed to ask God to help you believe in His love and power. It's through those times of deepest suffering that He lovingly draws you into a more intimate relationship with Him.

TOP 3 PRIORITIES:

- ☐ ....
- ☐ ....
- ☐ ....

SCHEDULE/TO-DO LIST:

- ☐ ....
- ☐ ....
- ☐ ....
- ☐

REFLECTIONS ON TODAY'S BIBLE READING

8 glasses a day: ▯ ▯ ▯ ▯ ▯ ▯ ▯ ▯

March

S	M	T	W	T	F	S
			1	2	3	4
5	6	7	8	9	10	11
12	13	14	15	16	17	18
19	20	21	22	23	24	25
26	27	28	29	30	31	

REMEMBER

Today's Bible Reading:

NUMBERS 4; MARK 10:1–34; PSALM 48:9–14

For this God is our God for ever and ever:
he will be our guide even unto death.
PSALM 48:14

It is a beautiful thing to serve a God who has lived on this earth as a human, has suffered temptation and loss, has died the death of a mortal, and has risen victorious over it all. There is nowhere you can go and nothing you can do that Christ won't be able to guide you through. Christ has even gone before you in death so that you need not fear that dreaded inevitability. He will hold your hand and walk you through into everlasting glory on the other side. He is your God forever and ever.

REFLECTIONS ON TODAY'S BIBLE READING

TOP 3 PRIORITIES:

☐ ....
☐ ....
☐ ....

SCHEDULE/TO-DO LIST:

☐ ....
☐ ....
☐ ....
☐ ....

8 glasses a day: ▢ ▢ ▢ ▢ ▢ ▢ ▢ ▢

REMEMBER

April

S	M	T	W	T	F	S
						1
2	3	4	5	6	7	8
9	10	11	12	13	14	15
16	17	18	19	20	21	22
23	24	25	26	27	28	29
30						

Today's Bible Reading:

NUMBERS 5:1–6:21; MARK 10:35–52; PSALM 49:1–9

And whosoever of you will be the chiefest, shall be servant of all. For even the Son of man came not to be ministered unto, but to minister, and to give his life a ransom for many.
MARK 10:44–45

Christ turned the values and expectations of His society upside down. Instead of the conquering King that the Jews expected, the Messiah came as a lowly servant whose ultimate act on this earth was a cursed death. Instead of raising up an army of courageous men, Christ sought followers who would humbly serve others. His kingdom is one where the attitude of a child is honored and where weakness is used to greater advantage than strength. His ways are still countercultural and still capable of changing lives and moving mountains.

TOP 3 PRIORITIES:

- ☐ ....
- ☐ ....
- ☐ ....

SCHEDULE/TO-DO LIST:

- ☐ ....
- ☐ ....
- ☐ ....
- ☐ ....

REFLECTIONS ON TODAY'S BIBLE READING

8 glasses a day: ☐ ☐ ☐ ☐ ☐ ☐ ☐ ☐

March

S	M	T	W	T	F	S
			1	2	3	4
5	6	7	8	9	10	11
12	13	14	15	16	17	18
19	20	21	22	23	24	25
26	27	28	29	30	31	

REMEMBER

Today's Bible Reading:

NUMBERS 6:22–7:47; MARK 11; PSALM 49:10–20

Like sheep they are laid in the grave; death shall feed on them; and the upright shall have dominion over them in the morning; and their beauty shall consume in the grave from their dwelling. But God will redeem my soul from the power of the grave: for he shall receive me. Selah.
PSALM 49:14–15

For those who don't acknowledge Christ as Lord there will always be a nagging feeling of meaninglessness and futility to life. They may try to ignore this feeling by building for themselves an empire here on earth or by drowning themselves in pleasure. And yet, that gnawing knowledge will always remain. But for those who are in Christ, a far greater reality awaits us than anything this earth can offer. Once our work here is done, the grave is only an entryway into the matchless glory that will receive us in heaven.

REFLECTIONS ON TODAY'S BIBLE READING

8 glasses a day:

TOP 3 PRIORITIES:

- ☐ ....
- ☐ ....
- ☐ ....

SCHEDULE/TO-DO LIST:

- ☐ ....
- ☐ ....
- ☐ ....
- ☐

REMEMBER

April

S	M	T	W	T	F	S
						1
2	3	4	5	6	7	8
9	10	11	12	13	14	15
16	17	18	19	20	21	22
23	24	25	26	27	28	29
30						

Today's Bible Reading:

NUMBERS 7:48–8:4; MARK 12:1–27; PSALM 50:1–15

If I were hungry, I would not tell thee: for the world is mine, and the fulness thereof. . . . Offer unto God thanksgiving; and pay thy vows unto the most High.
PSALM 50:12, 14

The nature of your relationship with God is one that can be hard to comprehend because it is like no other relationship that you have. There is literally nothing that you can offer God that He could not gain on His own. He owns the entire world. So many of our earthly relationships are based on what we can give and get. Our pride and self-sufficiency often leave us feeling uncomfortable if we believe that there is nothing we can give to a relationship. We like to be needed. But with God we have to lay the desire to be needed aside. All we can do is humbly give Him our service and praise.

TOP 3 PRIORITIES:

- ☐ ....
- ☐ ....
- ☐ ....

SCHEDULE/TO-DO LIST:

- ☐ ....
- ☐ ....
- ☐ ....
- ☐ ....

REFLECTIONS ON TODAY'S BIBLE READING

8 glasses a day: ☐ ☐ ☐ ☐ ☐ ☐ ☐ ☐

March

S	M	T	W	T	F	S
			1	2	3	4
5	6	7	8	9	10	11
12	13	14	15	16	17	18
19	20	21	22	23	24	25
26	27	28	29	30	31	

REMEMBER

Today's Bible Reading:

NUMBERS 8:5–9:23; MARK 12:28–44; PSALM 50:16–23

And so it was, when the cloud abode from even unto the morning, and that the cloud was taken up in the morning, then they journeyed: whether it was by day or by night that the cloud was taken up, they journeyed.
NUMBERS 9:21

The Israelites had to live day by day, watching and waiting for the cloud or pillar of fire to move from its place. Once the presence of God moved, they had to follow it without delay. Are you as willing to pack up your life and your comforts to follow God wherever He may lead? We would probably grumble and complain to be forced to live in such limbo. And yet, aren't we only sojourners and nomads on this earth? Beware of getting so attached to the things and places of this world that you would grumble to follow the pillar of fire wherever it may lead.

REFLECTIONS ON TODAY'S BIBLE READING

TOP 3 PRIORITIES:

SCHEDULE/TO-DO LIST:

8 glasses a day:

REMEMBER

April

S	M	T	W	T	F	S
						1
2	3	4	5	6	7	8
9	10	11	12	13	14	15
16	17	18	19	20	21	22
23	24	25	26	27	28	29
30						

Today's Bible Reading:

NUMBERS 10-11; MARK 13:1-8; PSALM 51:1-9

Against thee, thee only, have I sinned, and done
this evil in thy sight: that thou mightest be justified
when thou speakest, and be clear when thou judgest.
PSALM 51:4

In this psalm, David understood the true nature of sin. Every sin is an insult to God and grieves Him deeply. We are often so nonchalant with our sins, imagining that they are pretty much harmless. But Christ didn't die for something inconsequential and harmless. It is important to recognize the weight of each and every sin. Only when we see how abhorrent sin is can we truly come to appreciate the sacrifice Christ made for us.

TOP 3 PRIORITIES:

- ☐ ....
- ☐ ....
- ☐ ....

SCHEDULE/TO-DO LIST:

- ☐ ....
- ☐ ....
- ☐ ....
- ☐ ....

REFLECTIONS ON TODAY'S BIBLE READING

8 glasses a day: ☐ ☐ ☐ ☐ ☐ ☐ ☐ ☐

March

S	M	T	W	T	F	S
			1	2	3	4
5	6	7	8	9	10	11
12	13	14	15	16	17	18
19	20	21	22	23	24	25
26	27	28	29	30	31	

REMEMBER

Today's Bible Reading:

NUMBERS 12–13; MARK 13:9–37; PSALM 51:10–19

*(Now the man Moses was very meek, above all
the men which were upon the face of the earth.)*
NUMBERS 12:3

A fascinating little phrase is tucked into Numbers 12:3–Moses was the meekest man on earth. At first this may seem surprising. Moses was, after all, the leader of a multitude of people, a direct correspondent with God, and someone who had performed miracles. But rather than making him arrogant, the fact that he had seen and spoken with God was the very thing that made him humble. Throughout the Bible an encounter with God never puffs up but inevitably brings people to their knees. Our smallness, inconsequence, and transience is recognized so much more clearly when seen in the radiance of the person of God. No wonder Moses was the meekest man on earth since he knew his God better than any man on earth.

REFLECTIONS ON TODAY'S BIBLE READING

8 glasses a day: ▽ ▽ ▽ ▽ ▽ ▽ ▽ ▽

REMEMBER

TOP 3 PRIORITIES:

- ☐ ....
- ☐ ....
- ☐ ....

SCHEDULE/TO-DO LIST:

- ☐ ....
- ☐ ....
- ☐ ....
- ☐ ....

April

S	M	T	W	T	F	S
						1
2	3	4	5	6	7	8
9	10	11	12	13	14	15
16	17	18	19	20	21	22
23	24	25	26	27	28	29
30						

Today's Bible Reading:

NUMBERS 14; MARK 14:1–31; PSALM 52

If the LORD delight in us, then he will bring us into this land,
and give it us; a land which floweth with milk and honey.
NUMBERS 14:8

Joshua and Caleb had remarkable courage and faith. They believed in the power and faithfulness of God in spite of terrifying enemies and faithless, complaining friends. It would have been easy for them to have conformed to the crowd and sided with the majority. But they had enough faith in God to speak up against the majority. How often do we shy away from speaking up for our beliefs because we're scared? Or maybe we're just not fully convinced that He actually is a promise keeper. Fortunately, our faithlessness does not affect His faithfulness.

TOP 3 PRIORITIES:

- ☐ ....
- ☐ ....
- ☐ ....

SCHEDULE/TO-DO LIST:

- ☐ ....
- ☐ ....
- ☐ ....
- ☐ ....

REFLECTIONS ON TODAY'S BIBLE READING

8 glasses a day: ☐ ☐ ☐ ☐ ☐ ☐ ☐ ☐

March

S	M	T	W	T	F	S
			1	2	3	4
5	6	7	8	9	10	11
12	13	14	15	16	17	18
19	20	21	22	23	24	25
26	27	28	29	30	31	

REMEMBER

Today's Bible Reading:

NUMBERS 15; MARK 14:32–72; PSALM 53

*The fool hath said in his heart, There is no God. Corrupt are they,
and have done abominable iniquity: there is none that doeth good.*
PSALM 53:1

Psalm 53:1 says that they are fools who believe that there is no God. It seems that today's culture is increasingly asserting the belief that those who believe there *is* a God are the foolish ones. And yet, all creation points to a thoughtful, creative engineer. Could it really be that those who find a depth of peace beyond anything this world can offer, those who give their lives for the sake of others and their faith, those whose greatest desire is to please God. . .could it really be that they are the fools? No, those who deprive themselves of a life-giving relationship with God are truly the fools.

REFLECTIONS ON TODAY'S BIBLE READING

TOP 3 PRIORITIES:

SCHEDULE/TO-DO LIST:

8 glasses a day:

REMEMBER

April

S	M	T	W	T	F	S
						1
2	3	4	5	6	7	8
9	10	11	12	13	14	15
16	17	18	19	20	21	22
23	24	25	26	27	28	29
30						

Today's Bible Reading:

NUMBERS 16; MARK 15:1–32; PSALM 54

*Likewise also the chief priests mocking said among themselves
with the scribes, He saved others; himself he cannot save.*
MARK 15:31

Jesus could have silenced the taunts by coming down off the cross or by calling down legions of angels that would have shocked and awed His murderers. Though doing this would likely have converted much of the watching crowd, the story would have inevitably become legend after a few generations. Instead of saving Himself, Christ bore the shame, insults, and utter humiliation to become so much more than a legend. By keeping silent before His false accusers He became a Savior to everlasting generations. God so often doesn't use the flashy, eye-catching techniques we might use to accomplish His will. Instead, He uses the relentless endurance of His servants whose greatest desire is to have His will supersede their own. Christ was clearly the ultimate example of this.

TOP 3 PRIORITIES:

- [ ] ....
- [ ] ....
- [ ] ....

SCHEDULE/TO-DO LIST:

- [ ] ....
- [ ] ....
- [ ] ....
- [ ] ....

REFLECTIONS ON TODAY'S BIBLE READING

8 glasses a day: ▭ ▭ ▭ ▭ ▭ ▭ ▭ ▭

REMEMBER

March

S	M	T	W	T	F	S
				1	2	3	4
5	6	7	8	9	10	11
12	13	14	15	16	17	18
19	20	21	22	23	24	25
26	27	28	29	30	31	

Today's Bible Reading:

NUMBERS 17–18; MARK 15:33–47; PSALM 55

Joseph of Arimathaea, an honourable counsellor, which also waited for the kingdom of God, came, and went in boldly unto Pilate, and craved the body of Jesus.
MARK 15:43

Joseph of Arimathaea was bold enough to align himself with the crucified King when he came to take His body for burial. When the majority of Christ's disciples were in hiding, Joseph was publicly honoring Jesus. This was a risky move on his part. He could have easily been ostracized or worse. But the impact that Christ had on him was great enough to overcome the fear of men. Would you be as bold to align yourself with Someone who was just killed by hateful mobs?

REFLECTIONS ON TODAY'S BIBLE READING

8 glasses a day:

TOP 3 PRIORITIES:

- ☐ ....
- ☐ ....
- ☐ ....

SCHEDULE/TO-DO LIST:

- ☐ ....
- ☐ ....
- ☐ ....
- ☐ ....

REMEMBER

April

S	M	T	W	T	F	S
						1
2	3	4	5	6	7	8
9	10	11	12	13	14	15
16	17	18	19	20	21	22
23	24	25	26	27	28	29
30						

Today's Bible Reading:

NUMBERS 19–20; MARK 16; PSALM 56:1–7

Now when Jesus was risen early the first day of the week, he appeared first to Mary Magdalene, out of whom he had cast seven devils.
MARK 16:9

Even in His resurrection Christ was showing the world His heart for the weak and those without status. The first person He appeared to was not a chief priest or even one of the twelve disciples. He showed Himself first to a woman. In the culture of the day, women were not highly esteemed. But this woman loved her Savior enough to be the first one at the grave very early in the morning. The hearts of those who love Him are so much more precious to Christ than any earthly status.

TOP 3 PRIORITIES:

- [ ] ....
- [ ] ....
- [ ] ....

SCHEDULE/TO-DO LIST:

- [ ] ....
- [ ] ....
- [ ] ....
- [ ] ....

REFLECTIONS ON TODAY'S BIBLE READING

8 glasses a day:

March

S	M	T	W	T	F	S
			1	2	3	4
5	6	7	8	9	10	11
12	13	14	15	16	17	18
19	20	21	22	23	24	25
26	27	28	29	30	31	

REMEMBER

Today's Bible Reading:

NUMBERS 21:1–22:20; LUKE 1:1–25; PSALM 56:8–13

*When I cry unto thee, then shall mine enemies
turn back: this I know; for God is for me.*
PSALM 56:9

Do you believe that God is for you? Or do you believe that maybe He likes you or at least tolerates you when you do what He wants? To believe that God is for you is to have an unshakable confidence that everything that happens in your life is orchestrated by God for your good and His glory. This certainly can be a hard thing to believe during times of personal struggles or heartbreak. But God is for you. And one day, in this life or the next, you'll be able to look back and see the beautiful tapestry that He's woven of your life where each thread of struggle leads to matchless joy.

REFLECTIONS ON TODAY'S BIBLE READING

8 glasses a day:

TOP 3 PRIORITIES:

- ☐ ....
- ☐ ....
- ☐ ....

SCHEDULE/TO-DO LIST:

- ☐ ....
- ☐ ....
- ☐ ....
- ☐

REMEMBER

April

S	M	T	W	T	F	S
						1
2	3	4	5	6	7	8
9	10	11	12	13	14	15
16	17	18	19	20	21	22
23	24	25	26	27	28	29
30						

First Day of Spring

Today's Bible Reading:

NUMBERS 22:21–23:30; LUKE 1:26–56; PSALM 57

And the ass saw me, and turned from me these three times: unless she had turned from me, surely now also I had slain thee, and saved her alive.
NUMBERS 22:33

You never know what seemingly frustrating thing in your life is actually God's way of saving you from harm. In the story of Balaam's donkey in Numbers 22, Balaam was angry at his donkey for continually turning away from the path. Most of us could easily put ourselves in his shoes with his anger building as things continued to not go his way. But the angel of the Lord eventually told him that the very thing he was angry about was what saved his life. An annoying, frustrating, or even very trying situation in life may just be God protecting and guiding you.

TOP 3 PRIORITIES:

☐ ....
☐ ....
☐ ....

SCHEDULE/TO-DO LIST:

☐ ....
☐ ....
☐ ....
☐ ....

REFLECTIONS ON TODAY'S BIBLE READING

8 glasses a day: ☐ ☐ ☐ ☐ ☐ ☐ ☐ ☐

March

S	M	T	W	T	F	S
			1	2	3	4
5	6	7	8	9	10	11
12	13	14	15	16	17	18
19	20	21	22	23	24	25
26	27	28	29	30	31	

REMEMBER

Today's Bible Reading:

NUMBERS 24–25; LUKE 1:57–2:20; PSALM 58

And she brought forth her firstborn son, and wrapped him in swaddling clothes, and laid him in a manger; because there was no room for them in the inn.
LUKE 2:7

God orchestrates history in such an exquisitely unique way. Centuries-old prophecies of a Messiah being born in Bethlehem were fulfilled because of the seemingly mundane act of having to travel for a census. The Savior of the world was born into a world that apparently had no room for Him, forcing Him to be born in a stable. Shepherds, a very lowly class in their culture, were the first to enter the courts of the King. Given the opportunity, it's doubtful that any of us would have written the story of the most important birth in history this way. But in that is the awesome beauty of it all. This is not a man-made story; this is the story of the Creator and Sustainer of the universe.

REFLECTIONS ON TODAY'S BIBLE READING

8 glasses a day:

TOP 3 PRIORITIES:

- [ ]
- [ ]
- [ ]

SCHEDULE/TO-DO LIST:

- [ ]
- [ ]
- [ ]
- [ ]

REMEMBER

April

S	M	T	W	T	F	S
						1
2	3	4	5	6	7	8
9	10	11	12	13	14	15
16	17	18	19	20	21	22
23	24	25	26	27	28	29
30						

Today's Bible Reading:

NUMBERS 26:1–27:11; LUKE 2:21–38; PSALM 59:1–8

Lord, now lettest thou thy servant depart in peace, according to thy word: for mine eyes have seen thy salvation, which thou hast prepared before the face of all people; a light to lighten the Gentiles, and the glory of thy people Israel.
LUKE 2:29–32

God gives His servant Simeon a marvelous blessing to allow him to see the Messiah before he died. Simeon understood the prophecies and plan of God and recognized Jesus for what He was–God's salvation to Israel and the Gentiles. How glorious that he could behold the Savior who would soon bring to fruition all the promises of God that Simeon knew and held to as his hope.

TOP 3 PRIORITIES:

- ☐ ....
- ☐ ....
- ☐ ....

SCHEDULE/TO-DO LIST:

- ☐ ....
- ☐ ....
- ☐ ....
- ☐

REFLECTIONS ON TODAY'S BIBLE READING

8 glasses a day: ☐ ☐ ☐ ☐ ☐ ☐ ☐ ☐

REMEMBER

March

S	M	T	W	T	F	S
			1	2	3	4
5	6	7	8	9	10	11
12	13	14	15	16	17	18
19	20	21	22	23	24	25
26	27	28	29	30	31	

Today's Bible Reading:

NUMBERS 27:12–29:11; LUKE 2:39–52; PSALM 59:9–17

But I will sing of thy power; yea, I will sing aloud of thy mercy in the morning: for thou hast been my defence and refuge in the day of my trouble.
PSALM 59:16

How often do you openly praise God for His power and mercy? He sustains us every day of our lives, and yet we sometimes fail to acknowledge that. We often struggle to praise Him privately in our own hearts for all He's done for us, let alone proclaim aloud His praise to others. No matter what happens in your life, you still have ample reason to praise God at the end of the day.

REFLECTIONS ON TODAY'S BIBLE READING

8 glasses a day:

TOP 3 PRIORITIES:

SCHEDULE/TO-DO LIST:

REMEMBER

April

S	M	T	W	T	F	S
						1
2	3	4	5	6	7	8
9	10	11	12	13	14	15
16	17	18	19	20	21	22
23	24	25	26	27	28	29
30						

Today's Bible Reading:

NUMBERS 29:12–30:16; LUKE 3; PSALM 60:1–5

Which was the son of Enos, which was the son of Seth,
which was the son of Adam, which was the son of God.
LUKE 3:38

What a splendid and inexplicable mystery it is that Jesus was both fully man and fully God when He came to earth. He had a traceable genealogy. He came from a line of humans from which He would have inherited strengths, weaknesses, and physical traits. When God chose to come to earth to dwell among men, He didn't show up with a fancy entrance or a doting entourage proclaiming His deity. Instead, He chose to come as part of a family.

TOP 3 PRIORITIES:

- ☐ ....
- ☐ ....
- ☐ ....

SCHEDULE/TO-DO LIST:

- ☐ ....
- ☐ ....
- ☐ ....
- ☐ ....

REFLECTIONS ON TODAY'S BIBLE READING

8 glasses a day: ☐ ☐ ☐ ☐ ☐ ☐ ☐ ☐

March

S	M	T	W	T	F	S
			1	2	3	4
5	6	7	8	9	10	11
12	13	14	15	16	17	18
19	20	21	22	23	24	25
26	27	28	29	30	31	

REMEMBER

Today's Bible Reading:

NUMBERS 31; LUKE 4; PSALM 60:6-12

Give us help from trouble: for vain is the help of man. Through God we shall do valiantly: for he it is that shall tread down our enemies.
PSALM 60:11–12

Where do you turn first when you are struggling with something? Have you ever had the experience where you realize hours after anxiously working through a problem that you still haven't asked the Lord for help? In this psalm, we're told that the help of man is vain. Your only completely trustworthy source of help is your heavenly Father. While He can (and does) graciously use the people around you to give you sound wisdom and advice, you should still always turn to Him before anyone else with your troubles.

REFLECTIONS ON TODAY'S BIBLE READING

8 glasses a day:

REMEMBER

TOP 3 PRIORITIES:

- [ ] ....
- [ ] ....
- [ ] ....

SCHEDULE/TO-DO LIST:

- [ ] ....
- [ ] ....
- [ ] ....
- [ ]

April

S	M	T	W	T	F	S
						1
2	3	4	5	6	7	8
9	10	11	12	13	14	15
16	17	18	19	20	21	22
23	24	25	26	27	28	29
30						

Today's Bible Reading:

NUMBERS 32–33; LUKE 5:1–16; PSALM 61

*When Simon Peter saw it, he fell down at Jesus' knees,
saying, Depart from me; for I am a sinful man, O Lord.*
LUKE 5:8

Peter truly understood his standing before God. In Luke 5:8, he is so aware of his sinfulness and Jesus' holiness that he asks that Jesus would depart from him. Are we as aware of how filthy our sins are in the light of God's perfection? Or do we generally think we have it pretty well together?

TOP 3 PRIORITIES:

- ☐ ....
- ☐ ....
- ☐ ....

SCHEDULE/TO-DO LIST:

- ☐ ....
- ☐ ....
- ☐ ....
- ☐ ....

REFLECTIONS ON TODAY'S BIBLE READING

8 glasses a day: ☐ ☐ ☐ ☐ ☐ ☐ ☐ ☐

March

S	M	T	W	T	F	S
			1	2	3	4
5	6	7	8	9	10	11
12	13	14	15	16	17	18
19	20	21	22	23	24	25
26	27	28	29	30	31	

REMEMBER

Today's Bible Reading:

NUMBERS 34–36; LUKE 5:17–32; PSALM 62:1–6

He only is my rock and my salvation:
he is my defence; I shall not be moved.
PSALM 62:6

David understood that with God as his refuge he could not be moved. He calls God his rock. This would not have meant a stone or even a boulder but rather a mountain. Just as mountains are unshakably solid, so is God for those who seek refuge in Him. Run to the Rock and hide yourself in His shadow.

REFLECTIONS ON TODAY'S BIBLE READING

8 glasses a day:

TOP 3 PRIORITIES:

- [ ] ....
- [ ] ....
- [ ] ....

SCHEDULE/TO-DO LIST:

- [ ] ....
- [ ] ....
- [ ] ....
- [ ] ....

REMEMBER

April

S	M	T	W	T	F	S
						1
2	3	4	5	6	7	8
9	10	11	12	13	14	15
16	17	18	19	20	21	22
23	24	25	26	27	28	29
30						

Today's Bible Reading:

DEUTERONOMY 1:1–2:25; LUKE 5:33–6:11; PSALM 62:7–12

Yet in this thing ye did not believe the L<small>ORD</small> your God, who went in the way before you, to search you out a place to pitch your tents in, in fire by night, to shew you by what way ye should go, and in a cloud by day.
D<small>EUTERONOMY</small> 1:32–33

Moses rebukes the people for not believing God about the land He had promised them. This was the God who had dwelled with them for the entire journey, showing them the way in a cloud by day and as their light at night. This was the God who had proven Himself over and over again. And yet, they chose fear instead of faith. Is your first reaction to a difficult situation fear or faith? Hasn't God "proven" Himself to you as well?

TOP 3 PRIORITIES:

- ☐ ....
- ☐ ....
- ☐ ....

SCHEDULE/TO-DO LIST:

- ☐ ....
- ☐ ....
- ☐ ....
- ☐

REFLECTIONS ON TODAY'S BIBLE READING

8 glasses a day: ☐ ☐ ☐ ☐ ☐ ☐ ☐ ☐

March

S	M	T	W	T	F	S
			1	2	3	4
5	6	7	8	9	10	11
12	13	14	15	16	17	18
19	20	21	22	23	24	25
26	27	28	29	30	31	

REMEMBER

Today's Bible Reading:

DEUTERONOMY 2:26–4:14; LUKE 6:12–35; PSALM 63:1–5

And he lifted up his eyes on his disciples, and said,
Blessed be ye poor: for yours is the kingdom of God.
LUKE 6:20

Earthly success is not at all synonymous with spiritual success. In His sermon, Jesus called those who are poor, hungry, weeping, and hated by men blessed–hardly attributes that we would use to describe a "successful" life. If someone doesn't fit into our nicely defined version of earthly success, it does not in any way mean that God is not blessing that person. So much can be learned from passionate followers of Christ who use their poverty, hunger, sorrow, and persecution for the glory of their God.

REFLECTIONS ON TODAY'S BIBLE READING

TOP 3 PRIORITIES:

- ☐ ....
- ☐ ....
- ☐ ....

SCHEDULE/TO-DO LIST:

- ☐ ....
- ☐ ....
- ☐ ....
- ☐

8 glasses a day: ☐ ☐ ☐ ☐ ☐ ☐ ☐ ☐

REMEMBER

April

S	M	T	W	T	F	S
						1
2	3	4	5	6	7	8
9	10	11	12	13	14	15
16	17	18	19	20	21	22
23	24	25	26	27	28	29
30						

Today's Bible Reading:

DEUTERONOMY 4:15–5:22; LUKE 6:36–49; PSALM 63:6–11

But if from thence thou shalt seek the LORD thy God, thou shalt find
him, if thou seek him with all thy heart and with all thy soul.
DEUTERONOMY 4:29

God is not a God who makes Himself hard to find. He does not try to hide Himself from us or veil Himself so that we can't know Him. In times when God seems far off or it feels like He's abandoned you, maybe you have not been seeking Him as you need to. He promises to be found by those who seek Him—therefore, you have a 100 percent chance of success when searching to know God.

TOP 3 PRIORITIES:

- ☐ ....
- ☐ ....
- ☐ ....

SCHEDULE/TO-DO LIST:

- ☐ ....
- ☐ ....
- ☐ ....
- ☐ ....

REFLECTIONS ON TODAY'S BIBLE READING

8 glasses a day: ☐ ☐ ☐ ☐ ☐ ☐ ☐ ☐

March

S	M	T	W	T	F	S
			1	2	3	4
5	6	7	8	9	10	11
12	13	14	15	16	17	18
19	20	21	22	23	24	25
26	27	28	29	30	31	

REMEMBER

Today's Bible Reading:

DEUTERONOMY 5:23–7:26; LUKE 7:1–17; PSALM 64:1–5

Now when he came nigh to the gate of the city, behold, there was a dead man carried out, the only son of his mother, and she was a widow: and much people of the city was with her. And when the Lord saw her, he had compassion on her, and said unto her, Weep not.
LUKE 7:12–13

Christ's ministry is defined by so much compassion. His actions were inspired not by a people-pleasing, surface-level compassion but a deep-seated love for people, even people that He didn't know. Pray that God would instill in you the same kind of compassion that Christ so beautifully displayed. In this passage, Jesus very dramatically changed the life of this woman, but even a small act of compassion and kindness has the power to turn a life around.

REFLECTIONS ON TODAY'S BIBLE READING

8 glasses a day:

TOP 3 PRIORITIES:

- [ ] ....
- [ ] ....
- [ ] ....

SCHEDULE/TO-DO LIST:

- [ ] ....
- [ ] ....
- [ ] ....
- [ ]

REMEMBER

April

S	M	T	W	T	F	S
						1
2	3	4	5	6	7	8
9	10	11	12	13	14	15
16	17	18	19	20	21	22
23	24	25	26	27	28	29
30						

Today's Bible Reading:

DEUTERONOMY 8–9; LUKE 7:18–35; PSALM 64:6–10

And thou shalt remember all the way which the LORD thy God led thee these forty years in the wilderness, to humble thee, and to prove thee, to know what was in thine heart, whether thou wouldest keep his commandments, or no.
DEUTERONOMY 8:2

Moses called the people to remember–to remember their trying journey through the wilderness. They were to remember the humbling times, the proving grounds, and the heart-revealing struggles. They were to remember that God was leading them through those times every step of the way. It is a worthwhile endeavor to record the paths that God has led you down. Remember how faithfully He has led you so that you can boldly step into the future entrusting yourself to Him as your guide.

TOP 3 PRIORITIES:

- ☐ ....
- ☐ ....
- ☐ ....

SCHEDULE/TO-DO LIST:

- ☐ ....
- ☐ ....
- ☐ ....
- ☐ ....

REFLECTIONS ON TODAY'S BIBLE READING

8 glasses a day: ☐ ☐ ☐ ☐ ☐ ☐ ☐ ☐

REMEMBER

April

S	M	T	W	T	F	S
						1
2	3	4	5	6	7	8
9	10	11	12	13	14	15
16	17	18	19	20	21	22
23	24	25	26	27	28	29
30						

Today's Bible Reading:

DEUTERONOMY 10–11; LUKE 7:36–8:3; PSALM 65:1–8

Now when the Pharisee which had bidden him saw it, he spake within himself, saying, This man, if he were a prophet, would have known who and what manner of woman this is that toucheth him: for she is a sinner.
Luke 7:39

The irony of Luke 7:39 is almost comic. In his heart the Pharisee was scoffing at Jesus for not knowing that the woman who was showering Him with honor was a sinner. Meanwhile, Jesus not only knew exactly what this woman had done in the past and the repentance that was now in her heart, but He also knew the disrespectful thoughts that the Pharisee was thinking. The Pharisee had grossly underestimated the insight and power of the Man he was dining with.

REFLECTIONS ON TODAY'S BIBLE READING

8 glasses a day:

TOP 3 PRIORITIES:

- ☐ ....
- ☐ ....
- ☐ ....

SCHEDULE/TO-DO LIST:

- ☐ ....
- ☐ ....
- ☐ ....
- ☐

REMEMBER

May

S	M	T	W	T	F	S
	1	2	3	4	5	6
7	8	9	10	11	12	13
14	15	16	17	18	19	20
21	22	23	24	25	26	27
28	29	30	31			

Today's Bible Reading:

DEUTERONOMY 12–13; LUKE 8:4–21; PSALM 65:9–13

*They drop upon the pastures of the wilderness: and the little hills rejoice
on every side. The pastures are clothed with flocks; the valleys also
are covered over with corn; they shout for joy, they also sing.*
PSALM 65:12–13

Have you ever been outside on one of those days where you can almost hear nature praising its Maker? Have you ever seen a sight so heart-wrenchingly gorgeous that you have to start praising Him as well? What a wonderful thing that God has so blessed us by putting His beauty and creativity on full display for our pleasure. May we never take His creation for granted.

TOP 3 PRIORITIES:

- [ ] ....
- [ ] ....
- [ ] ....

SCHEDULE/TO-DO LIST:

- [ ] ....
- [ ] ....
- [ ] ....
- [ ] ....

REFLECTIONS ON TODAY'S BIBLE READING

8 glasses a day: ☐ ☐ ☐ ☐ ☐ ☐ ☐ ☐

REMEMBER

April

S	M	T	W	T	F	S
						1
2	3	4	5	6	7	8
9	10	11	12	13	14	15
16	17	18	19	20	21	22
23	24	25	26	27	28	29
30						

Today's Bible Reading:

DEUTERONOMY 14:1–16:8; LUKE 8:22–39; PSALM 66:1–7

And he said unto them, Where is your faith? And they being afraid wondered, saying one to another, What manner of man is this! for he commandeth even the winds and water, and they obey him.
LUKE 8:25

Are you ever surprised when God does something amazing in your life? The disciples in today's passage were in fearful awe when Jesus calmed the wind and the waves. Christ rebuked them for this, asking them, "Where is your faith?" Why is it that we are sometimes surprised when we see God's goodness in our lives? Is our faith so weak or our knowledge of God so limited that we doubt His power and love?

REFLECTIONS ON TODAY'S BIBLE READING

8 glasses a day: ▢ ▢ ▢ ▢ ▢ ▢ ▢ ▢

REMEMBER

TOP 3 PRIORITIES:

☐ ....
☐ ....
☐ ....

SCHEDULE/TO-DO LIST:

☐ ....
☐ ....
☐ ....
☐

May

S	M	T	W	T	F	S
	1	2	3	4	5	6
7	8	9	10	11	12	13
14	15	16	17	18	19	20
21	22	23	24	25	26	27
28	29	30	31			

Passover begins at Sundown

Today's Bible Reading:

DEUTERONOMY 16:9–18:22; LUKE 8:40–56; PSALM 66:8–15

And her spirit came again, and she arose straightway:
and he commanded to give her meat.
LUKE 8:55

Today's passage in Luke is a lovely example of how God uses both miraculous and ordinary means to complete His work. Jesus miraculously healed the girl, but then He instructed her parents to give her something to eat. This seems like an oddly mundane thing to instruct them to do after He just performed the phenomenal feat of bringing her back from the dead. But we shouldn't be surprised when God uses ordinary means to advance His kingdom.

TOP 3 PRIORITIES:

- ☐ ....
- ☐ ....
- ☐ ....

SCHEDULE/TO-DO LIST:

- ☐ ....
- ☐ ....
- ☐ ....
- ☐ ....

REFLECTIONS ON TODAY'S BIBLE READING

8 glasses a day: ☐ ☐ ☐ ☐ ☐ ☐ ☐ ☐

April

S	M	T	W	T	F	S
						1
2	3	4	5	6	7	8
9	10	11	12	13	14	15
16	17	18	19	20	21	22
23	24	25	26	27	28	29
30						

REMEMBER

Today's Bible Reading:

DEUTERONOMY 19:1–21:9; LUKE 9:1–22; PSALM 66:16–20

And shall say unto them, Hear, O Israel, ye approach this day unto battle against your enemies: let not your hearts faint, fear not, and do not tremble, neither be ye terrified because of them; for the Lord your God is he that goeth with you, to fight for you against your enemies, to save you.
DEUTERONOMY 20:3–4

Though the majority of us aren't facing enemy armies on a daily basis, we still have battles to fight nearly every day. Some may be more difficult than others, but we all at some point need courage to face the next step in life. Go forward with confidence knowing that it is God who fights for you. Fear not, for the all-powerful God is on your side.

REFLECTIONS ON TODAY'S BIBLE READING

8 glasses a day:

TOP 3 PRIORITIES:

SCHEDULE/TO-DO LIST:

REMEMBER

May

S	M	T	W	T	F	S
	1	2	3	4	5	6
7	8	9	10	11	12	13
14	15	16	17	18	19	20
21	22	23	24	25	26	27
28	29	30	31			

Today's Bible Reading:

DEUTERONOMY 21:10–23:8; LUKE 9:23–42; PSALM 67

God be merciful unto us, and bless us; and cause his face to shine upon us; Selah.
That thy way may be known upon earth, thy saving health among all nations.
PSALM 67:1–2

We all certainly want God to bless us. But why do we want Him to bless us? Merely for our own good, comfort, or security? In today's psalm, the author asked to be blessed so that others may know of the greatness of God. Use the blessings that God has bestowed on you to talk of and magnify Him. Strive to always be enthusiastic to speak of God and all that He has done for you so that others may be blessed by Him as well.

TOP 3 PRIORITIES:

- ☐ ....
- ☐ ....
- ☐ ....

SCHEDULE/TO-DO LIST:

- ☐ ....
- ☐ ....
- ☐ ....
- ☐ ....

REFLECTIONS ON TODAY'S BIBLE READING

8 glasses a day: ☐ ☐ ☐ ☐ ☐ ☐ ☐ ☐

April

S	M	T	W	T	F	S
						1
2	3	4	5	6	7	8
9	10	11	12	13	14	15
16	17	18	19	20	21	22
23	24	25	26	27	28	29
30						

REMEMBER

Today's Bible Reading:

DEUTERONOMY 23:9–25:19; LUKE 9:43–62; PSALM 68:1–6

A father of the fatherless, and a judge of the widows, is God in his holy habitation. God setteth the solitary in families: he bringeth out those which are bound with chains: but the rebellious dwell in a dry land.
PSALM 68:5–6

God is a relational God. So much so that even in His own person He is not one but three. It's no wonder, then, that He feels so strongly for the orphan, the widow, and those who don't belong anywhere. His heart for these people is so apparent throughout all of scripture. He is the Father to those who have none and the protector of the widow. He places those without a home into families. If God is so concerned about these children of His, shouldn't we be as well? And in times when you feel as though you don't belong anywhere, remember that God is always by your side as your loving Father.

REFLECTIONS ON TODAY'S BIBLE READING

TOP 3 PRIORITIES:

- [ ] ....
- [ ] ....
- [ ] ....

SCHEDULE/TO-DO LIST:

- [ ] ....
- [ ] ....
- [ ] ....
- [ ]

8 glasses a day:

REMEMBER

May

S	M	T	W	T	F	S
	1	2	3	4	5	6
7	8	9	10	11	12	13
14	15	16	17	18	19	20
21	22	23	24	25	26	27
28	29	30	31			

Today's Bible Reading:

DEUTERONOMY 26:1–28:14; LUKE 10:1–20; PSALM 68:7–14

Notwithstanding in this rejoice not, that the spirits are subject unto you;
but rather rejoice, because your names are written in heaven.
LUKE 10:20

Jesus presents an interesting challenge in today's passage. He adjured the disciples to rejoice, not in the power that they had through Him but in the fact that their names were written in the book of life. How often do we rejoice in earthly pursuits or successes and forget that the single most important thing for which to be grateful is our salvation? While we absolutely should rejoice in the gifts that God has given us on earth, it would benefit us to think more often on the greatest gift of all that God has given us—eternal life through His Son.

TOP 3 PRIORITIES:

- ☐ ....
- ☐ ....
- ☐ ....

SCHEDULE/TO-DO LIST:

- ☐ ....
- ☐ ....
- ☐ ....
- ☐ ....

REFLECTIONS ON TODAY'S BIBLE READING

8 glasses a day: ☐ ☐ ☐ ☐ ☐ ☐ ☐ ☐

REMEMBER

April

S	M	T	W	T	F	S
						1
2	3	4	5	6	7	8
9	10	11	12	13	14	15
16	17	18	19	20	21	22
23	24	25	26	27	28	29
30						

Today's Bible Reading:

DEUTERONOMY 28:15–68; LUKE 10:21–37; PSALM 68:15–19

Blessed be the Lord, who daily loadeth us with benefits,
even the God of our salvation. Selah.
Psalm 68:19

The Lord "daily loadeth us with benefits." What marvelous imagery that is. It implies that the blessings that God gives us on a daily basis are so bountiful as to almost be too much to carry. Our lives overflowing with the goodness of God. Take a moment to ponder and write down some of the benefits that God has given you in the past week.

REFLECTIONS ON TODAY'S BIBLE READING

8 glasses a day:

TOP 3 PRIORITIES:

SCHEDULE/TO-DO LIST:

REMEMBER

May

S	M	T	W	T	F	S
	1	2	3	4	5	6
7	8	9	10	11	12	13
14	15	16	17	18	19	20
21	22	23	24	25	26	27
28	29	30	31			

Today's Bible Reading:

DEUTERONOMY 29–30; LUKE 10:38–11:23; PSALM 68:20–27

I call heaven and earth to record this day against you, that I have set before you life and death, blessing and cursing: therefore choose life, that both thou and thy seed may live.
DEUTERONOMY 30:19

Just like the Israelites, every day we are faced with a choice: Will we choose death and a curse or life and a blessing. The choice seems simple enough–as Moses said, choose life. And yet, don't we often choose death when we continually go back to old patterns of sinful thought or behavior? We purposefully neglect our life-giving time with God for other worthless pursuits. Think about ways in which you can choose life on a daily basis, and then wait for the beautiful ways in which God will pour that abundant life into you.

TOP 3 PRIORITIES:

- ☐ ....
- ☐ ....
- ☐ ....

SCHEDULE/TO-DO LIST:

- ☐ ....
- ☐ ....
- ☐ ....
- ☐ ....

REFLECTIONS ON TODAY'S BIBLE READING

8 glasses a day: ☐ ☐ ☐ ☐ ☐ ☐ ☐ ☐

REMEMBER

April

S	M	T	W	T	F	S
						1
2	3	4	5	6	7	8
9	10	11	12	13	14	15
16	17	18	19	20	21	22
23	24	25	26	27	28	29
30						

Today's Bible Reading:

DEUTERONOMY 31:1–32:22; LUKE 11:24–36; PSALM 68:28–35

Be strong and of a good courage, fear not, nor be afraid of them: for the LORD thy God, he it is that doth go with thee; he will not fail thee, nor forsake thee.
DEUTERONOMY 31:6

Moses spoke such beautiful words to the Israelites before his death. He encouraged them to be courageous because God would go with them and would never fail or forsake them. You serve the same God today. He will never fail you, forsake you, or leave your side. How can you be confident that this is true? Because He forsook His own Son so that He would never have to turn His face from you. What a humbling and glorious truth. There is no one who can be trusted more fully than a God who has sacrificed so much to redeem you. So be courageous. Your God will never fail or forsake you.

REFLECTIONS ON TODAY'S BIBLE READING

8 glasses a day:

TOP 3 PRIORITIES:

SCHEDULE/TO-DO LIST:

REMEMBER

May

S	M	T	W	T	F	S
	1	2	3	4	5	6
7	8	9	10	11	12	13
14	15	16	17	18	19	20
21	22	23	24	25	26	27
28	29	30	31			

Thursday
APRIL 13

Today's Bible Reading:

DEUTERONOMY 32:23–33:29; LUKE 11:37–54; PSALM 69:1–9

Save me, O God; for the waters are come in unto my soul.
PSALM 69:1

The Bible is an incredibly attainable book. It's filled with stories of people we can relate to–it's not filled with stories of perfect human beings whose faith is so strong that they never struggle or doubt God. Psalm 69 is just one example of a child of God in deep, overwhelming turmoil. Don't ever be afraid or ashamed to cry out to God in this way. Your faith or standing with Him is not lessened because you feel like the waters are encompassing you and you desperately need His help. Take courage from these very real humans in the Bible and speak to God with as much candor as they did.

TOP 3 PRIORITIES:

- ☐ ....
- ☐ ....
- ☐ ....

SCHEDULE/TO-DO LIST:

- ☐ ....
- ☐ ....
- ☐ ....
- ☐ ....

REFLECTIONS ON TODAY'S BIBLE READING

8 glasses a day: ☐ ☐ ☐ ☐ ☐ ☐ ☐ ☐

April

S	M	T	W	T	F	S
						1
2	3	4	5	6	7	8
9	10	11	12	13	14	15
16	17	18	19	20	21	22
23	24	25	26	27	28	29
30						

REMEMBER

Today's Bible Reading:

DEUTERONOMY 34–JOSHUA 2; LUKE 12:1–15; PSALM 69:10–17

And I say unto you my friends, Be not afraid of them that kill the body, and after that have no more that they can do. But I will forewarn you whom ye shall fear: fear him, which after he hath killed hath power to cast into hell; yea, I say unto you, Fear him.
LUKE 12:4–5

Luke 12:4–5 may sound like a threat at first glance. But in these words of Christ is actually glorious comfort. In the whole scheme of eternity, we really have nothing to fear from man. And for those who are in Christ, we have nothing to fear from God because we have already been adopted into His family and redeemed for eternal life in heaven. Therefore, we have nothing to fear at all because, in the end, all man can do is hasten us on to a beautiful eternity with God in glory.

REFLECTIONS ON TODAY'S BIBLE READING

TOP 3 PRIORITIES:

-
-
-

SCHEDULE/TO-DO LIST:

-
-
-
-

8 glasses a day:

REMEMBER

May

S	M	T	W	T	F	S
	1	2	3	4	5	6
7	8	9	10	11	12	13
14	15	16	17	18	19	20
21	22	23	24	25	26	27
28	29	30	31			

Saturday
APRIL 15

Today's Bible Reading:

JOSHUA 3:1–5:12; LUKE 12:16–40; PSALM 69:18–28

And Joshua said unto the people, Sanctify yourselves:
for to morrow the Lord will do wonders among you.
JOSHUA 3:5

The faith of Joshua in this verse is so inspiring. He didn't tell the people to sanctify themselves just in case God decided to do something amazing. He didn't tell the people to hope and pray that God would show up. No, he told them to sanctify themselves because God *will* do wonders tomorrow. There is no doubting or second-guessing. Joshua knew His God. He knew Him to be an absolutely faithful promise keeper.

TOP 3 PRIORITIES:

- ☐ ....
- ☐ ....
- ☐ ....

SCHEDULE/TO-DO LIST:

- ☐ ....
- ☐ ....
- ☐ ....
- ☐ ....

REFLECTIONS ON TODAY'S BIBLE READING

8 glasses a day: ⬛ ⬛ ⬛ ⬛ ⬛ ⬛ ⬛ ⬛

REMEMBER

April

S	M	T	W	T	F	S
						1
2	3	4	5	6	7	8
9	10	11	12	13	14	15
16	17	18	19	20	21	22
23	24	25	26	27	28	29
30						

Today's Bible Reading:

JOSHUA 5:13–7:26; LUKE 12:41–48; PSALM 69:29–36

Blessed is that servant, whom his lord when he cometh shall find so doing.
LUKE 12:43

Do you live every day in anticipation of Christ's coming? Or do you put off ministry and service for God's kingdom, reasoning that you'll do that when you have more time in the future? Our time on earth is the only chance we'll get to share Christ with others. It's the only chance we have to serve the needy and hurting. Don't wait for this time to pass. Live for Christ's kingdom and His coming today and every day.

REFLECTIONS ON TODAY'S BIBLE READING

8 glasses a day:

TOP 3 PRIORITIES:

- ☐ ....
- ☐ ....
- ☐ ....

SCHEDULE/TO-DO LIST:

- ☐ ....
- ☐ ....
- ☐ ....
- ☐ ....

REMEMBER

May

S	M	T	W	T	F	S
	1	2	3	4	5	6
7	8	9	10	11	12	13
14	15	16	17	18	19	20
21	22	23	24	25	26	27
28	29	30	31			

Today's Bible Reading:

JOSHUA 8–9; LUKE 12:49–59; PSALM 70

Suppose ye that I am come to give peace on earth?
I tell you, Nay; but rather division.
LUKE 12:51

Christ told His disciples that He did not come to bring peace but division. This is not exactly a heartwarming concept. But it can certainly be encouraging for you if you are facing opposition simply because you align yourself with Christ. Christ promised that where He was and where He was proclaimed there would be resistance. Sometimes facing opposition for the sake of Christ is a sign that you are doing exactly what you should be doing and following faithfully in the steps of Jesus who went before you.

TOP 3 PRIORITIES:

- ☐ ....
- ☐ ....
- ☐ ....

SCHEDULE/TO-DO LIST:

- ☐ ....
- ☐ ....
- ☐ ....
- ☐ ....

REFLECTIONS ON TODAY'S BIBLE READING

8 glasses a day: ☐ ☐ ☐ ☐ ☐ ☐ ☐ ☐

REMEMBER

April

S	M	T	W	T	F	S
						1
2	3	4	5	6	7	8
9	10	11	12	13	14	15
16	17	18	19	20	21	22
23	24	25	26	27	28	29
30						

Today's Bible Reading:

JOSHUA 10:1–11:15; LUKE 13:1–21; PSALM 71:1–6

For thou art my hope, O Lord GOD:
thou art my trust from my youth.
PSALM 71:5

Where is your hope found? In your job? Family? Financial security? Social status? In today's psalm, the author wrote that his hope is grounded firmly in his Lord. Hope and trust in God and you won't be disappointed. This certainly doesn't mean that hoping in God is a way to avoid hardships and struggles. Instead, God will prove His trustworthiness through those times so that you can learn to hope in Him all the more.

REFLECTIONS ON TODAY'S BIBLE READING

8 glasses a day:

TOP 3 PRIORITIES:

- [ ] ....
- [ ] ....
- [ ] ....

SCHEDULE/TO-DO LIST:

- [ ] ....
- [ ] ....
- [ ] ....
- [ ] ....

REMEMBER

May

S	M	T	W	T	F	S
	1	2	3	4	5	6
7	8	9	10	11	12	13
14	15	16	17	18	19	20
21	22	23	24	25	26	27
28	29	30	31			

Today's Bible Reading:

JOSHUA 11:16–13:33; LUKE 13:22–35; PSALM 71:7–16

*But I will hope continually, and will
yet praise thee more and more.*
PSALM 71:14

The resilience of those who truly know God is remarkable. We see examples of this all through the Bible in God's prophets, disciples, apostles, and followers. In today's passage we see it in David. In this psalm, his life situation does not sound like anything to be happy about—even his enemies thought that God had forsaken him. And yet, he continued to hope in God, praise Him, and speak of His righteousness. Only the Lord can grant this kind of strength and perseverance in His children.

TOP 3 PRIORITIES:

- ☐ ....
- ☐ ....
- ☐ ....

SCHEDULE/TO-DO LIST:

- ☐ ....
- ☐ ....
- ☐ ....
- ☐ ....

REFLECTIONS ON TODAY'S BIBLE READING

8 glasses a day: ☐ ☐ ☐ ☐ ☐ ☐ ☐ ☐

April

S	M	T	W	T	F	S
						1
2	3	4	5	6	7	8
9	10	11	12	13	14	15
16	17	18	19	20	21	22
23	24	25	26	27	28	29
30						

REMEMBER

Today's Bible Reading:

JOSHUA 14–16; LUKE 14:1–15; PSALM 71:17–21

Thou, which hast shewed me great and sore troubles, shalt quicken me again, and shalt bring me up again from the depths of the earth. Thou shalt increase my greatness, and comfort me on every side.
PSALM 71:20–21

At times God may bring you through hard trials and "sore troubles." But you can be as confident as David was in this psalm that God will raise you up again from the depths of despair. David used beautiful imagery of God comforting him on every side–His comfort surrounds and protects His people. Even in (and often *especially* in) the darkest moments, you can feel His comfort and strength sustaining you.

REFLECTIONS ON TODAY'S BIBLE READING

8 glasses a day:

TOP 3 PRIORITIES:

SCHEDULE/TO-DO LIST:

REMEMBER

May

S	M	T	W	T	F	S
	1	2	3	4	5	6
7	8	9	10	11	12	13
14	15	16	17	18	19	20
21	22	23	24	25	26	27
28	29	30	31			

Friday
APRIL 21

Today's Bible Reading:

JOSHUA 17:1–19:16; LUKE 14:16–35; PSALM 71:22–24

*So likewise, whosoever he be of you that forsaketh
not all that he hath, he cannot be my disciple.*
LUKE 14:33

Would you qualify to be one of Jesus' disciples? It's a sobering question. Jesus said that only those who forsake everything they have can be His disciples. While God is not asking you to all of a sudden give away everything you have, would you be willing to if He did ask? What if your earthly comforts and treasures were taken away? How would you react? If your faith in Jesus is not dependent on earthly possessions and relationships, then you are worthy of being His disciple. Seek to know Him better so that you will have this kind of faith.

TOP 3 PRIORITIES:

- ☐ ....
- ☐ ....
- ☐ ....

SCHEDULE/TO-DO LIST:

- ☐ ....
- ☐ ....
- ☐ ....
- ☐ ....

REFLECTIONS ON TODAY'S BIBLE READING

8 glasses a day: ☐ ☐ ☐ ☐ ☐ ☐ ☐ ☐

April

S	M	T	W	T	F	S
						1
2	3	4	5	6	7	8
9	10	11	12	13	14	15
16	17	18	19	20	21	22
23	24	25	26	27	28	29
30						

REMEMBER

Today's Bible Reading:

JOSHUA 19:17–21:42; LUKE 15:1–10; PSALM 72:1–11

*Likewise, I say unto you, there is joy in the presence
of the angels of God over one sinner that repenteth.*
LUKE 15:10

When someone comes to know the Lord, it is no small thing in heaven. In fact, Jesus declared that the angels rejoice when someone prays to receive Christ. What a marvelous thing that heaven rejoiced when you were adopted into God's family. You are a valuable part of His kingdom, worth being celebrated.

REFLECTIONS ON TODAY'S BIBLE READING

8 glasses a day:

TOP 3 PRIORITIES:

SCHEDULE/TO-DO LIST:

REMEMBER

May

S	M	T	W	T	F	S
	1	2	3	4	5	6
7	8	9	10	11	12	13
14	15	16	17	18	19	20
21	22	23	24	25	26	27
28	29	30	31			

Today's Bible Reading:

JOSHUA 21:43–22:34; LUKE 15:11–32; PSALM 72:12–20

*There failed not ought of any good thing which the L*ORD *had spoken unto the house of Israel; all came to pass.*
JOSHUA 21:45

All of God's promises will come to pass. No good gift from Him will fail. God does not promise us things to manipulate, control, or distract. He promises us good things because He loves us in a way that we can't even comprehend. It is an entirely selfless, self-sacrificing love, the kind which we cannot fully know on earth apart from Him. So cling to His promises as truth, and look forward to their fulfillment. Just as He was faithful to the Israelites, He will be faithful to you.

TOP 3 PRIORITIES:

- ☐ ....
- ☐ ....
- ☐ ....

SCHEDULE/TO-DO LIST:

- ☐ ....
- ☐ ....
- ☐ ....
- ☐ ....

REFLECTIONS ON TODAY'S BIBLE READING

8 glasses a day:

REMEMBER

April

S	M	T	W	T	F	S
						1
2	3	4	5	6	7	8
9	10	11	12	13	14	15
16	17	18	19	20	21	22
23	24	25	26	27	28	29
30						

Today's Bible Reading:

JOSHUA 23-24; LUKE 16:1-18; PSALM 73:1-9

*If therefore ye have not been faithful in the unrighteous mammon,
who will commit to your trust the true riches?*
LUKE 16:11

It's easy to compartmentalize our lives into tidy little boxes that separate the spiritual from the everyday and earthly. Today's passage in Luke is an excellent reminder that we need to be faithful in every aspect of our lives whether or not it seems to directly relate to the kingdom. Honor God in the way you treat your family, perform at your job or school, do your finances, etc. Be faithful in these things so that you can be entrusted with far more precious riches.

REFLECTIONS ON TODAY'S BIBLE READING

TOP 3 PRIORITIES:

- [ ] ....
- [ ] ....
- [ ] ....

SCHEDULE/TO-DO LIST:

- [ ] ....
- [ ] ....
- [ ] ....
- [ ] ....

8 glasses a day: ☐ ☐ ☐ ☐ ☐ ☐ ☐ ☐

REMEMBER

May

S	M	T	W	T	F	S
	1	2	3	4	5	6
7	8	9	10	11	12	13
14	15	16	17	18	19	20
21	22	23	24	25	26	27
28	29	30	31			

Today's Bible Reading:

JUDGES 1–2; LUKE 16:19–17:10; PSALM 73:10–20

Until I went into the sanctuary of God;
then understood I their end.
PSALM 73:17

The first part of Psalm 73 is an anxiety-ridden, somewhat cynical view of the world. David was so overcome with the undeserved prosperity of the wicked that he began to doubt whether following a righteous path was worthwhile. He became so worked up that his thoughts were too painful to even consider. But the turning point of the psalm comes in verse 17–"Until I went into the sanctuary of God. . . ." When you are anxious and overwhelmed, run to God's sanctuary. Don't neglect your time with His people, and savor the times in His courts in your own personal devotions. Being in God's presence fixes cynical perspectives and soothes anxiety.

TOP 3 PRIORITIES:

- [ ] ....
- [ ] ....
- [ ] ....

SCHEDULE/TO-DO LIST:

- [ ] ....
- [ ] ....
- [ ] ....
- [ ] ....

REFLECTIONS ON TODAY'S BIBLE READING

8 glasses a day: ▢ ▢ ▢ ▢ ▢ ▢ ▢ ▢

REMEMBER

April

S	M	T	W	T	F	S
						1
2	3	4	5	6	7	8
9	10	11	12	13	14	15
16	17	18	19	20	21	22
23	24	25	26	27	28	29
30						

Today's Bible Reading:

JUDGES 3–4; LUKE 17:11–37; PSALM 73:21–28

*And one of them, when he saw that he was healed, turned back,
and with a loud voice glorified God, and fell down on his face at
his feet, giving him thanks: and he was a Samaritan.*
LUKE 17:15–16

Why did the one former leper return? He returned because he knew where he had been and he knew that God was solely responsible for his present state. Are we as aware of who we are without God's grace? If we were, we would probably be as grateful as the man in today's passage. We, too, would fall at His feet so overcome with what God has done in our lives.

REFLECTIONS ON TODAY'S BIBLE READING

8 glasses a day:

TOP 3 PRIORITIES:

- ☐ ....
- ☐ ....
- ☐ ....

SCHEDULE/TO-DO LIST:

- ☐ ....
- ☐ ....
- ☐ ....
- ☐ ....

REMEMBER

May

S	M	T	W	T	F	S
	1	2	3	4	5	6
7	8	9	10	11	12	13
14	15	16	17	18	19	20
21	22	23	24	25	26	27
28	29	30	31			

Today's Bible Reading:

JUDGES 5:1–6:24; LUKE 18:1–17; PSALM 74:1–3

And the publican, standing afar off, would not lift up so much as his eyes unto heaven, but smote upon his breast, saying, God be merciful to me a sinner.
LUKE 18:13

The publican in today's passage had the right perspective on who he was and who God is. His unworthiness to stand in the presence of a perfectly holy God was painfully apparent to him. All he could do was humbly beg for God's mercy. In our culture that praises the bold, unhindered, and self-sufficient, the publican's behavior may seem weak. But actually, it is through this kind of weakness that we become more powerful than we could imagine. For when we empty ourselves before God, He fills us up fully with His own strength.

TOP 3 PRIORITIES:

- [ ] ....
- [ ] ....
- [ ] ....

SCHEDULE/TO-DO LIST:

- [ ] ....
- [ ] ....
- [ ] ....
- [ ] ....

REFLECTIONS ON TODAY'S BIBLE READING

8 glasses a day:

April

S	M	T	W	T	F	S
						1
2	3	4	5	6	7	8
9	10	11	12	13	14	15
16	17	18	19	20	21	22
23	24	25	26	27	28	29
30						

REMEMBER

Today's Bible Reading:

JUDGES 6:25–7:25; LUKE 18:18–43; PSALM 74:4–11

And the Lord said unto Gideon, The people that are with thee are too many for me to give the Midianites into their hands, lest Israel vaunt themselves against me, saying, Mine own hand hath saved me.
Judges 7:2

God knows our natures so well. He was fully aware that He had to make Gideon's army absurdly small and weak in order for them to understand that the victory was only from God. How often do we take credit for all our successes in life? When things are going well, we pat ourselves on the back for a job well done. It's often because of our assumed self-sufficiency that God will bring challenges into our lives that force us to realize that we are sustained through Him and Him alone.

REFLECTIONS ON TODAY'S BIBLE READING

TOP 3 PRIORITIES:

- ☐ ....
- ☐ ....
- ☐ ....

SCHEDULE/TO-DO LIST:

- ☐ ....
- ☐ ....
- ☐ ....
- ☐

8 glasses a day: ☐ ☐ ☐ ☐ ☐ ☐ ☐ ☐

REMEMBER

May

S	M	T	W	T	F	S
	1	2	3	4	5	6
7	8	9	10	11	12	13
14	15	16	17	18	19	20
21	22	23	24	25	26	27
28	29	30	31			

Today's Bible Reading:

JUDGES 8:1–9:23; LUKE 19:1–28; PSALM 74:12–17

And Zacchaeus stood, and said unto the Lord: Behold, Lord, the half of my goods I give to the poor; and if I have taken any thing from any man by false accusation, I restore him fourfold.
LUKE 19:8

Zacchaeus could attest to the fact that encounters with Christ change people. Zacchaeus was a selfish criminal who stole from those he levied taxes from. In the course of his career he would have hurt many families for his own comfort and leisure. But his heart and lifestyle changed when Christ sought him out and came to his house. Don't ever imagine that such a self-absorbed and cruel sinner is past the saving power of Jesus. Christ came to earth to seek out the lost. He continues on that mission today.

TOP 3 PRIORITIES:

- ☐ ....
- ☐ ....
- ☐ ....

SCHEDULE/TO-DO LIST:

- ☐ ....
- ☐ ....
- ☐ ....
- ☐ ....

REFLECTIONS ON TODAY'S BIBLE READING

8 glasses a day: ☐ ☐ ☐ ☐ ☐ ☐ ☐ ☐

REMEMBER

April

S	M	T	W	T	F	S
						1
2	3	4	5	6	7	8
9	10	11	12	13	14	15
16	17	18	19	20	21	22
23	24	25	26	27	28	29
30						

Today's Bible Reading:

JUDGES 9:24–10:18; LUKE 19:29–48; PSALM 74:18–23

*And they that were sent went their way,
and found even as he had said unto them.*
LUKE 19:32

The Gospel writers recorded this story of finding a donkey right where Christ had told them it would be. It may seem like an insignificant little tidbit to include in the stories of when God walked on earth. But it records a valuable story of how God ordains every detail of our lives. Even the minute details of your life matter to your God.

REFLECTIONS ON TODAY'S BIBLE READING

8 glasses a day:

TOP 3 PRIORITIES:

- ☐ ....
- ☐ ....
- ☐ ....

SCHEDULE/TO-DO LIST:

- ☐ ....
- ☐ ....
- ☐ ....
- ☐

REMEMBER

May

S	M	T	W	T	F	S
	1	2	3	4	5	6
7	8	9	10	11	12	13
14	15	16	17	18	19	20
21	22	23	24	25	26	27
28	29	30	31			

Today's Bible Reading:

JUDGES 11:1–12:7; LUKE 20:1–26; PSALM 75:1–7

*For promotion cometh neither from the east, nor from
the west, nor from the south. But God is the judge:
he putteth down one, and setteth up another.*
PSALM 75:6–7

God is ultimately the one who promotes or demotes. Therefore, work and live as for the Lord. When your job, homework, or housework seems insignificant or thankless, remember that it is God for whom you work. He's the one who sees your efforts. He will reward you. So continue to labor hard for Him.

TOP 3 PRIORITIES:

- ☐ ....
- ☐ ....
- ☐ ....

SCHEDULE/TO-DO LIST:

- ☐ ....
- ☐ ....
- ☐ ....
- ☐ ....

REFLECTIONS ON TODAY'S BIBLE READING

8 glasses a day: ☐ ☐ ☐ ☐ ☐ ☐ ☐ ☐

REMEMBER

May

S	M	T	W	T	F	S
	1	2	3	4	5	6
7	8	9	10	11	12	13
14	15	16	17	18	19	20
21	22	23	24	25	26	27
28	29	30	31			

Today's Bible Reading:

JUDGES 12:8–14:20; LUKE 20:27–47; PSALM 75:8–10

*Beware of the scribes, which desire to walk in long robes,
and love greetings in the markets, and the highest seats
in the synagogues, and the chief rooms at feasts.*
LUKE 20:46

It's a probing question that should be asked: What are your motives for doing good? Do your good works stem from a desire to be praised or a desire for God to be praised? While God can certainly use deeds done for the wrong motives to His glory, you will be abundantly more blessed when your work comes from a humble desire to faithfully and fully serve your God.

REFLECTIONS ON TODAY'S BIBLE READING

TOP 3 PRIORITIES:
- [ ]
- [ ]
- [ ]

SCHEDULE/TO-DO LIST:
- [ ]
- [ ]
- [ ]
- [ ]

8 glasses a day:

REMEMBER

June

S	M	T	W	T	F	S
				1	2	3
4	5	6	7	8	9	10
11	12	13	14	15	16	17
18	19	20	21	22	23	24
25	26	27	28	29	30	

Today's Bible Reading:

JUDGES 15–16; LUKE 21:1–19; PSALM 76:1–7

And he said, Of a truth I say unto you, that this poor widow hath cast in more than they all: for all these have of their abundance cast in unto the offerings of God: but she of her penury hath cast in all the living that she had.
LUKE 21:3–4

Have you ever put kingdom work on hold because you felt like you didn't have enough to offer? Today's story in Luke completely negates that excuse. The poor widow in this passage gave an offering that by the world's standards was worthless. But by God's standards it was the most valuable offering that she could have given. Fortunately, God's kingdom does not function on the same economy as our worldly kingdoms. So bring your offerings of time, talents, and treasure to Him no matter how insignificant they may seem to you.

TOP 3 PRIORITIES:

- ☐ ....
- ☐ ....
- ☐ ....

SCHEDULE/TO-DO LIST:

- ☐ ....
- ☐ ....
- ☐ ....
- ☐ ....

REFLECTIONS ON TODAY'S BIBLE READING

8 glasses a day: ☐ ☐ ☐ ☐ ☐ ☐ ☐ ☐

REMEMBER

May

S	M	T	W	T	F	S
	1	2	3	4	5	6
7	8	9	10	11	12	13
14	15	16	17	18	19	20
21	22	23	24	25	26	27
28	29	30	31			

Today's Bible Reading:

JUDGES 17–18; LUKE 21:20–22:6; PSALM 76:8-12

Heaven and earth shall pass away:
but my words shall not pass away.
Luke 21:33

This world is entirely transitory, unpredictable, and mortal. You may have painfully experienced firsthand how often things in this life change and how quickly lives, relationships, and status can be extinguished. Life can feel very much like an unmoored sailboat in a vast, choppy ocean. But in God you have the firmest foundation possible. He anchors you securely to Himself and to His plans for you. Even if this entire world were to pass away and slip into oblivion, His Word will remain steadfast. And in His Word we have hope for eternal life that is not affected by the fate of this earth.

REFLECTIONS ON TODAY'S BIBLE READING

TOP 3 PRIORITIES:

- ☐ ....
- ☐ ....
- ☐ ....

SCHEDULE/TO-DO LIST:

- ☐ ....
- ☐ ....
- ☐ ....
- ☐ ....

8 glasses a day: ☐ ☐ ☐ ☐ ☐ ☐ ☐ ☐

REMEMBER

June

S	M	T	W	T	F	S
				1	2	3
4	5	6	7	8	9	10
11	12	13	14	15	16	17
18	19	20	21	22	23	24
25	26	27	28	29	30	

Today's Bible Reading:

JUDGES 19:1–20:23; LUKE 22:7–30; PSALM 77:1–11

> *Hath God forgotten to be gracious? hath he in anger shut up*
> *his tender mercies? Selah. . . . I will remember the works of*
> *the* Lord: *surely I will remember thy wonders of old.*
> Psalm 77:9, 11

We have all (including today's psalmist) been in situations that cause us to question the very goodness and sovereignty of God. But instead of being spiritually nearsighted and writing God off when the here and now isn't going the way you deem it should be, expand your vision to remember His wonders of old. Call to mind the way He has cared for and sustained you (and centuries of His children) in the past. It is likely that the very struggle you're enduring now will later become one that you will look back on to recall God's faithfulness.

TOP 3 PRIORITIES:

- ☐ ....
- ☐ ....
- ☐ ....

SCHEDULE/TO-DO LIST:

- ☐ ....
- ☐ ....
- ☐ ....
- ☐ ....

REFLECTIONS ON TODAY'S BIBLE READING

8 glasses a day: ☐ ☐ ☐ ☐ ☐ ☐ ☐ ☐

May

S	M	T	W	T	F	S
	1	2	3	4	5	6
7	8	9	10	11	12	13
14	15	16	17	18	19	20
21	22	23	24	25	26	27
28	29	30	31			

REMEMBER

Today's Bible Reading:

JUDGES 20:24–21:25; LUKE 22:31–54; PSALM 77:12–20

*Saying, Father, if thou be willing, remove this cup from me:
nevertheless not my will, but thine, be done.*
LUKE 22:42

"Not my will, but thine, be done." This is a remarkably difficult attitude to have even in minor, everyday struggles. We have no problem abiding with God's will when it lines up perfectly with ours. As soon as God's plan veers away from the course that we've set for our lives, we often begin to doubt that He's really got it right after all. It's only through the power of Christ that we can superhumanly bend our will and desire to rest in God's perfect plan for us.

REFLECTIONS ON TODAY'S BIBLE READING

TOP 3 PRIORITIES:

- ☐ ....
- ☐ ....
- ☐ ....

SCHEDULE/TO-DO LIST:

- ☐ ....
- ☐ ....
- ☐ ....
- ☐

8 glasses a day: ☐ ☐ ☐ ☐ ☐ ☐ ☐ ☐

REMEMBER

June

S	M	T	W	T	F	S
				1	2	3
4	5	6	7	8	9	10
11	12	13	14	15	16	17
18	19	20	21	22	23	24
25	26	27	28	29	30	

Today's Bible Reading:

RUTH 1–2; LUKE 22:55–23:25; PSALM 78:1–4

And Peter said, Man, I know not what thou sayest. And immediately, while he yet spake, the cock crew. And the Lord turned, and looked upon Peter. And Peter remembered the word of the Lord, how he had said unto him, Before the cock crow, thou shalt deny me thrice.
LUKE 22:60–61

Do we deny God in our daily lives? Maybe without even consciously realizing it? Maybe a better question is, do we feel the kind of remorse that Peter felt over denying our Lord? Our God is so merciful that even when we deny and disappoint Him time and time again, He will forgive us and not alter His love for us. The frightened, overwhelmed Peter became so courageous in his proclamation of Christ that he was willing even to die for the cause of His Savior. You are never too weak to be out of God's love or plans.

TOP 3 PRIORITIES:

- [ ] ....
- [ ] ....
- [ ] ....

SCHEDULE/TO-DO LIST:

- [ ] ....
- [ ] ....
- [ ] ....
- [ ] ....

REFLECTIONS ON TODAY'S BIBLE READING

8 glasses a day: ▢ ▢ ▢ ▢ ▢ ▢ ▢ ▢

May

S	M	T	W	T	F	S
	1	2	3	4	5	6
7	8	9	10	11	12	13
14	15	16	17	18	19	20
21	22	23	24	25	26	27
28	29	30	31			

REMEMBER

Today's Bible Reading:

RUTH 3-4; LUKE 23:26-24:12; PSALM 78:5-8

And the women her neighbours gave it a name, saying, There is a son born to Naomi; and they called his name Obed: he is the father of Jesse, the father of David.
RUTH 4:17

Ruth beautifully embodied God's pursuit of those outside the nation of Israel and foreshadowed the time when all nations would be included in God's people. Here was this foreigner from a pagan land who ended up as an ancestor of David and, therefore, an ancestor of Christ. The glorious story of God's redemption of people from every tribe and nation was already being threaded into the genealogy of His Son. If you look back at the genealogy of Christ in Matthew 1, you'll notice that only a generation or so before Ruth, Rahab (the harlot from Jericho) was also engrafted into the line of Christ. One can only wonder if Ruth and Rahab may have known each other as foreigners brought into the fold of God's people.

REFLECTIONS ON TODAY'S BIBLE READING

TOP 3 PRIORITIES:

☐ ....
☐ ....
☐ ....

SCHEDULE/TO-DO LIST:

☐ ....
☐ ....
☐ ....
☐

8 glasses a day: ☐ ☐ ☐ ☐ ☐ ☐ ☐ ☐

REMEMBER

June

S	M	T	W	T	F	S
				1	2	3
4	5	6	7	8	9	10
11	12	13	14	15	16	17
18	19	20	21	22	23	24
25	26	27	28	29	30	

Today's Bible Reading:

1 SAMUEL 1:1–2:21; LUKE 24:13–53; PSALM 78:9–16

But Hannah went not up; for she said unto her husband,
I will not go up until the child be weaned, and then I will bring him,
that he may appear before the Lord, and there abide for ever.
1 Samuel 1:22

Hannah had an astonishingly selfless understanding of how Samuel was completely a gift from God. She had begged for a child, and then when God granted her wish, she decided to give Samuel to serve in the temple of God his whole life. This is remarkable. We often grip so tightly to what God has given us freely that we forget where it came from in the first place. But Hannah was so grateful to God that she humbly loosened her grip on this good gift to return her son to the Lord.

TOP 3 PRIORITIES:

- ☐ ....
- ☐ ....
- ☐ ....

SCHEDULE/TO-DO LIST:

- ☐ ....
- ☐ ....
- ☐ ....
- ☐ ....

REFLECTIONS ON TODAY'S BIBLE READING

8 glasses a day: ☐ ☐ ☐ ☐ ☐ ☐ ☐ ☐

May

S	M	T	W	T	F	S
	1	2	3	4	5	6
7	8	9	10	11	12	13
14	15	16	17	18	19	20
21	22	23	24	25	26	27
28	29	30	31			

REMEMBER

Today's Bible Reading:

1 SAMUEL 2:22–4:22; JOHN 1:1–28; PSALM 78:17–24

In the beginning was the Word, and the Word was with God, and the Word was God. . . . And the Word was made flesh, and dwelt among us, (and we beheld his glory, the glory as of the only begotten of the Father,) full of grace and truth.
JOHN 1:1, 14

In the Greek philosophy of the day, the word *Logos* (translated as "Word") carried the connotation of the reason for life. So John very boldly proclaims that the Word, the reason for life, became flesh and dwelled among us. The reason for life is not a philosophy, a job, or a goal that must be attained with effort. Instead, the Logos is a Man. Life finds its deepest fulfillment in relationship with Him. He dwelled with John and now dwells in you.

REFLECTIONS ON TODAY'S BIBLE READING

TOP 3 PRIORITIES:

- ☐ ....
- ☐ ....
- ☐ ....

SCHEDULE/TO-DO LIST:

- ☐ ....
- ☐ ....
- ☐ ....
- ☐

8 glasses a day: ▢ ▢ ▢ ▢ ▢ ▢ ▢ ▢

REMEMBER

June

S	M	T	W	T	F	S
					1	2	3
4	5	6	7	8	9	10
11	12	13	14	15	16	17
18	19	20	21	22	23	24
25	26	27	28	29	30

Today's Bible Reading:

1 SAMUEL 5–7; JOHN 1:29–51; PSALM 78:25–33

*And when they arose early on the morrow morning, behold, Dagon
was fallen upon his face to the ground before the ark of the Lord;
and the head of Dagon and both the palms of his hands were cut
off upon the threshold; only the stump of Dagon was left to him.*
1 Samuel 5:4

The story at the start of 1 Samuel 5 is almost comical as time and time again the city's idol is found on its face in front of the ark of God. But what is not comical at all is the truth demonstrated in this story: No other god is a match for our God. No idol that we may cling to today can stand up to the power of God. All will come crashing down at His feet. Stop holding on to things that can't possibly replace God.

TOP 3 PRIORITIES:

- ☐ ....
- ☐ ....
- ☐ ....

SCHEDULE/TO-DO LIST:

- ☐ ....
- ☐ ....
- ☐ ....
- ☐ ....

REFLECTIONS ON TODAY'S BIBLE READING

8 glasses a day: ☐ ☐ ☐ ☐ ☐ ☐ ☐ ☐

REMEMBER

May

S	M	T	W	T	F	S
	1	2	3	4	5	6
7	8	9	10	11	12	13
14	15	16	17	18	19	20
21	22	23	24	25	26	27
28	29	30	31			

Today's Bible Reading:

1 SAMUEL 8:1–9:26; JOHN 2; PSALM 78:34–41

And Saul answered and said, Am not I a Benjamite, of the smallest of the tribes of Israel? and my family the least of all the families of the tribe of Benjamin? wherefore then speakest thou so to me?
1 SAMUEL 9:21

In 1 Samuel 9:21, Saul tried to counter what Samuel was telling him by explaining to Samuel that he was from the smallest tribe and most insignificant family in Israel. He argued that because of this God couldn't possibly mean to anoint him king. Clearly, God must have made a mistake. Little did Saul know that choosing the most unlikely is God's usual strategy. Time and again, God uses the weak, the small, or the inhibited to do His work. Since power comes solely from Him, He does not need to choose the strong, powerful, or influential to accomplish His will.

REFLECTIONS ON TODAY'S BIBLE READING

8 glasses a day:

TOP 3 PRIORITIES:

- [ ] ....
- [ ] ....
- [ ] ....

SCHEDULE/TO-DO LIST:

- [ ] ....
- [ ] ....
- [ ] ....
- [ ]

REMEMBER

June

S	M	T	W	T	F	S
				1	2	3
4	5	6	7	8	9	10
11	12	13	14	15	16	17
18	19	20	21	22	23	24
25	26	27	28	29	30	

Today's Bible Reading:

1 SAMUEL 9:27–11:15; JOHN 3:1–22; PSALM 78:42–55

And this is the condemnation, that light is come into the world, and men loved darkness rather than light, because their deeds were evil. For every one that doeth evil hateth the light, neither cometh to the light, lest his deeds should be reproved.
JOHN 3:19–20

Don't be surprised if you encounter opposition for the sake of Christ. Sadly, too many in this world love the darkness more than the life-giving Light. It is tragic that someone would prefer to stumble in the darkness than walk in the brilliant light of God. It is your job to shine that light of God into the darkest corners of the world so that because of you others (even if just a few) may learn to bask in the light of the Son.

TOP 3 PRIORITIES:

- [ ] ....
- [ ] ....
- [ ] ....

SCHEDULE/TO-DO LIST:

- [ ] ....
- [ ] ....
- [ ] ....
- [ ] ....

REFLECTIONS ON TODAY'S BIBLE READING

8 glasses a day: ⬜ ⬜ ⬜ ⬜ ⬜ ⬜ ⬜ ⬜

May

S	M	T	W	T	F	S
	1	2	3	4	5	6
7	8	9	10	11	12	13
14	15	16	17	18	19	20
21	22	23	24	25	26	27
28	29	30	31			

REMEMBER

Mother's Day

Today's Bible Reading:

1 SAMUEL 12–13; JOHN 3:23–4:10; PSALM 78:56–66

He gave his people over also unto the sword;
and was wroth with his inheritance.
PSALM 78:62

How could a loving God give His people over to nations that hate them? God is a jealous God. He so desires us to follow Him that He will go to great lengths to make that happen. This is an incredibly good thing for us. Ease and prosperity have a way of making us forget God. Sometimes He has to remind us that our true life source can only be found in Him. And sometimes He must use hard circumstances to actually get through to us. It is, in fact, a sure sign of His love when He rebukes His people. For Him to not care and to allow you to fill your existence with deadening activities devoid of Him would be far, far worse than any trial He will lead you through.

REFLECTIONS ON TODAY'S BIBLE READING

TOP 3 PRIORITIES:

- [ ] ....
- [ ] ....
- [ ] ....

SCHEDULE/TO-DO LIST:

- [ ] ....
- [ ] ....
- [ ] ....
- [ ]

8 glasses a day: ☐ ☐ ☐ ☐ ☐ ☐ ☐ ☐

REMEMBER

June

S	M	T	W	T	F	S
				1	2	3
4	5	6	7	8	9	10
11	12	13	14	15	16	17
18	19	20	21	22	23	24
25	26	27	28	29	30	

Today's Bible Reading:

1 SAMUEL 14; JOHN 4:11–38; PSALM 78:67–72

*Jesus saith unto them, My meat is to do the will
of him that sent me, and to finish his work.*
JOHN 4:34

Food is essential to life. Without it we die. In John 4:34, Christ declared that His food was to do the will of His Father. Fulfilling God's will for His life was His very sustenance. Is doing God's will as important to you as your daily food? You would notice if you went a day without food. Would you notice if you went a day without seeking God? Don't starve yourself of the necessary spiritual nourishment of seeking after God and doing His will.

TOP 3 PRIORITIES:

- [ ]
- [ ]
- [ ]

SCHEDULE/TO-DO LIST:

- [ ]
- [ ]
- [ ]
- [ ]

REFLECTIONS ON TODAY'S BIBLE READING

8 glasses a day:

REMEMBER

May

S	M	T	W	T	F	S
	1	2	3	4	5	6
7	8	9	10	11	12	13
14	15	16	17	18	19	20
21	22	23	24	25	26	27
28	29	30	31			

Today's Bible Reading:

1 SAMUEL 15–16; JOHN 4:39–54; PSALM 79:1–7

*And it came to pass, when they were come, that he looked on Eliab,
and said, Surely the Lord's anointed is before him. But the Lord said unto
Samuel, Look not on his countenance, or on the height of his stature;
because I have refused him: for the Lord seeth not as man seeth; for man
looketh on the outward appearance, but the Lord looketh on the heart.*
1 Samuel 16:6–7

Our human perspectives and mind-sets so often blind us to an eternal and God-given perspective. We see examples of this in today's passage. The fear of the opinion of his fellow man was more powerful to Saul than his fear of God. Samuel looked at the impressive outward appearance of David's brothers and had to be reminded by God that his earthly perspective was limited. Ask God for an eternal perspective. It will certainly change the way you see things.

REFLECTIONS ON TODAY'S BIBLE READING

8 glasses a day:

TOP 3 PRIORITIES:

SCHEDULE/TO-DO LIST:

REMEMBER

June

S	M	T	W	T	F	S
				1	2	3
4	5	6	7	8	9	10
11	12	13	14	15	16	17
18	19	20	21	22	23	24
25	26	27	28	29	30	

Today's Bible Reading:

1 SAMUEL 17; JOHN 5:1–24; PSALM 79:8–13

Then said David to the Philistine, Thou comest to me with a sword,
and with a spear, and with a shield: but I come to thee in the name of
the Lord of hosts, the God of the armies of Israel, whom thou hast defied.
1 Samuel 17:45

David faced a terrifying enemy with the added pressure of the welfare of his entire nation resting on him. He stood up to Goliath with a courage that can only stem from a true and full knowledge of God's power and love for His people. David knew without a shadow of a doubt that God had a plan for His people and that He would deliver the Philistines into his hand that day. It's much easier to be brave when you know going in that the battle ends in your favor. Through Christ we, too, can be confident that the war ends in our favor with complete victory over death and sin. Face the world armed with the name of the Lord of hosts.

TOP 3 PRIORITIES:

- ☐ ....
- ☐ ....
- ☐ ....

SCHEDULE/TO-DO LIST:

- ☐ ....
- ☐ ....
- ☐ ....
- ☐ ....

REFLECTIONS ON TODAY'S BIBLE READING

8 glasses a day: ☐ ☐ ☐ ☐ ☐ ☐ ☐ ☐

May

S	M	T	W	T	F	S
	1	2	3	4	5	6
7	8	9	10	11	12	13
14	15	16	17	18	19	20
21	22	23	24	25	26	27
28	29	30	31			

REMEMBER

Today's Bible Reading:

1 SAMUEL 18–19; JOHN 5:25–47; PSALM 80:1–7

*Turn us again, O God of hosts, and cause
thy face to shine; and we shall be saved.*
PSALM 80:7

One of the most magnificent sights in nature is when, after a storm, the clouds break to let rays of sunshine through. It's almost as if the very light of heaven has broken through the dark clouds. The language of God's face shining upon His people calls to mind a similar image. Even in the most violent of tempests, God's face is turned toward you and His everlasting light breaks through the clouds.

REFLECTIONS ON TODAY'S BIBLE READING

8 glasses a day:

TOP 3 PRIORITIES:

- [ ] ....
- [ ] ....
- [ ] ....

SCHEDULE/TO-DO LIST:

- [ ] ....
- [ ] ....
- [ ] ....
- [ ]

REMEMBER

June

S	M	T	W	T	F	S
				1	2	3
4	5	6	7	8	9	10
11	12	13	14	15	16	17
18	19	20	21	22	23	24
25	26	27	28	29	30	

Today's Bible Reading:

1 SAMUEL 20–21; JOHN 6:1–21; PSALM 80:8–19

When Jesus then lifted up his eyes, and saw a great company come unto him, he saith unto Philip, Whence shall we buy bread, that these may eat? And this he said to prove him: for he himself knew what he would do.
JOHN 6:5–6

In this passage in John, Jesus asked Philip a question. But He didn't ask it in order to learn the answer. In fact, John tells us that Jesus already knew what He was going to do. When God asks you to walk through a difficult situation, or places questions in front of you that are difficult and painful to answer, take comfort in the fact that He already knows what He is going to do. Stand firmly rooted with faith in His sovereignty.

TOP 3 PRIORITIES:

- ☐ ....
- ☐ ....
- ☐ ....

SCHEDULE/TO-DO LIST:

- ☐ ....
- ☐ ....
- ☐ ....
- ☐ ....

REFLECTIONS ON TODAY'S BIBLE READING

8 glasses a day: ☐ ☐ ☐ ☐ ☐ ☐ ☐ ☐

REMEMBER

May

S	M	T	W	T	F	S
	1	2	3	4	5	6
7	8	9	10	11	12	13
14	15	16	17	18	19	20
21	22	23	24	25	26	27
28	29	30	31			

Today's Bible Reading:

1 SAMUEL 22–23; JOHN 6:22–42; PSALM 81:1–10

Jesus answered them and said, Verily, verily, I say unto you,
Ye seek me, not because ye saw the miracles, but because
ye did eat of the loaves, and were filled.
JOHN 6:26

It is so easy to be lulled into the trap of desiring and seeking God for what He gives rather than for who He is. Like the people in Jesus' time who sought Him because of the tangible food that they ate, we too can often seek Him for the gifts He gives. But there is so much more beauty and fulfillment to be found in seeking God to know Him. Just as Jesus went on to say, don't seek earthly bread from God but rather spiritual bread and an everlasting relationship with Him.

REFLECTIONS ON TODAY'S BIBLE READING

8 glasses a day:

TOP 3 PRIORITIES:

- [ ] ....
- [ ] ....
- [ ] ....

SCHEDULE/TO-DO LIST:

- [ ] ....
- [ ] ....
- [ ] ....
- [ ] ....

REMEMBER

June

S	M	T	W	T	F	S
				1	2	3
4	5	6	7	8	9	10
11	12	13	14	15	16	17
18	19	20	21	22	23	24
25	26	27	28	29	30	

Today's Bible Reading:

1 SAMUEL 24:1–25:31; JOHN 6:43–71; PSALM 81:11–16

*Then Simon Peter answered him, Lord, to whom
shall we go? thou hast the words of eternal life.*
JOHN 6:68

What a beautiful perspective Peter had in today's passage. Having tasted of the words of eternal life that Christ offered, he couldn't imagine ever leaving Jesus for something else. Have you been so touched by Christ as to not be able to fathom life without Him? Or is He merely a supplement to your life to be brought out on the weekends? A true relationship with Him is life changing, so strive to get to know Him more intimately.

TOP 3 PRIORITIES:

- ☐ ....
- ☐ ....
- ☐ ....

SCHEDULE/TO-DO LIST:

- ☐ ....
- ☐ ....
- ☐ ....
- ☐ ....

REFLECTIONS ON TODAY'S BIBLE READING

8 glasses a day: ☐ ☐ ☐ ☐ ☐ ☐ ☐ ☐

REMEMBER

May

S	M	T	W	T	F	S
	1	2	3	4	5	6
7	8	9	10	11	12	13
14	15	16	17	18	19	20
21	22	23	24	25	26	27
28	29	30	31			

Today's Bible Reading:

1 SAMUEL 25:32–27:12; JOHN 7:1–24; PSALM 82

And David said to Abishai, Destroy him not: for who can stretch forth his hand against the LORD's anointed, and be guiltless? David said furthermore, As the LORD liveth, the LORD shall smite him; or his day shall come to die; or he shall descend into battle, and perish.
1 SAMUEL 26:9–10

David had learned to let God work His perfect plan instead of assuming that God's plan lined up completely with his plan. It's easy for us to decide that we know God's will only because it's what we want. Beware of trying to impose your will on His; disappointment and anger are sure to follow. Rest in God's perfect timing instead of trying to accomplish His work for Him.

REFLECTIONS ON TODAY'S BIBLE READING

TOP 3 PRIORITIES:

SCHEDULE/TO-DO LIST:

8 glasses a day:

REMEMBER

June

S	M	T	W	T	F	S
				1	2	3
4	5	6	7	8	9	10
11	12	13	14	15	16	17
18	19	20	21	22	23	24
25	26	27	28	29	30	

Tuesday
MAY 23

Today's Bible Reading:

1 SAMUEL 28–29; JOHN 7:25–8:11; PSALM 83

When Jesus had lifted up himself, and saw none but the woman, he said unto her, Woman, where are those thine accusers? hath no man condemned thee?
JOHN 8:10

The woman in today's passage in John must have been terrified to be dragged in front of a known expert in the Law with a crowd of men desperate to see her stoned. But instead of meeting her accuser in that unofficial courtroom, she came face to face with her Savior. May we be more aware of and more disgusted by our own sin than anyone else's sin. But in our sin, may we always realize that in Christ we have an advocate and Savior, not an accuser.

TOP 3 PRIORITIES:

- ☐ ....
- ☐ ....
- ☐ ....

SCHEDULE/TO-DO LIST:

- ☐ ....
- ☐ ....
- ☐ ....
- ☐ ....

REFLECTIONS ON TODAY'S BIBLE READING

8 glasses a day: ☐ ☐ ☐ ☐ ☐ ☐ ☐ ☐

REMEMBER

May

S	M	T	W	T	F	S
	1	2	3	4	5	6
7	8	9	10	11	12	13
14	15	16	17	18	19	20
21	22	23	24	25	26	27
28	29	30	31			

Today's Bible Reading:

1 SAMUEL 30–31; JOHN 8:12–47; PSALM 84:1–4

My soul longeth, yea, even fainteth for the courts of the LORD:
my heart and my flesh crieth out for the living God.
PSALM 84:2

Do we long for God's presence as though it were the very thing sustaining us? Do we cry out for God as the psalmist does in today's passage? It is an awe-inspiring and humbling thing to be allowed into the presence of a ruler of any nation. And yet, we are invited to come freely into the throne room of the King of kings. This is not something that should be taken for granted. But rather, we should take advantage of this invitation and daily enter into His courts.

REFLECTIONS ON TODAY'S BIBLE READING

8 glasses a day:

REMEMBER

TOP 3 PRIORITIES:

SCHEDULE/TO-DO LIST:

June

S	M	T	W	T	F	S
				1	2	3
4	5	6	7	8	9	10
11	12	13	14	15	16	17
18	19	20	21	22	23	24
25	26	27	28	29	30	

Thursday
MAY 25

Today's Bible Reading:

2 SAMUEL 1–2; JOHN 8:48–9:12; PSALM 84:5–12

For the Lord God is a sun and shield: the Lord will give grace and glory:
no good thing will he withhold from them that walk uprightly.
PSALM 84:11

Whether or not we acknowledge it, we live in a battle of light versus darkness. God is our sun, never allowing the darkness to overtake or overwhelm us. He is also our shield, protecting us from the arrows of the enemy in the heat of battle.

TOP 3 PRIORITIES:

- [ ] ....
- [ ] ....
- [ ] ....

SCHEDULE/TO-DO LIST:

- [ ] ....
- [ ] ....
- [ ] ....
- [ ] ....

REFLECTIONS ON TODAY'S BIBLE READING

8 glasses a day: ▢ ▢ ▢ ▢ ▢ ▢ ▢ ▢

May

S	M	T	W	T	F	S
	1	2	3	4	5	6
7	8	9	10	11	12	13
14	15	16	17	18	19	20
21	22	23	24	25	26	27
28	29	30	31			

REMEMBER

Today's Bible Reading:

2 SAMUEL 3-4; JOHN 9:13-34; PSALM 85:1-7

*He answered and said, Whether he be a sinner or no, I know not:
one thing I know, that, whereas I was blind, now I see.*
JOHN 9:25

The formerly blind man in today's passage has a wonderful, simple testimony. He knew and testified to one thing—he once was blind but now could see. Christ had changed him in a visible and tangible way. What are some things in your life that clearly point to Christ's work in you?

REFLECTIONS ON TODAY'S BIBLE READING

8 glasses a day:

TOP 3 PRIORITIES:

- ☐ ....
- ☐ ....
- ☐ ....

SCHEDULE/TO-DO LIST:

- ☐ ....
- ☐ ....
- ☐ ....
- ☐ ....

REMEMBER

June

S	M	T	W	T	F	S
				1	2	3
4	5	6	7	8	9	10
11	12	13	14	15	16	17
18	19	20	21	22	23	24
25	26	27	28	29	30	

Today's Bible Reading:

2 SAMUEL 5:1–7:17; JOHN 9:35–10:10; PSALM 85:8–13

And David danced before the LORD with all his might;
and David was girded with a linen ephod.
2 SAMUEL 6:14

The total abandon of David in today's passage is refreshing. He was so in love with his God and so thrilled that the ark was returning home that he danced with all his might before God. He wasn't worried about his reputation or how he might look in front of all the people watching. He was simply overwhelmed with the goodness of his God that he couldn't help but show it.

TOP 3 PRIORITIES:

- [ ] ....
- [ ] ....
- [ ] ....

SCHEDULE/TO-DO LIST:

- [ ] ....
- [ ] ....
- [ ] ....
- [ ] ....

REFLECTIONS ON TODAY'S BIBLE READING

8 glasses a day:

REMEMBER

May

S	M	T	W	T	F	S
	1	2	3	4	5	6
7	8	9	10	11	12	13
14	15	16	17	18	19	20
21	22	23	24	25	26	27
28	29	30	31			

Today's Bible Reading:

2 SAMUEL 7:18–10:19; JOHN 10:11–30; PSALM 86:1–10

I am the good shepherd, and know my sheep, and am known of mine. As the Father knoweth me, even so know I the Father: and I lay down my life for the sheep.
JOHN 10:14–15

Do you ever fear that if you were truly known, you couldn't be loved? Your Good Shepherd both knows you and loves you in ways that you can't even fathom. He knew you perfectly before you were even born and continues to know each of your inward thoughts. But in spite of this, He still loves you. This is not a surface love either. It is a love that would drive Him to lay down His life for you. You are intimately known and deeply loved by the Person that matters the very most.

REFLECTIONS ON TODAY'S BIBLE READING

TOP 3 PRIORITIES:

- [ ] ....
- [ ] ....
- [ ] ....

SCHEDULE/TO-DO LIST:

- [ ] ....
- [ ] ....
- [ ] ....
- [ ] ....

8 glasses a day: ▢ ▢ ▢ ▢ ▢ ▢ ▢ ▢

REMEMBER

June

S	M	T	W	T	F	S
				1	2	3
4	5	6	7	8	9	10
11	12	13	14	15	16	17
18	19	20	21	22	23	24
25	26	27	28	29	30	

Memorial Day

Today's Bible Reading:

2 SAMUEL 11:1–12:25; JOHN 10:31–11:16; PSALM 86:11–17

And I am glad for your sakes that I was not there, to the
intent ye may believe; nevertheless let us go unto him.
JOHN 11:15

Sometimes God brings us through difficult circumstances for the purpose of increasing our faith. To those who knew and loved Lazarus, it probably would have felt like Jesus failed at this point. He had healed so many and yet He wasn't around to heal one of His friends. Little did they know that Jesus had an even bigger miracle in store. His plan was not merely to heal Lazarus but to raise him from the dead. When we feel as though God has missed an opportunity in our lives, we need to remember that His plan is perfect and He may just be preparing for something bigger than we could have imagined.

TOP 3 PRIORITIES:

- [ ] ....
- [ ] ....
- [ ] ....

SCHEDULE/TO-DO LIST:

- [ ] ....
- [ ] ....
- [ ] ....
- [ ] ....

REFLECTIONS ON TODAY'S BIBLE READING

8 glasses a day:

REMEMBER

May

S	M	T	W	T	F	S
	1	2	3	4	5	6
7	8	9	10	11	12	13
14	15	16	17	18	19	20
21	22	23	24	25	26	27
28	29	30	31			

Today's Bible Reading:

2 SAMUEL 12:26–13:39; JOHN 11:17–54; PSALM 87

Jesus therefore again groaning in himself cometh to the grave. It was a cave, and a stone lay upon it.
JOHN 11:38

Jesus groaned as He came to the grave where Lazarus was laid–a grave with a stone rolled over it, similar to the grave that He would be laid in shortly. He was deeply sorrowed over the death that He would soon conquer. Lazarus's resurrection was a skirmish in the ultimate battle of life over death–the battle that Christ would soon be victorious in. Even though we know the end of our story (a glorious eternal life with Christ), it is right and good to mourn over the pain and sorrow of this world as we wait for the fulfillment of God's promises.

REFLECTIONS ON TODAY'S BIBLE READING

8 glasses a day:

TOP 3 PRIORITIES:

SCHEDULE/TO-DO LIST:

REMEMBER

June

S	M	T	W	T	F	S
				1	2	3
4	5	6	7	8	9	10
11	12	13	14	15	16	17
18	19	20	21	22	23	24
25	26	27	28	29	30	

Today's Bible Reading:

2 SAMUEL 14:1–15:12; JOHN 11:55–12:19; PSALM 88:1–9

But the chief priests consulted that they might put Lazarus also to death; because that by reason of him many of the Jews went away, and believed on Jesus.
JOHN 12:10–11

The chief priests in the Jewish community plotted to kill not only Jesus but Lazarus as well. All throughout history and on into the future, people will oppose Christ and go to great lengths to disprove Him. Those who are walking testimonies of His power and love will be targeted also. But it is far better to live in His truth than to live in the fear of man.

TOP 3 PRIORITIES:

- ☐ ....
- ☐ ....
- ☐ ....

SCHEDULE/TO-DO LIST:

- ☐ ....
- ☐ ....
- ☐ ....
- ☐ ....

REFLECTIONS ON TODAY'S BIBLE READING

8 glasses a day: ☐ ☐ ☐ ☐ ☐ ☐ ☐ ☐

REMEMBER

May

S	M	T	W	T	F	S
	1	2	3	4	5	6
7	8	9	10	11	12	13
14	15	16	17	18	19	20
21	22	23	24	25	26	27
28	29	30	31			

Today's Bible Reading:

2 SAMUEL 15:13–16:23; JOHN 12:20–43; PSALM 88:10–18

*He that loveth his life shall lose it; and he that hateth
his life in this world shall keep it unto life eternal.*
JOHN 12:25

If you put too much time and effort into making your life exactly how you want it here on earth, you will certainly be disappointed. Holding on to the vision of a "perfect life" will cause you to lose that perfect life. A good life on earth can only be attained when lived out with the perspective of eternity. This perspective will radically change your priorities and the way you live your life.

REFLECTIONS ON TODAY'S BIBLE READING

8 glasses a day:

TOP 3 PRIORITIES:

- [ ] ....
- [ ] ....
- [ ] ....

SCHEDULE/TO-DO LIST:

- [ ] ....
- [ ] ....
- [ ] ....
- [ ] ....

REMEMBER

June

S	M	T	W	T	F	S
				1	2	3
4	5	6	7	8	9	10
11	12	13	14	15	16	17
18	19	20	21	22	23	24
25	26	27	28	29	30	

Friday
JUNE 2

Today's Bible Reading:

If I then, your Lord and Master, have washed your feet;
ye also ought to wash one another's feet. For I have given
you an example, that ye should do as I have done to you.
JOHN 13:14–15

Christ preached a very countercultural message. Here was a King who washed the feet of His followers and encouraged them to do the same. Is it any wonder that some people didn't believe that this could be the King and Conqueror that was prophesied of in the Old Testament? And yet, in all His humility, He was and is far more powerful than any earthly king and warrior could ever be. He didn't conquer the oppressive nation of Rome. Instead, He conquered death by being slaughtered as a sacrificial Lamb. This is the kind of King to follow.

TOP 3 PRIORITIES:

- ☐ ....
- ☐ ....
- ☐ ....

SCHEDULE/TO-DO LIST:

- ☐ ....
- ☐ ....
- ☐ ....
- ☐ ....

REFLECTIONS ON TODAY'S BIBLE READING

8 glasses a day: ☐ ☐ ☐ ☐ ☐ ☐ ☐ ☐

REMEMBER

June

S	M	T	W	T	F	S
				1	2	3
4	5	6	7	8	9	10
11	12	13	14	15	16	17
18	19	20	21	22	23	24
25	26	27	28	29	30	

Today's Bible Reading:

2 SAMUEL 18:19–19:39; JOHN 13:21–38; PSALM 89:7–13

*Thou rulest the raging of the sea: when the
waves thereof arise, thou stillest them.*
PSALM 89:9

God is the only one who can control the wind and the waves of the sea. He is praised for doing so in today's psalm. How poignant it would have been to the disciples when Jesus stilled the storm while they were at sea. They would have recognized that this was truly God walking among them.

REFLECTIONS ON TODAY'S BIBLE READING

8 glasses a day:

TOP 3 PRIORITIES:

☐ ....
☐ ....
☐ ....

SCHEDULE/TO-DO LIST:

☐ ....
☐ ....
☐ ....
☐ ....

REMEMBER

July

S	M	T	W	T	F	S
						1
2	3	4	5	6	7	8
9	10	11	12	13	14	15
16	17	18	19	20	21	22
23	24	25	26	27	28	29
30	31					

Today's Bible Reading:

2 SAMUEL 19:40–21:22; JOHN 14:1–17; PSALM 89:14–18

And I will pray the Father, and he shall give you another
Comforter, that he may abide with you for ever.
JOHN 14:16

God has been moving closer to His people all throughout history. But He couldn't possibly get any closer to His children than when He walked among them on earth, right? Christ's disciples may have thought this, which is why He told them about the Comforter that the Father would send to them. This Comforter doesn't just walk with us; He abides in us. He has no physical restrictions regarding space or time, meaning He can be with all of God's children simultaneously and continuously. He is ever present with you and will be so forever.

TOP 3 PRIORITIES:

☐ ....
☐ ....
☐ ....

SCHEDULE/TO-DO LIST:

☐ ....
☐ ....
☐ ....
☐ ....

REFLECTIONS ON TODAY'S BIBLE READING

8 glasses a day: ☐ ☐ ☐ ☐ ☐ ☐ ☐ ☐

REMEMBER

June

S	M	T	W	T	F	S
				1	2	3
4	5	6	7	8	9	10
11	12	13	14	15	16	17
18	19	20	21	22	23	24
25	26	27	28	29	30	

Today's Bible Reading:

2 SAMUEL 22:1–23:7; JOHN 14:18–15:27; PSALM 89:19–29

For thou art my lamp, O Lord:
and the Lord will lighten my darkness.
2 Samuel 22:29

David spoke from experience when he asserted that God was his lamp to lighten the darkness around him. His life was far from easy. He had friends and family turn against him and force him into a life of running and hiding. But through even the darkest of circumstances, God remained a faithful light by his side to illuminate his steps and keep him safe from harm. No matter the situation, God is your lamp as well. The darker it gets, the more brilliantly His light shines.

REFLECTIONS ON TODAY'S BIBLE READING

8 glasses a day:

TOP 3 PRIORITIES:

SCHEDULE/TO-DO LIST:

REMEMBER

July

S	M	T	W	T	F	S
						1
2	3	4	5	6	7	8
9	10	11	12	13	14	15
16	17	18	19	20	21	22
23	24	25	26	27	28	29
30	31					

Today's Bible Reading:

2 SAMUEL 23:8–24:25; JOHN 16:1–22; PSALM 89:30–37

My covenant will I not break, nor alter the thing that is gone out of my lips. Once have I sworn by my holiness that I will not lie unto David. His seed shall endure for ever, and his throne as the sun before me.
PSALM 89:34–36

God made a covenant with His servant David, and He has stood by that covenant through generations and generations. This covenant will stand forever since one of David's descendants sits on the eternal throne. God does not make His promises and covenants lightly because He will never go back on a promise He has made.

TOP 3 PRIORITIES:

- [ ] ....
- [ ] ....
- [ ] ....

SCHEDULE/TO-DO LIST:

- [ ] ....
- [ ] ....
- [ ] ....
- [ ] ....

REFLECTIONS ON TODAY'S BIBLE READING

8 glasses a day:

REMEMBER

June

S	M	T	W	T	F	S
				1	2	3
4	5	6	7	8	9	10
11	12	13	14	15	16	17
18	19	20	21	22	23	24
25	26	27	28	29	30	

Today's Bible Reading:

1 KINGS 1; JOHN 16:23–17:5; PSALM 89:38–52

These things I have spoken unto you, that in me ye might have peace. In the world ye shall have tribulation: but be of good cheer; I have overcome the world.
JOHN 16:33

As Jesus prepared to go to His death, He told His disciples that two things were certain: first, that in the world they would have trials and tribulations, but, second, that in these they would have a joyful peace because Christ had overcome the world. Don't be surprised when trials and difficulties surface in your life. Christ gave us fair warning that these would come. But in Him and in the knowledge of His victory over death, sin, and sorrow, you can have a peace that is unmatched by anything this world can offer. You can indeed face this world with good cheer.

REFLECTIONS ON TODAY'S BIBLE READING

8 glasses a day: ☐ ☐ ☐ ☐ ☐ ☐ ☐ ☐

TOP 3 PRIORITIES:

- ☐ ....
- ☐ ....
- ☐ ....

SCHEDULE/TO-DO LIST:

- ☐ ....
- ☐ ....
- ☐ ....
- ☐ ....

REMEMBER

July

S	M	T	W	T	F	S
						1
2	3	4	5	6	7	8
9	10	11	12	13	14	15
16	17	18	19	20	21	22
23	24	25	26	27	28	29
30	31					

Today's Bible Reading:

1 KINGS 2; JOHN 17:6–26; PSALM 90:1–12

*Neither pray I for these alone, but for them also
which shall believe on me through their word.*
JOHN 17:20

Isn't it remarkable that in the pages of the Bible is recorded for all time a prayer that Jesus prayed for you? While the inevitability of the cross loomed in front of Him, He prayed for His current followers and all those who would come after. As a follower of Christ, He prayed for you.

TOP 3 PRIORITIES:

- ☐ ....
- ☐ ....
- ☐ ....

SCHEDULE/TO-DO LIST:

- ☐ ....
- ☐ ....
- ☐ ....
- ☐ ....

REFLECTIONS ON TODAY'S BIBLE READING

8 glasses a day: ☐ ☐ ☐ ☐ ☐ ☐ ☐ ☐

June

S	M	T	W	T	F	S
				1	2	3
4	5	6	7	8	9	10
11	12	13	14	15	16	17
18	19	20	21	22	23	24
25	26	27	28	29	30	

REMEMBER

Today's Bible Reading:

1 KINGS 3–4; JOHN 18:1–27; PSALM 90:13–17

*Give therefore thy servant an understanding heart to judge
thy people, that I may discern between good and bad:
for who is able to judge this thy so great a people?*
1 KINGS 3:9

Wouldn't our prayers be so much more productive if we stopped praying for a situation to turn out specifically how we wanted it to and instead prayed for wisdom and discernment? We must humbly realize that God's plan, whatever that may be, is so much better than our plan. So ask Him for wisdom and patience to discern His will.

REFLECTIONS ON TODAY'S BIBLE READING

8 glasses a day:

TOP 3 PRIORITIES:

- [ ] ....
- [ ] ....
- [ ] ....

SCHEDULE/TO-DO LIST:

- [ ] ....
- [ ] ....
- [ ] ....
- [ ]

REMEMBER

July

S	M	T	W	T	F	S
						1
2	3	4	5	6	7	8
9	10	11	12	13	14	15
16	17	18	19	20	21	22
23	24	25	26	27	28	29
30	31					

Today's Bible Reading:

1 KINGS 5–6; JOHN 18:28–19:5; PSALM 91:1–10

A thousand shall fall at thy side, and ten thousand
at thy right hand; but it shall not come nigh thee.
PSALM 91:7

When you are one of God's children, held in His powerful hand, you are immortal until the day that He has ordained to bring you home. Nothing can touch you outside of His perfect plan. Even with ten thousand falling at your side, you will stand strong until the day when God has decided to bestow on you the glorious privilege of being admitted into heaven.

TOP 3 PRIORITIES:

- [ ] ....
- [ ] ....
- [ ] ....

SCHEDULE/TO-DO LIST:

- [ ] ....
- [ ] ....
- [ ] ....
- [ ] ....

REFLECTIONS ON TODAY'S BIBLE READING

8 glasses a day:

REMEMBER

June

S	M	T	W	T	F	S
				1	2	3
4	5	6	7	8	9	10
11	12	13	14	15	16	17
18	19	20	21	22	23	24
25	26	27	28	29	30	

Today's Bible Reading:

1 KINGS 7; JOHN 19:6–24; PSALM 91:11–16

This title then read many of the Jews: for the place where Jesus was crucified was nigh to the city: and it was written in Hebrew, and Greek, and Latin. Then said the chief priests of the Jews to Pilate, Write not, The King of the Jews; but that he said, I am King of the Jews. Pilate answered, What I have written I have written.
JOHN 19:20–22

The irony and stubborn truth displayed in what Pilate wrote for the cross of Christ is really very beautiful. Even during His humiliating death, it was being proclaimed to all who passed by that Jesus was King. The Gospel can never be silenced, not even by an angry mob who killed the very Son of God.

REFLECTIONS ON TODAY'S BIBLE READING

8 glasses a day:

TOP 3 PRIORITIES:

SCHEDULE/TO-DO LIST:

REMEMBER

July

S	M	T	W	T	F	S
						1
2	3	4	5	6	7	8
9	10	11	12	13	14	15
16	17	18	19	20	21	22
23	24	25	26	27	28	29
30	31					

Today's Bible Reading:

1 KINGS 8:1–53; JOHN 19:25–42; PSALM 92:1–9

*And it came to pass, when the priests were come out of the
holy place, that the cloud filled the house of the Lord.*
1 Kings 8:10

Imagine how awe inspiring it must have been to see the cloud of God's presence fill the holy place. How remarkable it would have been to be one of the people standing there, seeing the very presence of God and knowing that He dwelled with you. And yet, you have a greater gift than that. While the people were unable to enter the holy place, you can go right up to the very throne of God. The curtain that was torn in two at Christ's death will never be sewn together again. You have eternal access to your heavenly Father. His Spirit dwells in and with you.

TOP 3 PRIORITIES:

☐ ....
☐ ....
☐ ....

SCHEDULE/TO-DO LIST:

☐ ....
☐ ....
☐ ....
☐ ....

REFLECTIONS ON TODAY'S BIBLE READING

8 glasses a day: ☐ ☐ ☐ ☐ ☐ ☐ ☐ ☐

June

S	M	T	W	T	F	S
				1	2	3
4	5	6	7	8	9	10
11	12	13	14	15	16	17
18	19	20	21	22	23	24
25	26	27	28	29	30	

REMEMBER

Today's Bible Reading:

1 KINGS 8:54–10:13; JOHN 20:1–18; PSALM 92:10–15

They shall still bring forth fruit in old age;
they shall be fat and flourishing.
PSALM 92:14

Those who walk with Christ will still be fruitful even in their old age. Far from being forgotten members of society, the older generation has so much to offer about their long and faithful walk with Christ. As an elderly person, don't be afraid to share your testimony of God's faithfulness. As a younger person, seek out those from whom you can gain wisdom and the life perspective of a long life well lived.

REFLECTIONS ON TODAY'S BIBLE READING

8 glasses a day: ☐ ☐ ☐ ☐ ☐ ☐ ☐ ☐

TOP 3 PRIORITIES:

- ☐ ....
- ☐ ....
- ☐ ....

SCHEDULE/TO-DO LIST:

- ☐ ....
- ☐ ....
- ☐ ....
- ☐ ....

REMEMBER

July

S	M	T	W	T	F	S
						1
2	3	4	5	6	7	8
9	10	11	12	13	14	15
16	17	18	19	20	21	22
23	24	25	26	27	28	29
30	31					

Flag Day

Today's Bible Reading:

1 KINGS 10:14–11:43; JOHN 20:19–31; PSALM 93

*But these are written, that ye might believe that Jesus is the Christ,
the Son of God; and that believing ye might have life through his name.*
JOHN 20:31

There is not enough room in the Gospel accounts to tell the stories of all the people whose lives were radically changed by Christ. But the accounts of the real Man who touched and changed real people are there so that we too, generations later, can believe in Him. Write down your own accounts of how Christ changes and shapes your life. Remembering His faithfulness will strengthen your faith and give you abundant life through His name.

TOP 3 PRIORITIES:

- ☐ ....
- ☐ ....
- ☐ ....

SCHEDULE/TO-DO LIST:

- ☐ ....
- ☐ ....
- ☐ ....
- ☐ ....

REFLECTIONS ON TODAY'S BIBLE READING

8 glasses a day: ☐ ☐ ☐ ☐ ☐ ☐ ☐ ☐

June

S	M	T	W	T	F	S
				1	2	3
4	5	6	7	8	9	10
11	12	13	14	15	16	17
18	19	20	21	22	23	24
25	26	27	28	29	30	

REMEMBER

Today's Bible Reading:

1 KINGS 12:1–13:10; JOHN 21; PSALM 94:1–11

*But he forsook the counsel of the old men, which they had
given him, and consulted with the young men that were
grown up with him, and which stood before him.*
1 KINGS 12:8

Rehoboam very unwisely followed the counsel of his foolish friends rather than the counsel of the wise men who had far more experience with ruling people. Who are your counselors? Who are you surrounding yourself with whose thoughts and attitudes are rubbing off on you? Choose your friends and counselors wisely since those who are closest to you have a powerful say in your life.

REFLECTIONS ON TODAY'S BIBLE READING

TOP 3 PRIORITIES:

- ☐ ....
- ☐ ....
- ☐ ....

SCHEDULE/TO-DO LIST:

- ☐ ....
- ☐ ....
- ☐ ....
- ☐ ....

8 glasses a day: ☐ ☐ ☐ ☐ ☐ ☐ ☐ ☐

REMEMBER

July

S	M	T	W	T	F	S
						1
2	3	4	5	6	7	8
9	10	11	12	13	14	15
16	17	18	19	20	21	22
23	24	25	26	27	28	29
30	31					

Friday
JUNE 16

Today's Bible Reading:

1 KINGS 13:11–14:31; ACTS 1:1–11; PSALM 94:12–23

> *Blessed is the man whom thou chastenest,*
> *O LORD, and teachest him out of thy law.*
> PSALM 94:12

We rarely think that discipline and chastening are blessings. But when God teaches and rebukes you through His Word or through others in your life, you ought to be grateful. He is graciously pulling you back from a dangerous ledge and sparing you from a long fall. Sometimes God's discipline may seem harsher than at other times, but each correction ultimately brings you healing and guides you into a closer walk with God.

TOP 3 PRIORITIES:

- ☐ ....
- ☐ ....
- ☐ ....

SCHEDULE/TO-DO LIST:

- ☐ ....
- ☐ ....
- ☐ ....
- ☐ ....

REFLECTIONS ON TODAY'S BIBLE READING

8 glasses a day: ⊔ ⊔ ⊔ ⊔ ⊔ ⊔ ⊔ ⊔

June

S	M	T	W	T	F	S
				1	2	3
4	5	6	7	8	9	10
11	12	13	14	15	16	17
18	19	20	21	22	23	24
25	26	27	28	29	30	

REMEMBER

Today's Bible Reading:

1 KINGS 15:1–16:20; ACTS 1:12–26; PSALM 95

*Nevertheless for David's sake did the LORD his God give him a lamp
in Jerusalem, to set up his son after him, and to establish Jerusalem.*
1 KINGS 15:4

God does not abandon His plan. He covenanted with David that one of his descendants would always reign. Even with all the evil kings that reigned after David, He did not disregard His promise. And now Jesus, a descendant of David, will reign forever. You know that you serve a God who keeps His promises and doesn't change His mind. Therefore, you can have a sure confidence that no matter what is happening in your life right now it is definitely part of God's perfect plan.

REFLECTIONS ON TODAY'S BIBLE READING

8 glasses a day: ▢ ▢ ▢ ▢ ▢ ▢ ▢ ▢

TOP 3 PRIORITIES:

☐ ....
☐ ....
☐ ....

SCHEDULE/TO-DO LIST:

☐ ....
☐ ....
☐ ....
☐

REMEMBER

July

S	M	T	W	T	F	S
						1
2	3	4	5	6	7	8
9	10	11	12	13	14	15
16	17	18	19	20	21	22
23	24	25	26	27	28	29
30	31					

Today's Bible Reading:

1 KINGS 16:21–18:19; ACTS 2:1–21; PSALM 96:1–8

O sing unto the Lord a new song:
sing unto the Lord, all the earth.
PSALM 96:1

The psalmist desires all the earth to sing to the Lord. Generations later at Pentecost, this vision of the psalmist started to become a reality. The Holy Spirit descended, allowing people from many nations to hear the Gospel in their own language. The good news continued to spread from there into all the earth. One day people of every nation will be singing God's praise together in the throne room of their Savior.

TOP 3 PRIORITIES:

- ☐ ....
- ☐ ....
- ☐ ....

SCHEDULE/TO-DO LIST:

- ☐ ....
- ☐ ....
- ☐ ....
- ☐ ....

REFLECTIONS ON TODAY'S BIBLE READING

8 glasses a day: ☐ ☐ ☐ ☐ ☐ ☐ ☐ ☐

June

S	M	T	W	T	F	S
				1	2	3
4	5	6	7	8	9	10
11	12	13	14	15	16	17
18	19	20	21	22	23	24
25	26	27	28	29	30	

REMEMBER

Today's Bible Reading:

1 KINGS 18:20–19:21; ACTS 2:22–41; PSALM 96:9–13

Then the fire of the LORD fell, and consumed the burnt sacrifice, and the wood, and the stones, and the dust, and licked up the water that was in the trench.
1 KINGS 18:38

Elijah loudly taunted and ridiculed the prophets of Baal, who were enemies of God. But when it came time for him to show Israel who the true God was, his prayer was a beautiful picture of someone who walked humbly with God and had a personal relationship with Him. He asked that God would consume the sacrifice, not so he would look good but so the people would know who their God was. And then God answered the faithful prayer of His servant and shattered any disbelief in the crowd by sending down fire from heaven.

REFLECTIONS ON TODAY'S BIBLE READING

8 glasses a day:

TOP 3 PRIORITIES:

SCHEDULE/TO-DO LIST:

REMEMBER

July

S	M	T	W	T	F	S
						1
2	3	4	5	6	7	8
9	10	11	12	13	14	15
16	17	18	19	20	21	22
23	24	25	26	27	28	29
30	31					

Today's Bible Reading:

1 KINGS 20; ACTS 2:42–3:26; PSALM 97:1–6

*And he leaping up stood, and walked, and entered with them
into the temple, walking, and leaping, and praising God.*
ACTS 3:8

The transformation of the lame man in Acts is a testament to God's ability to completely transform a person. Not only did He fix what was wrong in the man's legs, but He also created muscle strength and coordination that the man would never have had due to his disability–no physical therapy and long rehabilitation necessary. Even with all the incredible medical and scientific advancements we have been blessed to make, we can never match the power of the Creator to restore His broken creation. That is a God who truly deserves to be praised.

TOP 3 PRIORITIES:

- [ ] ....
- [ ] ....
- [ ] ....

SCHEDULE/TO-DO LIST:

- [ ] ....
- [ ] ....
- [ ] ....
- [ ] ....

REFLECTIONS ON TODAY'S BIBLE READING

8 glasses a day: ▢ ▢ ▢ ▢ ▢ ▢ ▢ ▢

June

S	M	T	W	T	F	S
				1	2	3
4	5	6	7	8	9	10
11	12	13	14	15	16	17
18	19	20	21	22	23	24
25	26	27	28	29	30	

REMEMBER

First Day of Summer

Today's Bible Reading:

1 KINGS 21:1–22:28; ACTS 4:1–22; PSALM 97:7–12

Ye that love the LORD, hate evil: he preserveth the souls of his saints; he delivereth them out of the hand of the wicked.
PSALM 97:10

It's easy to become overwhelmed by the evil in this world and to loathe its very existence. While we have to live in this imperfect world until Christ brings us home or comes again, take heart that this hatred of evil is a sure sign that you love God. When you have aligned yourself with someone, you end up loving or hating the things that person loves or hates. God hates evil even more than you, and as your heart becomes more like His, you will see things even more vividly from His perspective. Ask Him to continue to mold your heart to be like His.

REFLECTIONS ON TODAY'S BIBLE READING

TOP 3 PRIORITIES:

- ☐ ....
- ☐ ....
- ☐ ....

SCHEDULE/TO-DO LIST:

- ☐ ....
- ☐ ....
- ☐ ....
- ☐ ....

8 glasses a day: ☐ ☐ ☐ ☐ ☐ ☐ ☐ ☐

REMEMBER

July

S	M	T	W	T	F	S
						1
2	3	4	5	6	7	8
9	10	11	12	13	14	15
16	17	18	19	20	21	22
23	24	25	26	27	28	29
30	31					

Today's Bible Reading:

1 KINGS 22:29–2 KINGS 1; ACTS 4:23–5:11; PSALM 98

Before the LORD; for he cometh to judge the earth: with righteousness shall he judge the world, and the people with equity.
PSALM 98:9

Injustice is rampant on this earth. But God judges with righteousness and equity. He does not judge based on personal bias or prejudice. He does not take into account skin color, age, nationality, or gender. His judgment is pure and holy. He is coming to judge the earth in a way that will finally bring true justice to the wicked and peace and reconciliation to the oppressed.

TOP 3 PRIORITIES:

- ☐ ....
- ☐ ....
- ☐ ....

SCHEDULE/TO-DO LIST:

- ☐ ....
- ☐ ....
- ☐ ....
- ☐ ....

REFLECTIONS ON TODAY'S BIBLE READING

8 glasses a day: ☐ ☐ ☐ ☐ ☐ ☐ ☐ ☐

June

S	M	T	W	T	F	S
				1	2	3
4	5	6	7	8	9	10
11	12	13	14	15	16	17
18	19	20	21	22	23	24
25	26	27	28	29	30	

REMEMBER

Today's Bible Reading:

2 KINGS 2–3; ACTS 5:12–28; PSALM 99

*Saying, Did not we straitly command you that ye should not teach
in this name? and, behold, ye have filled Jerusalem with your
doctrine, and intend to bring this man's blood upon us.*
ACTS 5:28

The apostles were accused of filling an entire city with their doctrine. Their relentless preaching of the Gospel was so pervasive that the officials of the city took note and felt like something had to be done to address the rapid spread of their teachings. Wouldn't it be amazing if we could fill the cities we live in with this same life-giving doctrine? To be accused of the same thing as these faithful and courageous apostles would truly be an honor.

REFLECTIONS ON TODAY'S BIBLE READING

8 glasses a day:

TOP 3 PRIORITIES:

- [ ] ....
- [ ] ....
- [ ] ....

SCHEDULE/TO-DO LIST:

- [ ] ....
- [ ] ....
- [ ] ....
- [ ] ....

REMEMBER

July

S	M	T	W	T	F	S
						1
2	3	4	5	6	7	8
9	10	11	12	13	14	15
16	17	18	19	20	21	22
23	24	25	26	27	28	29
30	31					

Today's Bible Reading:

2 KINGS 4; ACTS 5:29–6:15; PSALM 100

*Then he said, Go, borrow thee vessels abroad of all thy neighbours,
even empty vessels; borrow not a few. And when thou art come in,
thou shalt shut the door upon thee and upon thy sons, and shalt pour
out into all those vessels, and thou shalt set aside that which is full.*
2 KINGS 4:3–4

Could Elisha, through God's power, have solved all the widow's problems in today's passage without having her do anything? Of course he could have. But, instead, we're presented with a valuable model of helping those in need. The woman first worked to get empty vessels from all her neighbors, and then God performed the miracle. As God knew and demonstrated, it is often very constructive to allow the person in need to be part of the solution and not just a bystanding benefactor of it.

TOP 3 PRIORITIES:

- ☐ ....
- ☐ ....
- ☐ ....

SCHEDULE/TO-DO LIST:

- ☐ ....
- ☐ ....
- ☐ ....
- ☐ ....

REFLECTIONS ON TODAY'S BIBLE READING

8 glasses a day: ☐ ☐ ☐ ☐ ☐ ☐ ☐ ☐

REMEMBER

June

S	M	T	W	T	F	S
				1	2	3
4	5	6	7	8	9	10
11	12	13	14	15	16	17
18	19	20	21	22	23	24
25	26	27	28	29	30	

Today's Bible Reading:

2 KINGS 5:1–6:23; ACTS 7:1–16; PSALM 101

And he answered, Fear not: for they that be with us are more than they that be with them. And Elisha prayed, and said, Lord, I pray thee, open his eyes, that he may see. And the Lord opened the eyes of the young man; and he saw: and, behold, the mountain was full of horses and chariots of fire round about Elisha.
2 Kings 6:16–17

Oh, that God would open our eyes as He did the eyes of Elisha's servant that we too might see the mighty army arrayed to protect us and to carry out God's will. We are never in this battle alone. How much more courageously would you step into battle if you were aware that you are always surrounded by a victorious, heavenly army.

REFLECTIONS ON TODAY'S BIBLE READING

8 glasses a day:

TOP 3 PRIORITIES:

- [ ] ....
- [ ] ....
- [ ] ....

SCHEDULE/TO-DO LIST:

- [ ] ....
- [ ] ....
- [ ] ....
- [ ] ....

REMEMBER

July

S	M	T	W	T	F	S
						1
2	3	4	5	6	7	8
9	10	11	12	13	14	15
16	17	18	19	20	21	22
23	24	25	26	27	28	29
30	31					

Today's Bible Reading:

2 KINGS 6:24–8:15; ACTS 7:17–36; PSALM 102:1–7

And seeing one of them suffer wrong, he defended him,
and avenged him that was oppressed, and smote the Egyptian.
ACTS 7:24

God does not just save those who are already perfect and have their act together. In fact, the three men who wrote the most books of the Bible are all murderers—Moses (as we read about in today's passage), David (killed Uriah), and Paul (looked on in approval as Stephen was murdered). These three pillars of the faith were far from perfect men. And yet, God used them to carry out His flawless plan. If He could use them, He can certainly use you as well.

TOP 3 PRIORITIES:

- [ ] ....
- [ ] ....
- [ ] ....

SCHEDULE/TO-DO LIST:

- [ ] ....
- [ ] ....
- [ ] ....
- [ ] ....

REFLECTIONS ON TODAY'S BIBLE READING

8 glasses a day:

June

S	M	T	W	T	F	S
				1	2	3
4	5	6	7	8	9	10
11	12	13	14	15	16	17
18	19	20	21	22	23	24
25	26	27	28	29	30	

REMEMBER

Today's Bible Reading:

2 KINGS 8:16–9:37; ACTS 7:37–53; PSALM 102:8–17

*My days are like a shadow that declineth; and I am withered like grass. But thou,
O LORD, shall endure for ever; and thy remembrance unto all generations.*
PSALM 102:11–12

The psalmist in today's passage understood his own frailty. He knew that his life was like a flickering shadow and grass that withers rapidly. But he had faith in something greater than himself. While his life was merely a vapor, his God endures forever. While most of us are forgotten soon after we depart this earth, our God will be remembered and praised throughout all eternity. Put your effort into glorifying and magnifying Him during this life rather than magnifying yourself.

REFLECTIONS ON TODAY'S BIBLE READING

TOP 3 PRIORITIES:

SCHEDULE/TO-DO LIST:

8 glasses a day:

REMEMBER

July

S	M	T	W	T	F	S
						1
2	3	4	5	6	7	8
9	10	11	12	13	14	15
16	17	18	19	20	21	22
23	24	25	26	27	28	29
30	31					

Today's Bible Reading:

2 KINGS 10–11; ACTS 7:54–8:8; PSALM 102:18–28

Therefore they that were scattered abroad
went every where preaching the word.
ACTS 8:4

The people who led the persecution of the early Church must have felt like they were doing a good job of squelching the Gospel of Christ. After all, those who adhered to the teachings of Christ as the Messiah were scattering under the persecution. But God's plan and the inevitable advancement of the Gospel cannot be stopped so easily. In fact, God used the very persecution of His people to more quickly reach others for Christ. Had persecution not forced the Christians away from their homes it would have taken longer for the good news to spread around the world.

TOP 3 PRIORITIES:

☐ ....
☐ ....
☐ ....

SCHEDULE/TO-DO LIST:

☐ ....
☐ ....
☐ ....
☐ ....

REFLECTIONS ON TODAY'S BIBLE READING

8 glasses a day: ☐ ☐ ☐ ☐ ☐ ☐ ☐ ☐

REMEMBER

June

S	M	T	W	T	F	S
				1	2	3
4	5	6	7	8	9	10
11	12	13	14	15	16	17
18	19	20	21	22	23	24
25	26	27	28	29	30	

Today's Bible Reading:

2 KINGS 12–13; ACTS 8:9–40; PSALM 103:1–9

*And Philip said, If thou believest with all thine heart, thou mayest.
And he answered and said, I believe that Jesus Christ is the Son of God.*
ACTS 8:37

God has lovingly planned the steps of His children even down to the smallest details. The eunuch that Philip witnessed to in today's passage was reading in Isaiah 53. He came to embrace Christ that very day. We can only assume that this new believer would have kept reading in Isaiah. A few chapters later in Isaiah 56 he would have come across an exquisite passage specifically talking about the family that a eunuch has as a follower of God. How beautiful that God not only brought Philip to explain the Gospel to him, but that God also showed him through His Word that he was loved and had a place in God's family.

REFLECTIONS ON TODAY'S BIBLE READING

8 glasses a day:

TOP 3 PRIORITIES:

- [ ] ....
- [ ] ....
- [ ] ....

SCHEDULE/TO-DO LIST:

- [ ] ....
- [ ] ....
- [ ] ....
- [ ] ....

REMEMBER

July

S	M	T	W	T	F	S
						1
2	3	4	5	6	7	8
9	10	11	12	13	14	15
16	17	18	19	20	21	22
23	24	25	26	27	28	29
30	31					

Today's Bible Reading:

2 KINGS 14–15; ACTS 9:1–16; PSALM 103:10–14

For he knoweth our frame; he remembereth that we are dust.
PSALM 103:14

God knows that you are frail. He knows that you are prone to certain weaknesses and sins. He remembers that you were born in sin and must often fight your very sin nature to serve Him. You serve a God who, in His holiness, demands perfection–but who, in His love, has granted you that perfection based on no effort of your own. Don't let guilt or insecurities over your shortcomings have any place in your service to God.

TOP 3 PRIORITIES:

- ☐ ....
- ☐ ....
- ☐ ....

SCHEDULE/TO-DO LIST:

- ☐ ....
- ☐ ....
- ☐ ....
- ☐

REFLECTIONS ON TODAY'S BIBLE READING

8 glasses a day: ⬜ ⬜ ⬜ ⬜ ⬜ ⬜ ⬜ ⬜

June

S	M	T	W	T	F	S
				1	2	3
4	5	6	7	8	9	10
11	12	13	14	15	16	17
18	19	20	21	22	23	24
25	26	27	28	29	30	

REMEMBER

Today's Bible Reading:

2 KINGS 16–17; ACTS 9:17–31; PSALM 103:15–22

But Barnabas took him, and brought him to the apostles, and declared unto them how he had seen the Lord in the way, and that he had spoken to him, and how he had preached boldly at Damascus in the name of Jesus.
ACTS 9:27

God will build His Church. Sometimes He builds it through the miraculous conversion of enemies of the Gospel–people like Saul. But more often He builds it through the faithful, humble, and relentless service of His children–people like Barnabas and Ananias. Whether your conversion was an elaborate "Damascus road" experience or a simple acceptance of Christ at a young age, it was a miracle that day when God ushered you into the kingdom of His Son. He can and will use every sinner who has been saved by grace.

REFLECTIONS ON TODAY'S BIBLE READING

TOP 3 PRIORITIES:

- ☐ ....
- ☐ ....
- ☐ ....

SCHEDULE/TO-DO LIST:

- ☐ ....
- ☐ ....
- ☐ ....
- ☐ ....

8 glasses a day: ☐ ☐ ☐ ☐ ☐ ☐ ☐ ☐

REMEMBER

July

S	M	T	W	T	F	S
						1
2	3	4	5	6	7	8
9	10	11	12	13	14	15
16	17	18	19	20	21	22
23	24	25	26	27	28	29
30	31					

Today's Bible Reading:

2 KINGS 18:1–19:7; ACTS 9:32–10:16; PSALM 104:1–9

Then Peter arose and went with them. When he was come, they brought him into the upper chamber: and all the widows stood by him weeping, and shewing the coats and garments which Dorcas made, while she was with them.
ACTS 9:39

Peter—a miracle-working, mighty, and faithful servant of God—was called to Joppa because another mighty, faithful servant of God had died. This servant, Dorcas, had not restored sight to the blind or raised anyone from the dead, but her work was so significant that a group of people implored Peter to bring her back to life. And God chose to grant their supplication. God can work through miracles, but He can also work through a faithful daughter of His who made garments for those in need.

TOP 3 PRIORITIES:

- [ ] ....
- [ ] ....
- [ ] ....

SCHEDULE/TO-DO LIST:

- [ ] ....
- [ ] ....
- [ ] ....
- [ ] ....

REFLECTIONS ON TODAY'S BIBLE READING

8 glasses a day: ☐ ☐ ☐ ☐ ☐ ☐ ☐ ☐

REMEMBER

July

S	M	T	W	T	F	S
						1
2	3	4	5	6	7	8
9	10	11	12	13	14	15
16	17	18	19	20	21	22
23	24	25	26	27	28	29
30	31					

Today's Bible Reading:

2 KINGS 19:8–20:21; ACTS 10:17–33; PSALM 104:10–23

And Hezekiah received the letter of the hand of the messengers, and read it: and Hezekiah went up into the house of the LORD, and spread it before the LORD.
2 KINGS 19:14

Fear is a powerful weapon. The Assyrians understood this as they attempted to destroy the morale of God's people with terrifying taunts. But fear is no match for God. Hezekiah did what we all should do–when confronted with a seemingly indestructible enemy, Hezekiah laid the whole situation before God. He didn't try to figure it out on his own. Rather, he went to the one who was mightier than he or the Assyrians or fear itself.

REFLECTIONS ON TODAY'S BIBLE READING

8 glasses a day:

TOP 3 PRIORITIES:

- [ ] ....
- [ ] ....
- [ ] ....

SCHEDULE/TO-DO LIST:

- [ ] ....
- [ ] ....
- [ ] ....
- [ ]

REMEMBER

August

S	M	T	W	T	F	S
		1	2	3	4	5
6	7	8	9	10	11	12
13	14	15	16	17	18	19
20	21	22	23	24	25	26
27	28	29	30	31		

Today's Bible Reading:

2 KINGS 21:1–22:20; ACTS 10:34–11:18; PSALM 104:24–30

Now while Peter doubted in himself what this vision which he had seen should mean, behold, the men which were sent from Cornelius had made enquiry for Simon's house, and stood before the gate, and called, and asked whether Simon, which was surnamed Peter, were lodged there.
ACTS 10:17–18

Cornelius sent men to go visit Peter. This seems like a fairly simple story in the book of Acts. But, it is a glorious step for God's kingdom as it is the official inclusion of the Gentiles into the Gospel of Christ. God made it clear to Peter that there was no longer any national distinction of God's people. People from all nations and languages were made clean and granted the blessing to be adopted as God's children.

TOP 3 PRIORITIES:

- [ ] ....
- [ ] ....
- [ ] ....

SCHEDULE/TO-DO LIST:

- [ ] ....
- [ ] ....
- [ ] ....
- [ ] ....

REFLECTIONS ON TODAY'S BIBLE READING

8 glasses a day: ⬜ ⬜ ⬜ ⬜ ⬜ ⬜ ⬜ ⬜

REMEMBER

July

S	M	T	W	T	F	S
						1
2	3	4	5	6	7	8
9	10	11	12	13	14	15
16	17	18	19	20	21	22
23	24	25	26	27	28	29
30	31					

Today's Bible Reading:

2 KINGS 23; ACTS 11:19–12:17; PSALM 104:31–35

*And like unto him was there no king before him, that turned to the LORD
with all his heart, and with all his soul, and with all his might, according
to all the law of Moses; neither after him arose there any like him.*
2 KINGS 23:25

Josiah understood who he was and who God was. The title and position of king did not make him think that he was equal to his heavenly King. He understood that all understanding and guidance comes from the Lord. Therefore, he turned to God with all his heart, soul, and might. Have you done the same?

REFLECTIONS ON TODAY'S BIBLE READING

TOP 3 PRIORITIES:

☐ ....
☐ ....
☐ ....

SCHEDULE/TO-DO LIST:

☐ ....
☐ ....
☐ ....
☐ ....

8 glasses a day:

REMEMBER

August

S	M	T	W	T	F	S
		1	2	3	4	5
6	7	8	9	10	11	12
13	14	15	16	17	18	19
20	21	22	23	24	25	26
27	28	29	30	31		

Today's Bible Reading:

2 KINGS 24–25; ACTS 12:18–13:13; PSALM 105:1–7

O give thanks unto the LORD; call upon his name: make known
his deeds among the people. Sing unto him, sing psalms
unto him: talk ye of all his wondrous works.
PSALM 105:1–2

Though your relationship with God is deeply personal, it should not be totally private. You should openly give thanks to God and declare to others what He has done for you. If you truly grasped the depth of His grace to you, you would not be able to contain His praise or keep your love of Him from others. So sing unto Him and talk of His wondrous works.

TOP 3 PRIORITIES:

- ☐ ....
- ☐ ....
- ☐ ....

SCHEDULE/TO-DO LIST:

- ☐ ....
- ☐ ....
- ☐ ....
- ☐ ....

REFLECTIONS ON TODAY'S BIBLE READING

8 glasses a day: ☐ ☐ ☐ ☐ ☐ ☐ ☐ ☐

REMEMBER

July

S	M	T	W	T	F	S
						1
2	3	4	5	6	7	8
9	10	11	12	13	14	15
16	17	18	19	20	21	22
23	24	25	26	27	28	29
30	31					

Today's Bible Reading:

1 CHRONICLES 1–2; ACTS 13:14–43; PSALM 105:8–15

He hath remembered his covenant for ever, the word which he commanded to a thousand generations. . . . When they were but a few men in number; yea, very few, and strangers in it.
PSALM 105:8, 12

When God made His covenant with Abraham and promised him that his descendants would be as numerous as the stars, Abraham probably never could have imagined how immensely God would fulfill that promise. God has remembered His covenant and brought to Himself innumerable spiritual descendants of Abraham from all over the earth. Because of your faith in God, you are a direct fulfillment of God's promise.

REFLECTIONS ON TODAY'S BIBLE READING

8 glasses a day:

TOP 3 PRIORITIES:

- ☐ ....
- ☐ ....
- ☐ ....

SCHEDULE/TO-DO LIST:

- ☐ ....
- ☐ ....
- ☐ ....
- ☐

REMEMBER

August

S	M	T	W	T	F	S
		1	2	3	4	5
6	7	8	9	10	11	12
13	14	15	16	17	18	19
20	21	22	23	24	25	26
27	28	29	30	31		

Today's Bible Reading:

1 CHRONICLES 3:1–5:10; ACTS 13:44–14:10; PSALM 105:16–28

*And the disciples were filled with joy,
and with the Holy Ghost.*
ACTS 13:52

In 1 Chronicles 4:10, we read about Jabez, whose prayer for blessing, prosperity, and protection was granted. We can imagine that he would have lived a happy and joyful life. And yet, in Acts we read about followers of Christ who were being persecuted, beaten, and imprisoned. But even in these circumstances they were filled with joy. When it comes to living a joy-filled life, the circumstances don't matter. Whom you serve does.

TOP 3 PRIORITIES:

☐ ....
☐ ....
☐ ....

SCHEDULE/TO-DO LIST:

☐ ....
☐ ....
☐ ....
☐ ....

REFLECTIONS ON TODAY'S BIBLE READING

8 glasses a day: ☐ ☐ ☐ ☐ ☐ ☐ ☐ ☐

July

S	M	T	W	T	F	S
						1
2	3	4	5	6	7	8
9	10	11	12	13	14	15
16	17	18	19	20	21	22
23	24	25	26	27	28	29
30	31					

REMEMBER

Today's Bible Reading:

1 CHRONICLES 5:11–6:81; ACTS 14:11–28; PSALM 105:29–36

And saying, Sirs, why do ye these things? We also are men of like passions with you, and preach unto you that ye should turn from these vanities unto the living God, which made heaven, and earth, and the sea, and all things that are therein.
ACTS 14:15

Having been declared gods by the local people, it would have been easy for Paul and Barnabas to see this as their free ticket out of persecution and let the people continue to treat them as gods. But they did not deny their God to take the easy way out. Instead, they declared themselves as mere men. God could (and sometimes does) send impressive angels to declare His Word, but He most often uses flawed and weak humans. Through these broken vessels He can shine the light of His power more clearly.

REFLECTIONS ON TODAY'S BIBLE READING

8 glasses a day:

TOP 3 PRIORITIES:

- [ ] ....
- [ ] ....
- [ ] ....

SCHEDULE/TO-DO LIST:

- [ ] ....
- [ ] ....
- [ ] ....
- [ ] ....

REMEMBER

August

S	M	T	W	T	F	S
		1	2	3	4	5
6	7	8	9	10	11	12
13	14	15	16	17	18	19
20	21	22	23	24	25	26
27	28	29	30	31		

Today's Bible Reading:

1 CHRONICLES 7:1–9:9; ACTS 15:1–18; PSALM 105:37–45

And gave them the lands of the heathen: and they inherited the labour of the people; that they might observe his statutes, and keep his laws. Praise ye the LORD.
PSALM 105:44–45

God miraculously sustained the Israelites through the wilderness and brought them into a rich promised land. He did this so that they might serve and obey Him. But instead, the people more often disobeyed and disappointed Him. God has also brought you into the promised land of His kingdom. Don't make the same mistake as the Israelites who took His blessings and provision for granted. Thank God and serve Him for all He has done for you.

TOP 3 PRIORITIES:

- ☐ ....
- ☐ ....
- ☐ ....

SCHEDULE/TO-DO LIST:

- ☐ ....
- ☐ ....
- ☐ ....
- ☐ ....

REFLECTIONS ON TODAY'S BIBLE READING

8 glasses a day: ☐ ☐ ☐ ☐ ☐ ☐ ☐ ☐

REMEMBER

July

S	M	T	W	T	F	S
						1
2	3	4	5	6	7	8
9	10	11	12	13	14	15
16	17	18	19	20	21	22
23	24	25	26	27	28	29
30	31					

Today's Bible Reading:

1 CHRONICLES 9:10–11:9; ACTS 15:19–41; PSALM 106:1–12

And the contention was so sharp between them, that they departed asunder one from the other: and so Barnabas took Mark, and sailed unto Cyprus.
Acts 15:39

Today's passage in Acts 15 feels slightly uncomfortable. Two of the leading apostles who were working together to spread the Gospel had a disagreement so strong that they had to separate. This seems like a major setback in the advancement of the Gospel. But God used even this for His purposes. Instead of working side by side, Paul and Barnabas were able to reach more people by going their separate ways and spreading the Gospel to different countries and people.

REFLECTIONS ON TODAY'S BIBLE READING

TOP 3 PRIORITIES:

☐ ....
☐ ....
☐ ....

SCHEDULE/TO-DO LIST:

☐ ....
☐ ....
☐ ....
☐ ....

8 glasses a day: ☐ ☐ ☐ ☐ ☐ ☐ ☐ ☐

REMEMBER

August

S	M	T	W	T	F	S
		1	2	3	4	5
6	7	8	9	10	11	12
13	14	15	16	17	18	19
20	21	22	23	24	25	26
27	28	29	30	31		

Today's Bible Reading:

1 CHRONICLES 11:10-12:40; ACTS 16:1-15; PSALM 106:13-27

Thus they changed their glory into the similitude of an ox that eateth grass.
PSALM 106:20

It seems so absurd that the Israelites would have created an idol of a common animal to replace the God whose very presence they had witnessed in the pillar of fire and cloud. But don't we often do the same thing? We trade the rich bounties that are available to us in God's Word for worthless shows or games. Or we belittle the holy and mighty God into a mere genie whom we only talk to when we want something. Strive to recognize and know the glorious God for who He really is.

TOP 3 PRIORITIES:

- ☐ ....
- ☐ ....
- ☐ ....

SCHEDULE/TO-DO LIST:

- ☐ ....
- ☐ ....
- ☐ ....
- ☐ ....

REFLECTIONS ON TODAY'S BIBLE READING

8 glasses a day: ☐ ☐ ☐ ☐ ☐ ☐ ☐ ☐

July

S	M	T	W	T	F	S
						1
2	3	4	5	6	7	8
9	10	11	12	13	14	15
16	17	18	19	20	21	22
23	24	25	26	27	28	29
30	31					

REMEMBER

Today's Bible Reading:

1 CHRONICLES 13–15; ACTS 16:16–40; PSALM 106:28–33

And when her masters saw that the hope of their gains was gone, they caught Paul and Silas, and drew them into the marketplace unto the rulers.
Acts 16:19

The concept of Jesus may sound pretty nice, or at least nonthreatening, to most people. . .until He gets in the way of their comfort. We live in a world where comfort and prosperity are god. The Jesus that we preach may be offensive to people, as He forces them to come to terms with their sin and give up things that they have held to be precious. But the riches that are in Christ are far greater than any riches that this earth can offer. We can't dare risk not sharing such an important message because we're afraid of how it will be received.

REFLECTIONS ON TODAY'S BIBLE READING

TOP 3 PRIORITIES:

- ☐ ....
- ☐ ....
- ☐ ....

SCHEDULE/TO-DO LIST:

- ☐ ....
- ☐ ....
- ☐ ....
- ☐

8 glasses a day: ▢ ▢ ▢ ▢ ▢ ▢ ▢ ▢

REMEMBER

August

S	M	T	W	T	F	S
		1	2	3	4	5
6	7	8	9	10	11	12
13	14	15	16	17	18	19
20	21	22	23	24	25	26
27	28	29	30	31		

Friday
JULY 14

Today's Bible Reading:

1 CHRONICLES 16–17; ACTS 17:1–14; PSALM 106:34–43

And when they found them not, they drew Jason and certain brethren unto the rulers of the city, crying, These that have turned the world upside down are come hither also.
Acts 17:6

The apostles were accused of turning the world upside down. How incredible would it be if those words were spoken again of God's people? May we so unwaveringly stand for truth in the face of opposition and unabashedly proclaim Christ as the only way to true life that we turn the world on its head.

TOP 3 PRIORITIES:

☐ ....
☐ ....
☐ ....

SCHEDULE/TO-DO LIST:

☐ ....
☐ ....
☐ ....
☐ ....

REFLECTIONS ON TODAY'S BIBLE READING

8 glasses a day: ☐ ☐ ☐ ☐ ☐ ☐ ☐ ☐

REMEMBER

July

S	M	T	W	T	F	S
						1
2	3	4	5	6	7	8
9	10	11	12	13	14	15
16	17	18	19	20	21	22
23	24	25	26	27	28	29
30	31					

Today's Bible Reading:

1 CHRONICLES 18–20; ACTS 17:15–34; PSALM 106:44–48

*For in him we live, and move, and have our being; as certain also
of your own poets have said, For we are also his offspring.*
ACTS 17:28

Paul knew and understood the culture in which he was preaching. In today's passage, he even quoted the society's poets. It's important to know whom you are talking to when sharing the Gospel so that you can formulate your message to be the most understandable to your culture. This can be a powerful tool as long as the fundamental message and natural power of the Gospel are not softened or changed.

REFLECTIONS ON TODAY'S BIBLE READING

8 glasses a day:

TOP 3 PRIORITIES:

- ☐ ....
- ☐ ....
- ☐ ....

SCHEDULE/TO-DO LIST:

- ☐ ....
- ☐ ....
- ☐ ....
- ☐ ....

REMEMBER

August

S	M	T	W	T	F	S
		1	2	3	4	5
6	7	8	9	10	11	12
13	14	15	16	17	18	19
20	21	22	23	24	25	26
27	28	29	30	31		

Today's Bible Reading:

1 CHRONICLES 21–22; ACTS 18:1–23; PSALM 107:1–9

*And Satan stood up against Israel,
and provoked David to number Israel.*
1 CHRONICLES 21:1

Today's passage in 1 Chronicles is one of the few times that Satan is mentioned in the Old Testament. But even when he's not spoken of directly, you can recognize his scent as his evil work is woven throughout the narratives. It is vitally important that we remember that there is a spiritual battle raging in this world at all times. We will be ill-equipped if we don't train for such a battle. Our enemy is real; so be on your guard. But remember that our ally is stronger and can thwart any evil plans the devil can devise.

TOP 3 PRIORITIES:

- ☐ ....
- ☐ ....
- ☐ ....

SCHEDULE/TO-DO LIST:

- ☐ ....
- ☐ ....
- ☐ ....
- ☐ ....

REFLECTIONS ON TODAY'S BIBLE READING

8 glasses a day: ▯ ▯ ▯ ▯ ▯ ▯ ▯ ▯

REMEMBER

July

S	M	T	W	T	F	S
						1
2	3	4	5	6	7	8
9	10	11	12	13	14	15
16	17	18	19	20	21	22
23	24	25	26	27	28	29
30	31					

Today's Bible Reading:

1 CHRONICLES 23–25; ACTS 18:24–19:10; PSALM 107:10–16

*And he began to speak boldly in the synagogue: whom when
Aquila and Priscilla had heard, they took him unto them,
and expounded unto him the way of God more perfectly.*
ACTS 18:26

When Aquila and Priscilla heard Apollos speak, they realized that he did not have a completely full or accurate knowledge of the Gospel. In response to this, they did not spend their energy talking behind his back about how ignorant he was. Instead, they took him in and trained him in the fullness of the message of Christ. Wouldn't we spend our time so much more wisely by talking less about a problem and working more to fix it?

REFLECTIONS ON TODAY'S BIBLE READING

8 glasses a day:

TOP 3 PRIORITIES:

- ☐ ....
- ☐ ....
- ☐ ....

SCHEDULE/TO-DO LIST:

- ☐ ....
- ☐ ....
- ☐ ....
- ☐ ....

REMEMBER

August

S	M	T	W	T	F	S
		1	2	3	4	5
6	7	8	9	10	11	12
13	14	15	16	17	18	19
20	21	22	23	24	25	26
27	28	29	30	31		

Tuesday
JULY 18

Today's Bible Reading:

1 CHRONICLES 26–27; ACTS 19:11–22; PSALM 107:17–32

Then they cry unto the LORD in their trouble, and he saveth them out of their distresses. He sent his word, and healed them, and delivered them from their destructions. Oh that men would praise the LORD for his goodness, and for his wonderful works to the children of men!
PSALM 107:19–21

The writer of today's psalm had firsthand experience of the love and saving power of God. This personal knowledge drove him to wish that others would praise God and know of His wonderful works as well. Does God's goodness to you inspire you to tell others about Him and cause you to work hard to let others know of His wonderful works?

TOP 3 PRIORITIES:

- ☐ ....
- ☐ ....
- ☐ ....

SCHEDULE/TO-DO LIST:

- ☐ ....
- ☐ ....
- ☐ ....
- ☐ ....

REFLECTIONS ON TODAY'S BIBLE READING

8 glasses a day: ☐ ☐ ☐ ☐ ☐ ☐ ☐ ☐

July

S	M	T	W	T	F	S
						1
2	3	4	5	6	7	8
9	10	11	12	13	14	15
16	17	18	19	20	21	22
23	24	25	26	27	28	29
30	31					

REMEMBER

Today's Bible Reading:

1 CHRONICLES 28–29; ACTS 19:23–41; PSALM 107:33–38

*And David said to Solomon his son, Be strong and of good courage,
and do it: fear not, nor be dismayed: for the LORD God, even my God,
will be with thee; he will not fail thee, nor forsake thee, until thou hast
finished all the work for the service of the house of the LORD.*
1 CHRONICLES 28:20

In today's passage, David spoke beautifully personal words to his son Solomon, encouraging him to be strong and courageous and to rely on God. David knew that his God would continue to be faithful to the next generation. Are you passing on your faith to the next generation? It is a beautiful thing when the surpassing value of a personal relationship with God is passed down to the children's children and so on. It is the best possible inheritance.

REFLECTIONS ON TODAY'S BIBLE READING

TOP 3 PRIORITIES:

- ☐ ....
- ☐ ....
- ☐ ....

SCHEDULE/TO-DO LIST:

- ☐ ....
- ☐ ....
- ☐ ....
- ☐

8 glasses a day: ☐ ☐ ☐ ☐ ☐ ☐ ☐ ☐

REMEMBER

August

S	M	T	W	T	F	S
		1	2	3	4	5
6	7	8	9	10	11	12
13	14	15	16	17	18	19
20	21	22	23	24	25	26
27	28	29	30	31		

Thursday
JULY 20

Today's Bible Reading:

2 CHRONICLES 1–3; ACTS 20:1–16; PSALM 107:39–43

*He poureth contempt upon princes, and causeth them to wander
in the wilderness, where there is no way. Yet setteth he the poor
on high from affliction, and maketh him families like a flock.*
PSALM 107:40–41

God does not do things as the world does. While we celebrate the rich, beautiful, and powerful, He delights in the poor, lonely, and needy. It would do us good to see the world through His eyes and to value what He values.

TOP 3 PRIORITIES:

- ☐ ....
- ☐ ....
- ☐ ....

SCHEDULE/TO-DO LIST:

- ☐ ....
- ☐ ....
- ☐ ....
- ☐ ....

REFLECTIONS ON TODAY'S BIBLE READING

8 glasses a day: ☐ ☐ ☐ ☐ ☐ ☐ ☐ ☐

REMEMBER

July

S	M	T	W	T	F	S
						1
2	3	4	5	6	7	8
9	10	11	12	13	14	15
16	17	18	19	20	21	22
23	24	25	26	27	28	29
30	31					

Today's Bible Reading:

2 CHRONICLES 4:1–6:11; ACTS 20:17–38; PSALM 108

But none of these things move me, neither count I my life dear unto myself,
so that I might finish my course with joy, and the ministry, which I have
received of the Lord Jesus, to testify the gospel of the grace of God.
ACTS 20:24

Paul knew that bonds and afflictions waited for him in every city where he preached. This knowledge would cause many of us to give up. And yet, Paul talks about finishing his course with joy even in the face of this persecution. The only way that he could have this kind of joyful attitude amid unavoidable suffering was because he knew his God very well. His joy was entirely disconnected from his circumstances and completely rooted in his relationship with God and his hope in an eternity with his Savior.

REFLECTIONS ON TODAY'S BIBLE READING

8 glasses a day:

TOP 3 PRIORITIES:

- [ ] ....
- [ ] ....
- [ ] ....

SCHEDULE/TO-DO LIST:

- [ ] ....
- [ ] ....
- [ ] ....
- [ ] ....

REMEMBER

August

S	M	T	W	T	F	S
		1	2	3	4	5
6	7	8	9	10	11	12
13	14	15	16	17	18	19
20	21	22	23	24	25	26
27	28	29	30	31		

Saturday
JULY 22

Today's Bible Reading:

2 CHRONICLES 6:12–7:10; ACTS 21:1–14; PSALM 109:1–20

But will God in very deed dwell with men on the earth?
behold, heaven and the heaven of heavens cannot contain
thee; how much less this house which I have built!
2 CHRONICLES 6:18

Solomon spoke rightly that not even the highest heaven can contain God. Because of this he wondered that God could ever dwell on earth with men. And yet, He did dwell on earth, as a humble and self-sacrificing Man. And now He dwells in us. That the almighty God condescended to dwell among us and in us is a truth almost too beautiful to fathom.

TOP 3 PRIORITIES:

SCHEDULE/TO-DO LIST:

REFLECTIONS ON TODAY'S BIBLE READING

8 glasses a day:

July

S	M	T	W	T	F	S
						1
2	3	4	5	6	7	8
9	10	11	12	13	14	15
16	17	18	19	20	21	22
23	24	25	26	27	28	29
30	31					

REMEMBER

Today's Bible Reading:

2 CHRONICLES 7:11–9:28; ACTS 21:15–32; PSALM 109:21–31

Then Paul took the men, and the next day purifying himself with them entered into the temple, to signify the accomplishment of the days of purification, until that an offering should be offered for every one of them.
ACTS 21:26

It's important to make wise decisions about when to bend to cultural norms for the sake of the Gospel. In today's passage, Paul purified himself according to Jewish custom. This was not something that he as a Christian needed to do. He did this solely for the sake of the Gospel, believing that it would allow him to reach more people for Christ.

REFLECTIONS ON TODAY'S BIBLE READING

8 glasses a day:

TOP 3 PRIORITIES:

- [ ] ....
- [ ] ....
- [ ] ....

SCHEDULE/TO-DO LIST:

- [ ] ....
- [ ] ....
- [ ] ....
- [ ] ....

REMEMBER

August

S	M	T	W	T	F	S
		1	2	3	4	5
6	7	8	9	10	11	12
13	14	15	16	17	18	19
20	21	22	23	24	25	26
27	28	29	30	31		

Today's Bible Reading:

2 CHRONICLES 9:29–12:16; ACTS 21:33–22:16; PSALM 110:1–3

And he did evil, because he prepared not his heart to seek the Lord.
2 CHRONICLES 12:14

Rehoboam did evil because he did not prepare his heart to seek the Lord. What steps have you taken to prepare your heart to seek God? Do you have a regular devotional time? Do you faithfully attend church? Are you committed to reading and memorizing God's Word? If you have not humbled yourself to seek and serve God, nothing that you do can be righteous in His sight. Set your heart to seek God and you will find Him. He will reward you for seeking.

TOP 3 PRIORITIES:

- ☐ ....
- ☐ ....
- ☐ ....

SCHEDULE/TO-DO LIST:

- ☐ ....
- ☐ ....
- ☐ ....
- ☐ ....

REFLECTIONS ON TODAY'S BIBLE READING

8 glasses a day: ☐ ☐ ☐ ☐ ☐ ☐ ☐ ☐

REMEMBER

July

S	M	T	W	T	F	S
						1
2	3	4	5	6	7	8
9	10	11	12	13	14	15
16	17	18	19	20	21	22
23	24	25	26	27	28	29
30	31					

Today's Bible Reading:

2 CHRONICLES 13–15; ACTS 22:17–23:11; PSALM 110:4–7

And, behold, God himself is with us for our captain, and his priests with sounding trumpets to cry alarm against you. O children of Israel, fight ye not against the LORD God of your fathers; for ye shall not prosper.
2 CHRONICLES 13:12

Any battle fought against the living God is a losing battle. The battle to keep your indulgent sins is a battle where you are pitted against God and you will lose to His holiness. The battle of death over life has already been lost by the devil because he was foolish enough to go up against his Maker. Choose sides with your Savior—you will always be on the winning side.

REFLECTIONS ON TODAY'S BIBLE READING

8 glasses a day:

TOP 3 PRIORITIES:

- [ ] ....
- [ ] ....
- [ ] ....

SCHEDULE/TO-DO LIST:

- [ ] ....
- [ ] ....
- [ ] ....
- [ ]

REMEMBER

August

S	M	T	W	T	F	S
		1	2	3	4	5
6	7	8	9	10	11	12
13	14	15	16	17	18	19
20	21	22	23	24	25	26
27	28	29	30	31		

Today's Bible Reading:

2 CHRONICLES 16–17; ACTS 23:12–24:21; PSALM 111

For the eyes of the LORD run to and fro throughout the whole earth, to shew himself strong in the behalf of them whose heart is perfect toward him. Herein thou hast done foolishly: therefore from henceforth thou shalt have wars.
2 CHRONICLES 16:9

It may at times feel like God is not actively involved in the world or that He has given up on a creation that has strayed so far from Him. But this is not true. He is constantly watching the movement of His creation. He shows Himself as a strong defense to those whose hearts are His. God is not an inactive and disconnected observer. He is already aware of your circumstances, so call out to Him in your need.

TOP 3 PRIORITIES:

- ☐ ....
- ☐ ....
- ☐ ....

SCHEDULE/TO-DO LIST:

- ☐ ....
- ☐ ....
- ☐ ....
- ☐ ....

REFLECTIONS ON TODAY'S BIBLE READING

8 glasses a day: ☐ ☐ ☐ ☐ ☐ ☐ ☐ ☐

REMEMBER

July

S	M	T	W	T	F	S
						1
2	3	4	5	6	7	8
9	10	11	12	13	14	15
16	17	18	19	20	21	22
23	24	25	26	27	28	29
30	31					

Today's Bible Reading:

2 CHRONICLES 18–19; ACTS 24:22–25:12; PSALM 112

And the king of Israel said unto Jehoshaphat, There is yet one man, by whom we may enquire of the LORD: but I hate him; for he never prophesied good unto me, but always evil: the same is Micaiah the son of Imla. And Jehoshaphat said, Let not the king say so.
2 CHRONICLES 18:7

Micaiah was faithful in relaying messages from God and was, therefore, hated by the king of Israel because he never told the king what he wanted to hear. You may sometimes find yourself in the same situation where being faithful to the truth of God and His Word puts you at odds with those around you. May we have the same courage as God's faithful prophets to continue to speak His truth no matter what the reception.

REFLECTIONS ON TODAY'S BIBLE READING

8 glasses a day:

TOP 3 PRIORITIES:

- [ ] ....
- [ ] ....
- [ ] ....

SCHEDULE/TO-DO LIST:

- [ ] ....
- [ ] ....
- [ ] ....
- [ ] ....

REMEMBER

August

S	M	T	W	T	F	S
		1	2	3	4	5
6	7	8	9	10	11	12
13	14	15	16	17	18	19
20	21	22	23	24	25	26
27	28	29	30	31		

Today's Bible Reading:

2 CHRONICLES 20–21; ACTS 25:13–27; PSALM 113

And said, O Lord God of our fathers, art not thou God in heaven? and rulest not thou over all the kingdoms of the heathen? and in thine hand is there not power and might, so that none is able to withstand thee? Art not thou our God, who didst drive out the inhabitants of this land before thy people Israel, and gavest it to the seed of Abraham thy friend for ever?
2 Chronicles 20:6–7

We ought to pray remembering and relying on God's promises and faithfulness. Jehoshaphat prayed in the light of God's past work and His present promises. Because he knew his God to be a promise keeper, he was able to go into battle praising God (2 Chronicles 20:21). You can march into whatever battle you are facing praising God as well. When the outcome is already decided by the past work of Christ, there is no reason to fear. There is nothing left to do but praise.

TOP 3 PRIORITIES:

- ☐ ....
- ☐ ....
- ☐ ....

SCHEDULE/TO-DO LIST:

- ☐ ....
- ☐ ....
- ☐ ....
- ☐

REFLECTIONS ON TODAY'S BIBLE READING

8 glasses a day: ☐ ☐ ☐ ☐ ☐ ☐ ☐ ☐

July

S	M	T	W	T	F	S
						1
2	3	4	5	6	7	8
9	10	11	12	13	14	15
16	17	18	19	20	21	22
23	24	25	26	27	28	29
30	31					

REMEMBER

Today's Bible Reading:

2 CHRONICLES 22–23; ACTS 26; PSALM 114

And Paul said, I would to God, that not only thou, but also all that hear me this day, were both almost, and altogether such as I am, except these bonds.
ACTS 26:29

It's easy to dwell on the things in your life that are not going well. But are you aware of how blessed you are solely based on your relationship with Christ? No matter what circumstance you are in, you are beyond fortunate. Paul knew how blessed he was because of his walk with God and wished that others might also know the depths of the riches that he had every day. He had a truly good life that was not affected by chains or suffering.

REFLECTIONS ON TODAY'S BIBLE READING

TOP 3 PRIORITIES:

SCHEDULE/TO-DO LIST:

8 glasses a day:

REMEMBER

August

S	M	T	W	T	F	S
		1	2	3	4	5
6	7	8	9	10	11	12
13	14	15	16	17	18	19
20	21	22	23	24	25	26
27	28	29	30	31		

Today's Bible Reading:

2 CHRONICLES 24:1–25:16; ACTS 27:1–20; PSALM 115:1–10

Now after the death of Jehoiada came the princes of Judah, and made obeisance to the king. Then the king hearkened unto them.
2 CHRONICLES 24:17

A good mentor is remarkably valuable. When Jehoiada was alive, Joash did what was right in God's sight. When Jehoiada died, Joash began to be influenced by far less wise people and, tragically, turned from God. Don't be afraid to reach out to mentor someone–it could be the difference between that person choosing to follow God or not. At the same time seek out a mentor for yourself that will guide you in the way of Christ.

TOP 3 PRIORITIES:

- ☐ ....
- ☐ ....
- ☐ ....

SCHEDULE/TO-DO LIST:

- ☐ ....
- ☐ ....
- ☐ ....
- ☐

REFLECTIONS ON TODAY'S BIBLE READING

8 glasses a day: ☐ ☐ ☐ ☐ ☐ ☐ ☐ ☐

July

S	M	T	W	T	F	S
						1
2	3	4	5	6	7	8
9	10	11	12	13	14	15
16	17	18	19	20	21	22
23	24	25	26	27	28	29
30	31					

REMEMBER

Today's Bible Reading:

2 CHRONICLES 25:17–27:9; ACTS 27:21–28:6; PSALM 115:11–18

Wherefore, sirs, be of good cheer: for I believe God,
that it shall be even as it was told me.
ACTS 27:25

Paul knew the plan that God had for him and recognized that he was immortal until that plan was fulfilled. His faith in God's purposes was rock solid. Not even things as lethal as a shipwreck or poisonous snake could alter the course that God had set for him.

REFLECTIONS ON TODAY'S BIBLE READING

8 glasses a day: ▢ ▢ ▢ ▢ ▢ ▢ ▢ ▢

TOP 3 PRIORITIES:

☐ ....
☐ ....
☐ ....

SCHEDULE/TO-DO LIST:

☐ ....
☐ ....
☐ ....
☐ ....

REMEMBER

August

S	M	T	W	T	F	S
		1	2	3	4	5
6	7	8	9	10	11	12
13	14	15	16	17	18	19
20	21	22	23	24	25	26
27	28	29	30	31		

Tuesday
AUGUST 1

Today's Bible Reading:

2 CHRONICLES 28:1–29:19; ACTS 28:7–31; PSALM 116:1–5

*But we desire to hear of thee what thou thinkest: for as concerning
this sect, we know that every where it is spoken against.*
ACTS 28:22

The "sect" of Christianity was spoken against everywhere. The adherents to this sect preached of life that was released from the bonds of the Law. They preached of salvation based on no merit of one's own. They spoke of eternal life with God in heaven secured by the sacrifice of His Son. Isn't it remarkable that there could be so much resistance to such a beautiful message?

TOP 3 PRIORITIES:

- [ ] ....
- [ ] ....
- [ ] ....

SCHEDULE/TO-DO LIST:

- [ ]
- [ ]
- [ ]
- [ ]

REFLECTIONS ON TODAY'S BIBLE READING

8 glasses a day: ☐ ☐ ☐ ☐ ☐ ☐ ☐ ☐

REMEMBER

August

S	M	T	W	T	F	S
		1	2	3	4	5
6	7	8	9	10	11	12
13	14	15	16	17	18	19
20	21	22	23	24	25	26
27	28	29	30	31		

Today's Bible Reading:

2 CHRONICLES 29:20–30:27; ROMANS 1:1–17; PSALM 116:6–19

Precious in the sight of the LORD is the death of his saints.
PSALM 116:15

For those of us who have lost loved ones who are in Christ (or for those who are facing an imminent death), keep in mind that the death of God's saints is not the end. The death of His children is precious in His sight. We do not pass from this world into the next forgotten and on our own. Rather, we are led through by our faithful guide who overcame death on our behalf. A beautiful celebration awaits us on the other side. Celebrate the lives and deaths of God's children, for our Father does.

REFLECTIONS ON TODAY'S BIBLE READING

TOP 3 PRIORITIES:
- ☐ ....
- ☐ ....
- ☐ ....

SCHEDULE/TO-DO LIST:
- ☐ ....
- ☐ ....
- ☐ ....
- ☐ ....

8 glasses a day: ☐ ☐ ☐ ☐ ☐ ☐ ☐ ☐

REMEMBER

September

S	M	T	W	T	F	S
					1	2
3	4	5	6	7	8	9
10	11	12	13	14	15	16
17	18	19	20	21	22	23
24	25	26	27	28	29	30

Today's Bible Reading:

2 CHRONICLES 31–32; ROMANS 1:18–32; PSALM 117

Be strong and courageous, be not afraid nor dismayed for the king of Assyria, nor for all the multitude that is with him: for there be more with us than with him: with him is an arm of flesh; but with us is the LORD our God to help us, and to fight our battles. And the people rested themselves upon the words of Hezekiah king of Judah.
2 CHRONICLES 32:7–8

What a beautiful and inspiring speech we read from King Hezekiah in today's passage. The terrifying and brutal force of Assyria was threatening God's people. But instead of giving in to fear, Hezekiah relied on his God. No matter how big or fearful a force is up against you, you will always have more on your side because you have a heavenly army led by the everlasting God fighting for you. Being on God's side automatically puts you in the majority.

TOP 3 PRIORITIES:

- ☐ ....
- ☐ ....
- ☐ ....

SCHEDULE/TO-DO LIST:

- ☐ ....
- ☐ ....
- ☐ ....
- ☐ ....

REFLECTIONS ON TODAY'S BIBLE READING

8 glasses a day: ☐ ☐ ☐ ☐ ☐ ☐ ☐ ☐

REMEMBER

August

S	M	T	W	T	F	S
		1	2	3	4	5
6	7	8	9	10	11	12
13	14	15	16	17	18	19
20	21	22	23	24	25	26
27	28	29	30	31		

Today's Bible Reading:

2 CHRONICLES 33:1–34:7; ROMANS 2; PSALM 118:1–18

For when the Gentiles, which have not the law, do by nature the things contained in the law, these, having not the law, are a law unto themselves: which shew the work of the law written in their hearts, their conscience also bearing witness, and their thoughts the mean while accusing or else excusing one another.
ROMANS 2:14–15

We have an innate understanding of the moral law written on our hearts that proves the existence of a higher order. No matter how hard people may fight against the idea of a Creator, their very innermost conscience speaks and witnesses of Him. An instinctual knowledge of Him is inevitable. This means that however hard some people may work to harden their hearts and minds to Christ, they are without excuse on the day when they stand before their Maker.

REFLECTIONS ON TODAY'S BIBLE READING

8 glasses a day:

TOP 3 PRIORITIES:

SCHEDULE/TO-DO LIST:

REMEMBER

September

S	M	T	W	T	F	S
					1	2
3	4	5	6	7	8	9
10	11	12	13	14	15	16
17	18	19	20	21	22	23
24	25	26	27	28	29	30

Today's Bible Reading:

2 CHRONICLES 34:8–35:19; ROMANS 3:1–26; PSALM 118:19–23

*Even the righteousness of God which is by faith of Jesus Christ
unto all and upon all them that believe: for there is no difference:
for all have sinned, and come short of the glory of God.*
ROMANS 3:22–23

When it comes to our presalvation standing before God, we are all on an even playing field. We have all sinned and are in desperate need of His righteous covering. In God's eyes, there is no difference regarding race, gender, socioeconomic status, physical ability, or beauty. None of us can attain to His standards on our own. If God does not cater His message based on physical, financial, or social standards, then neither should we.

TOP 3 PRIORITIES:

- ☐ ....
- ☐ ....
- ☐ ....

SCHEDULE/TO-DO LIST:

- ☐ ....
- ☐ ....
- ☐ ....
- ☐

REFLECTIONS ON TODAY'S BIBLE READING

8 glasses a day: ▢ ▢ ▢ ▢ ▢ ▢ ▢ ▢

August

S	M	T	W	T	F	S
		1	2	3	4	5
6	7	8	9	10	11	12
13	14	15	16	17	18	19
20	21	22	23	24	25	26
27	28	29	30	31		

REMEMBER

Today's Bible Reading:

2 CHRONICLES 35:20–36:23; ROMANS 3:27–4:25; PSALM 118:24–29

This is the day which the LORD hath made;
we will rejoice and be glad in it.
PSALM 118:24

"This is the day which the Lord hath made; we will rejoice and be glad in it." This is a mind-set and a decision to be made each and every morning—*God has made today; therefore I will be glad*. If at the moment your life is such that it is hard to find things to rejoice in, at least you can be glad that God has given you another new day with new opportunities and new blessings from Him. He has planned out this day for you. Rejoice in the new day that God gives you.

REFLECTIONS ON TODAY'S BIBLE READING

TOP 3 PRIORITIES:

☐ ....
☐ ....
☐ ....

SCHEDULE/TO-DO LIST:

☐ ....
☐ ....
☐ ....
☐ ....

8 glasses a day:

REMEMBER

September

S	M	T	W	T	F	S
					1	2
3	4	5	6	7	8	9
10	11	12	13	14	15	16
17	18	19	20	21	22	23
24	25	26	27	28	29	30

Monday
AUGUST 7

Today's Bible Reading:

EZRA 1–3; ROMANS 5; PSALM 119:1–8

Therefore being justified by faith, we have peace with God through our Lord Jesus Christ: by whom also we have access by faith into this grace wherein we stand, and rejoice in hope of the glory of God.
ROMANS 5:1–2

Where does your peace come from? Not from relationships, physical healing, or more money. It comes from being justified before God. You know you stand clean and spotless before a holy God and that because of this you are guaranteed a life of eternity in His glory. This is true peace, to know that you have been saved by grace and that nothing can touch you outside of His will for you.

TOP 3 PRIORITIES:

- [ ] ....
- [ ] ....
- [ ] ....

SCHEDULE/TO-DO LIST:

- [ ] ....
- [ ] ....
- [ ] ....
- [ ]

REFLECTIONS ON TODAY'S BIBLE READING

8 glasses a day: ☐ ☐ ☐ ☐ ☐ ☐ ☐ ☐

August

S	M	T	W	T	F	S
		1	2	3	4	5
6	7	8	9	10	11	12
13	14	15	16	17	18	19
20	21	22	23	24	25	26
27	28	29	30	31		

REMEMBER

Today's Bible Reading:

EZRA 4–5; ROMANS 6:1–7:6; PSALM 119:9–16

*Thy word have I hid in mine heart,
that I might not sin against thee.*
PSALM 119:11

Memorize God's Word. Having God's Word in your heart and mind is remarkably powerful. It has the ability to keep you from sinning and to guide you in the will of God. When temptations arise, quote scripture to yourself and brandish the sword that God has given you in His Word. The devil will flee from a fight where the unerring Word of God is boldly used as a defense. Let God's Word reign in your heart to dethrone the sin that Christ sacrificed so much to conquer (Romans 6:12).

REFLECTIONS ON TODAY'S BIBLE READING

8 glasses a day:

TOP 3 PRIORITIES:

- [ ]
- [ ]
- [ ]

SCHEDULE/TO-DO LIST:

- [ ]
- [ ]
- [ ]
- [ ]

REMEMBER

September

S	M	T	W	T	F	S
					1	2
3	4	5	6	7	8	9
10	11	12	13	14	15	16
17	18	19	20	21	22	23
24	25	26	27	28	29	30

Wednesday
AUGUST 9

Today's Bible Reading:

EZRA 6:1–7:26; ROMANS 7:7–25; PSALM 119:17–32

Moreover I make a decree what ye shall do to the elders of these Jews for the building of this house of God: that of the king's goods, even of the tribute beyond the river, forthwith expenses be given unto these men, that they be not hindered.
EZRA 6:8

The stories recorded in Ezra and Nehemiah are a marvelous demonstration of how God is in control no matter how out of control a situation may appear to our eyes. The people's mission to rebuild the house of God was constantly facing the threat of termination. In today's passage, King Darius (a ruler from an enemy nation that had captured God's people) not only allowed them to continue work, but he even assisted them with their project. God has never lost control. He is always sovereign.

TOP 3 PRIORITIES:

REFLECTIONS ON TODAY'S BIBLE READING

SCHEDULE/TO-DO LIST:

8 glasses a day:

August

S	M	T	W	T	F	S
		1	2	3	4	5
6	7	8	9	10	11	12
13	14	15	16	17	18	19
20	21	22	23	24	25	26
27	28	29	30	31		

REMEMBER

Today's Bible Reading:

EZRA 7:27–9:4; ROMANS 8:1–27; PSALM 119:33–40

There is therefore now no condemnation to them which are in Christ Jesus, who walk not after the flesh, but after the Spirit.
ROMANS 8:1

There is no condemnation for you who are in Christ. Do you really grasp that? Covered by Christ's blood-washed robes, you cannot be condemned. You no longer need to live under the yoke of slavery to sin and the Law. Your freedom in Christ releases you from a life of desperately trying to attain to an unattainable standard. This doesn't mean that you shouldn't strive to live a righteous life. But now that righteous life is inspired not by a need to be right before God but by a gratefulness for what God has already done for you.

REFLECTIONS ON TODAY'S BIBLE READING

8 glasses a day:

TOP 3 PRIORITIES:

SCHEDULE/TO-DO LIST:

REMEMBER

September

S	M	T	W	T	F	S
					1	2
3	4	5	6	7	8	9
10	11	12	13	14	15	16
17	18	19	20	21	22	23
24	25	26	27	28	29	30

Today's Bible Reading:

EZRA 9:5–10:44; ROMANS 8:28–39; PSALM 119:41–64

*Nay, in all these things we are more than
conquerors through him that loved us.*
ROMANS 8:37

The end of Romans 8 is one of the most exquisitely victorious passages in the Bible. Bookmark it in your Bible so that anytime you feel as though you are caught in a losing battle, you can be reminded that in Christ you are more than a conqueror. Absolutely nothing has the power to separate you from the love of Christ. God alone is powerful enough to separate you from His love by deciding to take it away. But He has shown you through the sacrifice of His own Son that He will stop at nothing to be able to keep loving you. You are secure in His love and will be for eternity.

TOP 3 PRIORITIES:

- ☐ ....
- ☐ ....
- ☐ ....

SCHEDULE/TO-DO LIST:

- ☐ ....
- ☐ ....
- ☐ ....
- ☐ ....

REFLECTIONS ON TODAY'S BIBLE READING

8 glasses a day: ▽ ▽ ▽ ▽ ▽ ▽ ▽ ▽

August

S	M	T	W	T	F	S
		1	2	3	4	5
6	7	8	9	10	11	12
13	14	15	16	17	18	19
20	21	22	23	24	25	26
27	28	29	30	31		

REMEMBER

Today's Bible Reading:

NEHEMIAH 1:1–3:16; ROMANS 9:1–18; PSALM 119:65–72

Then the king said unto me, For what dost thou make request? So I prayed to the God of heaven.
NEHEMIAH 2:4

Nehemiah is standing in the courts of the king, and the king asks him what he requests. What would be your knee-jerk reaction in this intimidating situation? Nehemiah's reaction was to pray. Even in the middle of the king's court, his dialogue with God continued. Nehemiah was constantly in the court of his heavenly King. Prayer is too often a second or third resort for us. Strive to be more like Nehemiah where the natural thing to do is to pray.

REFLECTIONS ON TODAY'S BIBLE READING

8 glasses a day:

TOP 3 PRIORITIES:

- [ ] ....
- [ ] ....
- [ ] ....

SCHEDULE/TO-DO LIST:

- [ ] ....
- [ ] ....
- [ ] ....
- [ ] ....

REMEMBER

September

S	M	T	W	T	F	S
					1	2
3	4	5	6	7	8	9
10	11	12	13	14	15	16
17	18	19	20	21	22	23
24	25	26	27	28	29	30

Sunday
AUGUST 13

Today's Bible Reading:

NEHEMIAH 3:17–5:13; ROMANS 9:19–33; PSALM 119:73–80

Nay but, O man, who art thou that repliest against God? Shall the thing formed say to him that formed it, Why hast thou made me thus?
ROMANS 9:20

Romans 9:20 gives us an apt answer to a plethora of our doubting questions–who are we to reply to God? God's ways, thoughts, wisdom, and knowledge are so far above ours as to be incomprehensible to us. A dose of humility and trust in the love of God would do us good when facing life's hard questions.

TOP 3 PRIORITIES:

- ☐ ....
- ☐ ....
- ☐ ....

SCHEDULE/TO-DO LIST:

- ☐ ....
- ☐ ....
- ☐ ....
- ☐ ....

REFLECTIONS ON TODAY'S BIBLE READING

8 glasses a day: ☐ ☐ ☐ ☐ ☐ ☐ ☐ ☐

August

S	M	T	W	T	F	S
		1	2	3	4	5
6	7	8	9	10	11	12
13	14	15	16	17	18	19
20	21	22	23	24	25	26
27	28	29	30	31		

REMEMBER

Today's Bible Reading:

NEHEMIAH 5:14–7:73; ROMANS 10:1–13; PSALM 119:81–88

For they all made us afraid, saying, Their hands shall be weakened from the work, that it be not done. Now therefore, O God, strengthen my hands.
NEHEMIAH 6:9

Nehemiah 6:9 records a quick prayer that Nehemiah spoke to God in the face of fearful circumstances–"O God, strengthen my hands." We can probably assume that his life was punctuated perpetually with this type of prayer. He was in constant conversation with the One who was so much greater and more able than himself. May your thoughts be similarly inseparable from an inner conversation with your Father.

REFLECTIONS ON TODAY'S BIBLE READING

TOP 3 PRIORITIES:

- ☐ ....
- ☐ ....
- ☐ ....

SCHEDULE/TO-DO LIST:

- ☐ ....
- ☐ ....
- ☐ ....
- ☐

8 glasses a day: ☐ ☐ ☐ ☐ ☐ ☐ ☐ ☐

REMEMBER

September

S	M	T	W	T	F	S
					1	2
3	4	5	6	7	8	9
10	11	12	13	14	15	16
17	18	19	20	21	22	23
24	25	26	27	28	29	30

Tuesday
AUGUST 15

Today's Bible Reading:

NEHEMIAH 8:1–9:5; ROMANS 10:14–11:24; PSALM 119:89–104

Unless thy law had been my delights,
I should then have perished in mine affliction.
PSALM 119:92

David had learned to delight in the Word of God. It had become his sustenance. In today's reading, he cited his knowledge of and delight in God's law as the reason he didn't perish in his affliction. Knowing God's Word will keep you from falling, sustain your soul during grief, and bolster you with courage when you are afraid. It's through His Word that you can get to know God. Don't miss out on such a glorious opportunity.

TOP 3 PRIORITIES:

- [ ]
- [ ]
- [ ]

SCHEDULE/TO-DO LIST:

- [ ]
- [ ]
- [ ]
- [ ]

REFLECTIONS ON TODAY'S BIBLE READING

8 glasses a day:

REMEMBER

August

S	M	T	W	T	F	S
		1	2	3	4	5
6	7	8	9	10	11	12
13	14	15	16	17	18	19
20	21	22	23	24	25	26
27	28	29	30	31		

Today's Bible Reading:

NEHEMIAH 9:6–10:27; ROMANS 11:25–12:8; PSALM 119:105–120

Thy word is a lamp unto my feet, and a light unto my path.
PSALM 119:105

David asserted that God's Word was a lamp to his feet and a light to his path. If you are lacking direction in your life, go to God's Word. He has already provided you with the very light that you so crave to illuminate your future. Delve into this life-giving Word and seek to know all that you can from it. God will in turn use His Word to light your way. Use the lamp that He has provided.

REFLECTIONS ON TODAY'S BIBLE READING

TOP 3 PRIORITIES:

SCHEDULE/TO-DO LIST:

8 glasses a day:

REMEMBER

September

S	M	T	W	T	F	S
					1	2
3	4	5	6	7	8	9
10	11	12	13	14	15	16
17	18	19	20	21	22	23
24	25	26	27	28	29	30

Today's Bible Reading:

NEHEMIAH 10:28–12:26; ROMANS 12:9–13:7; PSALM 119:121–128

Be of the same mind one toward another. Mind not high things,
but condescend to men of low estate. Be not wise in your own conceits.
ROMANS 12:16

Why is it that knowledge of spiritual matters often makes us feel arrogant? This is unacceptable. We are not to be wise in our own eyes. If we feel arrogant that we know God better than someone else, then it's probably safe to say that we don't actually know Him at all. The God who humbled Himself to dwell and die on earth is not a God who takes delight in any form of arrogance or prejudice.

TOP 3 PRIORITIES:

☐ ....
☐ ....
☐ ....

SCHEDULE/TO-DO LIST:

☐ ....
☐ ....
☐ ....
☐ ....

REFLECTIONS ON TODAY'S BIBLE READING

8 glasses a day: ☐ ☐ ☐ ☐ ☐ ☐ ☐ ☐

August

S	M	T	W	T	F	S
		1	2	3	4	5
6	7	8	9	10	11	12
13	14	15	16	17	18	19
20	21	22	23	24	25	26
27	28	29	30	31		

REMEMBER

Today's Bible Reading:

NEHEMIAH 12:27–13:31; ROMANS 13:8–14:12; PSALM 119:129–136

Thy testimonies are wonderful:
therefore doth my soul keep them.
PSALM 119:129

It is astounding and convicting to read through Psalm 119 and see the immense love that David had for God's Word. As someone who was so intimately acquainted with God's laws and promises, it is no wonder that David was a man after God's own heart. His heart is displayed to us in His Word. We come to know and love Him more fully the more time we spend in it.

REFLECTIONS ON TODAY'S BIBLE READING

8 glasses a day: ☐ ☐ ☐ ☐ ☐ ☐ ☐ ☐

REMEMBER

TOP 3 PRIORITIES:

- ☐ ....
- ☐ ....
- ☐ ....

SCHEDULE/TO-DO LIST:

- ☐ ....
- ☐ ....
- ☐ ....
- ☐

September

S	M	T	W	T	F	S
					1	2
3	4	5	6	7	8	9
10	11	12	13	14	15	16
17	18	19	20	21	22	23
24	25	26	27	28	29	30

Today's Bible Reading:

ESTHER 1:1–2:18; ROMANS 14:13–15:13; PSALM 119:137–152

Now the God of hope fill you with all joy and peace in believing,
that ye may abound in hope, through the power of the Holy Ghost.
ROMANS 15:13

Biblical hope is not a vain wish for something that might happen but rather a steadfast faith in something that is sure to happen. God is the God of hope because He is the very author of our hope. Without His work and His promises, there would be nothing sure in which to have faith. Along with Paul in Romans 15:13, ask that God would fill you with joy and peace so that you would overflow with hope through the Holy Spirit.

TOP 3 PRIORITIES:

- [ ] ....
- [ ] ....
- [ ] ....

SCHEDULE/TO-DO LIST:

- [ ] ....
- [ ] ....
- [ ] ....
- [ ] ....

REFLECTIONS ON TODAY'S BIBLE READING

8 glasses a day: ⬜ ⬜ ⬜ ⬜ ⬜ ⬜ ⬜ ⬜

REMEMBER

August

S	M	T	W	T	F	S
			1	2	3	4	5
6	7	8	9	10	11	12
13	14	15	16	17	18	19
20	21	22	23	24	25	26
27	28	29	30	31		

Today's Bible Reading:

ESTHER 2:19–5:14; ROMANS 15:14–21; PSALM 119:153–168

For if thou altogether holdest thy peace at this time, then shall there enlargement and deliverance arise to the Jews from another place; but thou and thy father's house shall be destroyed: and who knoweth whether thou art come to the kingdom for such a time as this?
ESTHER 4:14

God is not directly referenced in the book of Esther. Still, the evidence of His work is woven throughout the entire narrative. Even if you don't acknowledge or notice God's work directly, be confident that He is constantly working out His will for you. Just like Esther, He may place you in a situation that does not seem to have any correlation with His will. And yet, you'll find that He has put you there for a very specific reason. . ."for such a time as this."

REFLECTIONS ON TODAY'S BIBLE READING

8 glasses a day:

TOP 3 PRIORITIES:

- [ ] ....
- [ ] ....
- [ ] ....

SCHEDULE/TO-DO LIST:

- [ ] ....
- [ ] ....
- [ ] ....
- [ ] ....

REMEMBER

September

S	M	T	W	T	F	S
					1	2
3	4	5	6	7	8	9
10	11	12	13	14	15	16
17	18	19	20	21	22	23
24	25	26	27	28	29	30

Today's Bible Reading:

ESTHER 6–8; ROMANS 15:22–33; PSALM 119:169–176

Let thine hand help me; for I have chosen thy precepts.
PSALM 119:173

David professed that he had chosen God's precepts. Desiring to know and follow God's Word is a choice and a commitment. Sometimes we get so caught up in avoiding legalism that we allow a healthy diligence and obedience to slide. Make a commitment to read, memorize, and meditate on God's Word. You will only ever be blessed by this kind of commitment.

TOP 3 PRIORITIES:

- [ ] ....
- [ ] ....
- [ ] ....

SCHEDULE/TO-DO LIST:

- [ ] ....
- [ ] ....
- [ ] ....
- [ ] ....

REFLECTIONS ON TODAY'S BIBLE READING

8 glasses a day: ▭ ▭ ▭ ▭ ▭ ▭ ▭ ▭

REMEMBER

August

S	M	T	W	T	F	S
		1	2	3	4	5
6	7	8	9	10	11	12
13	14	15	16	17	18	19
20	21	22	23	24	25	26
27	28	29	30	31		

Today's Bible Reading:

ESTHER 9–10; ROMANS 16; PSALM 120–122

*For your obedience is come abroad unto all men. I am glad
therefore on your behalf: but yet I would have you wise unto
that which is good, and simple concerning evil.*
ROMANS 16:19

Be wise in what is good and simple concerning evil. In today's culture, it often seems that we are more well versed in and familiar with what is evil than what is good. Yet Paul entreats the Romans to be simple concerning evil. Don't pursue knowledge of things that tear down, that promote violence or abuse, or that are simply worthless. Instead, do pursue knowledge of what is good and lovely and valuable. Be an expert in these things.

REFLECTIONS ON TODAY'S BIBLE READING

TOP 3 PRIORITIES:

- ☐ ....
- ☐ ....
- ☐ ....

SCHEDULE/TO-DO LIST:

- ☐ ....
- ☐ ....
- ☐ ....
- ☐ ....

8 glasses a day: ☐ ☐ ☐ ☐ ☐ ☐ ☐ ☐

REMEMBER

September

S	M	T	W	T	F	S
					1	2
3	4	5	6	7	8	9
10	11	12	13	14	15	16
17	18	19	20	21	22	23
24	25	26	27	28	29	30

Today's Bible Reading:

JOB 1–3; 1 CORINTHIANS 1:1–25; PSALM 123

And said, Naked came I out of my mother's womb, and naked shall I return thither: the Lord gave, and the Lord hath taken away; blessed be the name of the Lord.
JOB 1:21

Job understood that God is wiser than he could ever be and that if God could give immense blessing, He also had every right to take it away. He understood that he came into the world with nothing and that he could take nothing with him into the next life. He therefore had a loose hold on his earthly possessions and relationships. He chose to bless the name of the Lord even in the midst of unspeakable suffering.

TOP 3 PRIORITIES:

- ☐ ....
- ☐ ....
- ☐ ....

SCHEDULE/TO-DO LIST:

- ☐ ....
- ☐ ....
- ☐ ....
- ☐ ....

REFLECTIONS ON TODAY'S BIBLE READING

8 glasses a day: ☐ ☐ ☐ ☐ ☐ ☐ ☐ ☐

REMEMBER

August

S	M	T	W	T	F	S
		1	2	3	4	5
6	7	8	9	10	11	12
13	14	15	16	17	18	19
20	21	22	23	24	25	26
27	28	29	30	31		

Today's Bible Reading:

JOB 4–6; 1 CORINTHIANS 1:26–2:16; PSALM 124–125

*But God hath chosen the foolish things of the world to
confound the wise; and God hath chosen the weak things
of the world to confound the things which are mighty.*
1 CORINTHIANS 1:27

God uses the weak, broken, and foolish things of the world for His purposes. We see this concept all throughout scripture. Just as a piece of pottery can only let light through if it has cracks, so too God's light shines more clearly through those who do not have it all together. When God chooses to use us for His kingdom, it is our brokenness and weakness that allow God's power to become all the more visible to those around us.

REFLECTIONS ON TODAY'S BIBLE READING

8 glasses a day:

TOP 3 PRIORITIES:

SCHEDULE/TO-DO LIST:

REMEMBER

September

S	M	T	W	T	F	S
					1	2
3	4	5	6	7	8	9
10	11	12	13	14	15	16
17	18	19	20	21	22	23
24	25	26	27	28	29	30

Friday
AUGUST 25

Today's Bible Reading:

JOB 7-9; 1 CORINTHIANS 3; PSALM 126-127

*I know it is so of a truth: but how should man be just with God? If he
will contend with him, he cannot answer him one of a thousand.*
JOB 9:2-3

Job asked a very astute question in chapter 9: How can a man be just with God when he has nothing to bring to the table? The answer, of course, is Christ. Job obviously did not have the blessing of knowing what Christ would do on the cross, and so his standing before God seemed rather hopeless based solely on his own merit. We have the immense privilege of living in the new covenant, having been justified by our faith in Christ based solely on God's grace. Christ answered for God's wrath so that we would never have to.

TOP 3 PRIORITIES:

- [ ] ....
- [ ] ....
- [ ] ....

SCHEDULE/TO-DO LIST:

- [ ] ....
- [ ] ....
- [ ] ....
- [ ] ....

August

S	M	T	W	T	F	S
		1	2	3	4	5
6	7	8	9	10	11	12
13	14	15	16	17	18	19
20	21	22	23	24	25	26
27	28	29	30	31		

REFLECTIONS ON TODAY'S BIBLE READING

8 glasses a day:

REMEMBER

Today's Bible Reading:

JOB 10–13; 1 CORINTHIANS 4:1–13; PSALM 128–129

*For I know nothing by myself; yet am I not hereby
justified: but he that judgeth me is the Lord.*
1 CORINTHIANS 4:4

Paul knew of nothing against himself. Can you say the same of yourself? Do you strive to live a life where you can have a clear, guiltless conscience before God? You shouldn't strive for holiness as a way to be right before God, because you can never attain that on your own. Rather, your obedience should be a response to the grace that God has already shown you by making you clean before Him. You are already blameless in His eyes, so live that way.

REFLECTIONS ON TODAY'S BIBLE READING

8 glasses a day:

TOP 3 PRIORITIES:

- [ ] ....
- [ ] ....
- [ ] ....

SCHEDULE/TO-DO LIST:

- [ ] ....
- [ ] ....
- [ ] ....
- [ ] ....

REMEMBER

September

S	M	T	W	T	F	S
					1	2
3	4	5	6	7	8	9
10	11	12	13	14	15	16
17	18	19	20	21	22	23
24	25	26	27	28	29	30

Today's Bible Reading:

JOB 14–16; 1 CORINTHIANS 4:14–5:13; PSALM 130

I wrote unto you in an epistle not to company with fornicators: yet not altogether with the fornicators of this world, or with the covetous, or extortioners, or with idolaters; for then must ye needs go out of the world.
1 CORINTHIANS 5:9–10

In today's passage, Paul explained to the Corinthians that he never intended for them not to associate with sinners. He asserts that as Christians we ought to be in the world, getting to know the sexually immoral, greedy, and idolatrous. To not associate with these nonbelievers would be to miss the point of our pilgrimage here on earth. God's light shines the brightest when brought into the darker corners of the world.

TOP 3 PRIORITIES:

- ☐ ....
- ☐ ....
- ☐ ....

SCHEDULE/TO-DO LIST:

- ☐ ....
- ☐ ....
- ☐ ....
- ☐ ....

REFLECTIONS ON TODAY'S BIBLE READING

8 glasses a day: ☐ ☐ ☐ ☐ ☐ ☐ ☐ ☐

August

S	M	T	W	T	F	S
		1	2	3	4	5
6	7	8	9	10	11	12
13	14	15	16	17	18	19
20	21	22	23	24	25	26
27	28	29	30	31		

REMEMBER

Today's Bible Reading:

JOB 17–20; 1 CORINTHIANS 6; PSALM 131

*For I know that my redeemer liveth, and that he shall stand
at the latter day upon the earth: and though after my skin
worms destroy this body, yet in my flesh shall I see God.*
JOB 19:25–26

Job had a remarkably clear vision of God's coming to earth and the subsequent resurrection of his own body. How he knew that his Redeemer would one day stand on earth and that one day he would see God in his own body, we don't know. But God had provided him a priceless comfort in his suffering to know that this was not the end of his body and that his Redeemer would one day make all things right.

REFLECTIONS ON TODAY'S BIBLE READING

8 glasses a day:

TOP 3 PRIORITIES:

SCHEDULE/TO-DO LIST:

REMEMBER

September

S	M	T	W	T	F	S
					1	2
3	4	5	6	7	8	9
10	11	12	13	14	15	16
17	18	19	20	21	22	23
24	25	26	27	28	29	30

Tuesday
AUGUST 29

Today's Bible Reading:

JOB 21–23; 1 CORINTHIANS 7:1-16; PSALM 132

But he knoweth the way that I take:
when he hath tried me, I shall come forth as gold.
JOB 23:10

Job had a right understanding of suffering. He understood that through his trials God was polishing him as you would a dirty piece of priceless gold. Often it is the battering of trials that brings out the power of God that dwells in each of His children. We can all testify to knowing someone who has gone through immense trials but is all the stronger and more grounded in God because of them. The end result, a glittering piece of gold, is worth the process of polishing.

TOP 3 PRIORITIES:

- [ ] ....
- [ ] ....
- [ ] ....

SCHEDULE/TO-DO LIST:

- [ ] ....
- [ ] ....
- [ ] ....
- [ ] ....

August

S	M	T	W	T	F	S
		1	2	3	4	5
6	7	8	9	10	11	12
13	14	15	16	17	18	19
20	21	22	23	24	25	26
27	28	29	30	31		

REFLECTIONS ON TODAY'S BIBLE READING

8 glasses a day:

REMEMBER

Today's Bible Reading:

JOB 24-27; 1 CORINTHIANS 7:17-40; PSALM 133-134

*Behold, how good and how pleasant it is
for brethren to dwell together in unity!*
PSALM 133:1

It is a good and pleasant thing for God's people to dwell together in unity. Relationships are hard. People will disagree and cause contentions. But the value of having fellowship with other believers is precious enough that we should be striving to live in peace and unity with our brothers and sisters as much as possible. God has given us one another to bolster, uphold, soothe, convict, and encourage each other. Don't miss out on the value of spending time with His people.

REFLECTIONS ON TODAY'S BIBLE READING

TOP 3 PRIORITIES:

- [ ] ....
- [ ] ....
- [ ] ....

SCHEDULE/TO-DO LIST:

- [ ] ....
- [ ] ....
- [ ] ....
- [ ] ....

8 glasses a day:

REMEMBER

September

S	M	T	W	T	F	S
					1	2
3	4	5	6	7	8	9
10	11	12	13	14	15	16
17	18	19	20	21	22	23
24	25	26	27	28	29	30

Today's Bible Reading:

JOB 28–30; 1 CORINTHIANS 8; PSALM 135

And if any man think that he knoweth any thing, he knoweth nothing yet as he ought to know. But if any man love God, the same is known of him.
1 CORINTHIANS 8:2–3

In the whole scheme of things, we know so very little. It's true that the more we learn, the more we realize how little we know. So make it a priority to seek out the most valuable kind of knowledge. Seek to know your God. Though our knowledge of God will always be limited in this life because of our finite minds, we are known perfectly by Him. He knows us better than we know ourselves.

TOP 3 PRIORITIES:

- ☐ ....
- ☐ ....
- ☐ ....

SCHEDULE/TO-DO LIST:

- ☐ ....
- ☐ ....
- ☐ ....
- ☐ ....

REFLECTIONS ON TODAY'S BIBLE READING

8 glasses a day: ☐ ☐ ☐ ☐ ☐ ☐ ☐ ☐

August

S	M	T	W	T	F	S
		1	2	3	4	5
6	7	8	9	10	11	12
13	14	15	16	17	18	19
20	21	22	23	24	25	26
27	28	29	30	31		

REMEMBER

Today's Bible Reading:

JOB 31–33; 1 CORINTHIANS 9:1–18; PSALM 136:1–9

O give thanks unto the Lord; for he is good:
for his mercy endureth for ever.
PSALM 136:1

The refrain "for his mercy endureth for ever" occurs twenty-six times in Psalm 136. Each verse is punctuated by that phrase. Shouldn't our lives be punctuated by that refrain as well? After every chapter and verse of our lives, we can truthfully say, "His mercy endures forever." His mercy is woven all throughout the small, insignificant days as well as the life-changing events of our lives. It endures forever and will buoy us into the next life.

REFLECTIONS ON TODAY'S BIBLE READING

8 glasses a day:

TOP 3 PRIORITIES:

- ☐ ....
- ☐ ....
- ☐ ....

SCHEDULE/TO-DO LIST:

- ☐ ....
- ☐ ....
- ☐ ....
- ☐

REMEMBER

September

S	M	T	W	T	F	S
					1	2
3	4	5	6	7	8	9
10	11	12	13	14	15	16
17	18	19	20	21	22	23
24	25	26	27	28	29	30

Today's Bible Reading:

JOB 34–36; 1 CORINTHIANS 9:19–10:13; PSALM 136:10–26

*To the weak became I as weak, that I might gain the weak: I am made
all things to all men, that I might by all means save some. And this I do
for the gospel's sake, that I might be partaker thereof with you.*
1 CORINTHIANS 9:22–23

Paul strove to reach as many people as he possibly could for the sake of the Gospel. His own sense of self or personal reputation was of no concern compared to the need he felt to tell people of Christ. He became as a servant, as a Jew, as one under the Law, as one outside of the Law, and as weak in order to reach those in each category. The Gospel requires sacrifice and a giving up of oneself. But Paul would assert that this sacrifice was well worth it so that he could share in the riches of the Gospel with those he had reached.

TOP 3 PRIORITIES:

- [ ] ....
- [ ] ....
- [ ] ....

SCHEDULE/TO-DO LIST:

- [ ] ....
- [ ] ....
- [ ] ....
- [ ] ....

REFLECTIONS ON TODAY'S BIBLE READING

8 glasses a day: ☐ ☐ ☐ ☐ ☐ ☐ ☐ ☐

September

S	M	T	W	T	F	S
					1	2
3	4	5	6	7	8	9
10	11	12	13	14	15	16
17	18	19	20	21	22	23
24	25	26	27	28	29	30

REMEMBER

Today's Bible Reading:

JOB 37–39; 1 CORINTHIANS 10:14–11:1; PSALM 137

Where wast thou when I laid the foundations
of the earth? declare, if thou hast understanding.
Job 38:4

When God speaks back to Job, it is an awe-inspiring, terrifying, and humbling thing to read. Imagine being there and seeing and hearing the power of God. How could we ever begin to think that we know better than God? Were we there when He created the earth? Do we hold the universe together from day to day? It has taken us millennia to even begin to discover the depths of the mysteries of this world that He created by simply speaking it into existence. And yet, we sometimes dare to assume that our will is better than His.

REFLECTIONS ON TODAY'S BIBLE READING

TOP 3 PRIORITIES:

☐ ....
☐ ....
☐ ....

SCHEDULE/TO-DO LIST:

☐ ....
☐ ....
☐ ....
☐ ....

8 glasses a day: ☐ ☐ ☐ ☐ ☐ ☐ ☐ ☐

REMEMBER

October

S	M	T	W	T	F	S
1	2	3	4	5	6	7
8	9	10	11	12	13	14
15	16	17	18	19	20	21
22	23	24	25	26	27	28
29	30	31				

Today's Bible Reading:

JOB 40–42; 1 CORINTHIANS 11:2–34; PSALM 138

I know that thou canst do every thing, and that no thought can be withholden from thee. Who is he that hideth counsel without knowledge? therefore have I uttered that I understood not; things too wonderful for me, which I knew not.
JOB 42:2–3

Job's response to God is the only possible response to an encounter with God—complete and utter humility of oneself coupled with the utmost praise of God. Job's life would never have been the same after this. Imagine how radically your life would change after having been directly spoken to by God. And yet, He has given us access to Himself every single day. Listen for His voice as you read His Word and pray. May it humble you and cause you to praise and magnify Him.

TOP 3 PRIORITIES:

- ☐ ....
- ☐ ....
- ☐ ....

SCHEDULE/TO-DO LIST:

- ☐ ....
- ☐ ....
- ☐ ....
- ☐ ....

REFLECTIONS ON TODAY'S BIBLE READING

8 glasses a day: ☐ ☐ ☐ ☐ ☐ ☐ ☐ ☐

REMEMBER

September

S	M	T	W	T	F	S
					1	2
3	4	5	6	7	8	9
10	11	12	13	14	15	16
17	18	19	20	21	22	23
24	25	26	27	28	29	30

Today's Bible Reading:

ECCLESIASTES 1:1–3:15; 1 CORINTHIANS 12:1–26; PSALM 139:1–6

Vanity of vanities, saith the Preacher, vanity of vanities; all is vanity.
What profit hath a man of all his labour which he taketh under the sun?
ECCLESIASTES 1:2–3

Ecclesiastes is a remarkably apt description of life apart from God–life "under the sun." Apart from the purposes of God, all that we do on this earth is vanity and a passing shadow. God has put eternity in man's heart (Ecclesiastes 3:11) so that we inevitably realize that there has to be something more to life. Only a life that is lived with an "over the sun" perspective will provide true fulfillment and joy.

REFLECTIONS ON TODAY'S BIBLE READING

8 glasses a day: ☐ ☐ ☐ ☐ ☐ ☐ ☐ ☐

TOP 3 PRIORITIES:

☐ ....
☐ ....
☐ ....

SCHEDULE/TO-DO LIST:

☐ ....
☐ ....
☐ ....
☐

REMEMBER

October

S	M	T	W	T	F	S
1	2	3	4	5	6	7
8	9	10	11	12	13	14
15	16	17	18	19	20	21
22	23	24	25	26	27	28
29	30	31				

Wednesday
SEPTEMBER 6

Today's Bible Reading:

ECCLESIASTES 3:16–6:12; 1 CORINTHIANS 12:27–13:13; PSALM 139:7–18

Thine eyes did see my substance, yet being unperfect; and in thy book all my members were written, which in continuance were fashioned, when as yet there was none of them.
PSALM 139:16

God formed you in the womb and knew you before anyone else was even aware of your existence. Before the first beat of your heart, He planned out a life for you in which you would have the unmatchable privilege of knowing Him. For Him to have spent this much thought on your life means that you are exceptionally valuable to Him. The opinions that people on earth may have of you are nothing compared to the opinion and love that God has for you.

TOP 3 PRIORITIES:

☐ ....
☐ ....
☐ ....

SCHEDULE/TO-DO LIST:

☐ ....
☐ ....
☐ ....
☐ ....

REFLECTIONS ON TODAY'S BIBLE READING

8 glasses a day: ▽ ▽ ▽ ▽ ▽ ▽ ▽ ▽

September

S	M	T	W	T	F	S
					1	2
3	4	5	6	7	8	9
10	11	12	13	14	15	16
17	18	19	20	21	22	23
24	25	26	27	28	29	30

REMEMBER

Today's Bible Reading:

ECCLESIASTES 7:1–9:12; 1 CORINTHIANS 14:1–22; PSALM 139:19–24

Whatsoever thy hand findeth to do, do it with thy might; for there is no work, nor device, nor knowledge, nor wisdom, in the grave, whither thou goest.
ECCLESIASTES 9:10

Now is the time to work hard, to invest in people's lives, and to seek after wisdom and knowledge. In heaven we won't have the opportunity to speak of God to the lost. In heaven we won't have the opportunity to bind up the broken and heal the sick. Obviously, the perfection of heaven is incomparably preferable to the fallen state of this world, but you should make the most of your time here. It will be all the chance you get to be a light for God in the darkness.

REFLECTIONS ON TODAY'S BIBLE READING

8 glasses a day:

REMEMBER

TOP 3 PRIORITIES:

SCHEDULE/TO-DO LIST:

October

S	M	T	W	T	F	S
1	2	3	4	5	6	7
8	9	10	11	12	13	14
15	16	17	18	19	20	21
22	23	24	25	26	27	28
29	30	31				

Friday
SEPTEMBER 8

Today's Bible Reading:

ECCLESIASTES 9:13–12:14; 1 CORINTHIANS 14:23–15:11; PSALM 140:1–8

Let us hear the conclusion of the whole matter: Fear God,
and keep his commandments: for this is the whole duty of man.
ECCLESIASTES 12:13

The conclusion of Solomon's study into life is this: "Fear God, and keep his commandments." God is the one who will ultimately bring judgment on all that you have done in life. His opinion should be of the utmost concern to you. Your life should be lived to glorify and enjoy Him. Because in the end, the conclusion of your whole life will consist of what you have done for others and for the kingdom.

TOP 3 PRIORITIES:

- [ ]
- [ ]
- [ ]

SCHEDULE/TO-DO LIST:

- [ ]
- [ ]
- [ ]
- [ ]

REFLECTIONS ON TODAY'S BIBLE READING

8 glasses a day:

REMEMBER

September

S	M	T	W	T	F	S
					1	2
3	4	5	6	7	8	9
10	11	12	13	14	15	16
17	18	19	20	21	22	23
24	25	26	27	28	29	30

Today's Bible Reading:

SONG OF SOLOMON 1–4; 1 CORINTHIANS 15:12–34; PSALM 140:9–13

*If in this life only we have hope in Christ,
we are of all men most miserable.*
1 CORINTHIANS 15:19

Christianity hinges on the reality of Christ's death and resurrection. Without the person of Jesus, your faith is worthless. It would be the easiest religion to disprove if only someone would have found the bones of Jesus. And yet, no one did because Christ rose from the dead, appeared to many people on earth, and currently sits on His throne in heaven. We have hope in Christ not only in this life but in the next as well. Instead of the most miserable of all people, we are the most blessed and should be the most grateful.

REFLECTIONS ON TODAY'S BIBLE READING

TOP 3 PRIORITIES:

☐ ....
☐ ....
☐ ....

SCHEDULE/TO-DO LIST:

☐ ....
☐ ....
☐ ....
☐ ....

8 glasses a day: ☐ ☐ ☐ ☐ ☐ ☐ ☐ ☐

REMEMBER

October

S	M	T	W	T	F	S
1	2	3	4	5	6	7
8	9	10	11	12	13	14
15	16	17	18	19	20	21
22	23	24	25	26	27	28
29	30	31				

Sunday
SEPTEMBER 10

Today's Bible Reading:

SONG OF SOLOMON 5–8; 1 CORINTHIANS 15:35–58; PSALM 141

Set a watch, O Lord, before my mouth; keep the door of my lips.
PSALM 141:3

Psalm 141:3 is a prayer that we should pray every day–*Lord, set a watch on my mouth and keep the door of my lips.* How much less trouble would we get into if our thoughts and words were always filtered through the grace of God? What if everything we said built others up and glorified Him? What if our thoughts were always pure and lovely? Ask God to protect your words and even your very thoughts.

TOP 3 PRIORITIES:

- ☐ ....
- ☐ ....
- ☐ ....

SCHEDULE/TO-DO LIST:

- ☐ ....
- ☐ ....
- ☐ ....
- ☐

REFLECTIONS ON TODAY'S BIBLE READING

8 glasses a day: ▢ ▢ ▢ ▢ ▢ ▢ ▢ ▢

September

S	M	T	W	T	F	S
					1	2
3	4	5	6	7	8	9
10	11	12	13	14	15	16
17	18	19	20	21	22	23
24	25	26	27	28	29	30

REMEMBER

Today's Bible Reading:

ISAIAH 1–2; 1 CORINTHIANS 16; PSALM 142

Wash you, make you clean; put away the evil of your doings from before mine eyes; cease to do evil; learn to do well; seek judgment, relieve the oppressed, judge the fatherless, plead for the widow.
ISAIAH 1:16–17

Verse 16 is a beautiful turning point in chapter 1 of Isaiah. The start of the chapter is desolate as God recounts all the evil that His people have done and how they have not served Him as they should. Verses 16 and 17 are a call to repentance–wash, put away evil, do well, relieve the oppressed. And then verse 18 is a refreshing picture of redemption–our scarlet sins will be washed as clean as snow. This is how the Lord deals with His people. He does not leave us in our sin.

REFLECTIONS ON TODAY'S BIBLE READING

TOP 3 PRIORITIES:

- [ ] ....
- [ ] ....
- [ ] ....

SCHEDULE/TO-DO LIST:

- [ ] ....
- [ ] ....
- [ ] ....
- [ ]

8 glasses a day: ▢ ▢ ▢ ▢ ▢ ▢ ▢ ▢

REMEMBER

October

S	M	T	W	T	F	S
1	2	3	4	5	6	7
8	9	10	11	12	13	14
15	16	17	18	19	20	21
22	23	24	25	26	27	28
29	30	31				

Today's Bible Reading:

ISAIAH 3–5; 2 CORINTHIANS 1:1–11; PSALM 143:1–6

What could have been done more to my vineyard, that I have not done in it? wherefore, when I looked that it should bring forth grapes, brought it forth wild grapes?
ISAIAH 5:4

God told a tale of a vineyard in Isaiah 5 as an analogy of His people. It is a heartbreaking look into God's relationship with a sinful and ungrateful nation. He lovingly planted and tended to the vineyard only for it to rebel against Him. He then asked of the people, "What else could I have done for My vineyard?" God has poured out blessings on us, yet how often do we rebel against Him and bring forth the wild grapes of our rebellion instead of the fruit of our gratefulness?

TOP 3 PRIORITIES:

- ☐ ....
- ☐ ....
- ☐ ....

SCHEDULE/TO-DO LIST:

- ☐ ....
- ☐ ....
- ☐ ....
- ☐ ....

REFLECTIONS ON TODAY'S BIBLE READING

8 glasses a day: ☐ ☐ ☐ ☐ ☐ ☐ ☐ ☐

September

S	M	T	W	T	F	S
					1	2
3	4	5	6	7	8	9
10	11	12	13	14	15	16
17	18	19	20	21	22	23
24	25	26	27	28	29	30

REMEMBER

Today's Bible Reading:

ISAIAH 6–8; 2 CORINTHIANS 1:12–2:4; PSALM 143:7–12

*Also I heard the voice of the Lord, saying, Whom shall I send,
and who will go for us? Then said I, Here am I; send me.*
ISAIAH 6:8

Isaiah saw God in all His terrifying and majestic glory. When God asked whom He should send, Isaiah immediately and emphatically replied, "Here am I; send me." This is the only possible reaction of someone who has seen God enthroned on high. To know that God sits on His throne in victory should inspire us to respond to His call to go and spread His Gospel as enthusiastically and unhesitatingly as Isaiah did.

REFLECTIONS ON TODAY'S BIBLE READING

TOP 3 PRIORITIES:

SCHEDULE/TO-DO LIST:

8 glasses a day:

REMEMBER

October

S	M	T	W	T	F	S
1	2	3	4	5	6	7
8	9	10	11	12	13	14
15	16	17	18	19	20	21
22	23	24	25	26	27	28
29	30	31				

Today's Bible Reading:

ISAIAH 9–10; 2 CORINTHIANS 2:5–17; PSALM 144

Lord, what is man, that thou takest knowledge of him! or the son of man, that thou makest account of him! Man is like to vanity: his days are as a shadow that passeth away.
PSALM 144:3–4

Who are you that God should take notice of you? How is it that a life that is a mere shadow in the scheme of history could be intimately cared for by God? But He does care for you more than you even know. It is a remarkable and incomprehensible concept. If you could grasp how deeply God knows and loves you, would it change your life? We feel important if we know someone famous on earth whose life is of the same value as ours–how much more worthy should we feel that we know and are known by the almighty God? We should indeed be happy that God is our Lord.

TOP 3 PRIORITIES:

- [ ] ....
- [ ] ....
- [ ] ....

SCHEDULE/TO-DO LIST:

- [ ] ....
- [ ] ....
- [ ] ....
- [ ] ....

REFLECTIONS ON TODAY'S BIBLE READING

8 glasses a day: ⬚ ⬚ ⬚ ⬚ ⬚ ⬚ ⬚ ⬚

REMEMBER

September

S	M	T	W	T	F	S
					1	2
3	4	5	6	7	8	9
10	11	12	13	14	15	16
17	18	19	20	21	22	23
24	25	26	27	28	29	30

Today's Bible Reading:

ISAIAH 11–13; 2 CORINTHIANS 3; PSALM 145

Seeing then that we have such hope, we use great plainness of speech.
2 CORINTHIANS 3:12

In Christ we have an unmatchable hope and a glorious assurance of eternal life. Because of this, we should be bold to speak of it. How can we keep such a gift to ourselves? Do you not feel sufficient enough to share the Gospel? The good news is that you aren't sufficient in yourself, which is why you must rely on the impassable sufficiency of God (2 Corinthians 3:5). It's through His power that you can have the boldness to share His Word.

REFLECTIONS ON TODAY'S BIBLE READING

8 glasses a day: ▢ ▢ ▢ ▢ ▢ ▢ ▢ ▢

REMEMBER

TOP 3 PRIORITIES:

- ▢ ....
- ▢ ....
- ▢ ....

SCHEDULE/TO-DO LIST:

- ▢ ....
- ▢ ....
- ▢ ....
- ▢

October

S	M	T	W	T	F	S
1	2	3	4	5	6	7
8	9	10	11	12	13	14
15	16	17	18	19	20	21
22	23	24	25	26	27	28
29	30	31				

Today's Bible Reading:

ISAIAH 14–16; 2 CORINTHIANS 4; PSALM 146

Which made heaven, and earth, the sea, and all that therein is: which keepeth truth for ever: which executeth judgment for the oppressed: which giveth food to the hungry. The LORD looseth the prisoners.
PSALM 146:6–7

God's power, as demonstrated in His ability to create and sustain the entire universe, is incomparable to anything we know. But unlike so many humans who use power for personal gain or superiority, God uses His power to help the oppressed, release the prisoner, feed the hungry, and care for the orphan and widow. His power and justice are never separated from His love, kindness, and mercy.

TOP 3 PRIORITIES:

- ☐ ....
- ☐ ....
- ☐ ....

SCHEDULE/TO-DO LIST:

- ☐ ....
- ☐ ....
- ☐ ....
- ☐ ....

REFLECTIONS ON TODAY'S BIBLE READING

8 glasses a day: ▯ ▯ ▯ ▯ ▯ ▯ ▯ ▯

REMEMBER

September

S	M	T	W	T	F	S
					1	2
3	4	5	6	7	8	9
10	11	12	13	14	15	16
17	18	19	20	21	22	23
24	25	26	27	28	29	30

Today's Bible Reading:

ISAIAH 17–19; 2 CORINTHIANS 5; PSALM 147:1–11

He died for all, that they which live should not henceforth live unto themselves, but unto him which died for them, and rose again.
2 CORINTHIANS 5:15

Paul told the Corinthians that the love of Christ constrained (or compelled) him. What would it look like for Christ's love to compel you? Every action would be inspired by the love of Christ. Every word would seek to disperse His love to others. Every prayer would be said in the light of our standing before God, which was secured by His sacrificial love. You truly would no longer live for yourself but rather for Him who gave up His life so that you might live.

REFLECTIONS ON TODAY'S BIBLE READING

8 glasses a day:

TOP 3 PRIORITIES:

☐ ....
☐ ....
☐ ....

SCHEDULE/TO-DO LIST:

☐ ....
☐ ....
☐ ....
☐ ....

REMEMBER

October

S	M	T	W	T	F	S
1	2	3	4	5	6	7
8	9	10	11	12	13	14
15	16	17	18	19	20	21
22	23	24	25	26	27	28
29	30	31				

Today's Bible Reading:

ISAIAH 20–23; 2 CORINTHIANS 6; PSALM 147:12–20

For he hath strengthened the bars of thy gates;
he hath blessed thy children within thee.
PSALM 147:13

The psalmist in today's reading praised God for having strengthened his gates. In order to allow them to open and close, the gates would inevitably be the weakest part of a fortified city. Therefore, it was essential that the gates be strong. Have you identified what the weakest points are in your defense against the enemy? Where is it in your life that sin creeps in the easiest? Ask God to strengthen your gates and to help you be proactive in protecting those particular areas.

TOP 3 PRIORITIES:

- ☐ ....
- ☐ ....
- ☐ ....

SCHEDULE/TO-DO LIST:

- ☐ ....
- ☐ ....
- ☐ ....
- ☐ ....

REFLECTIONS ON TODAY'S BIBLE READING

8 glasses a day: ▢ ▢ ▢ ▢ ▢ ▢ ▢ ▢

REMEMBER

September

S	M	T	W	T	F	S
					1	2
3	4	5	6	7	8	9
10	11	12	13	14	15	16
17	18	19	20	21	22	23
24	25	26	27	28	29	30

Today's Bible Reading:

ISAIAH 24:1–26:19; 2 CORINTHIANS 7; PSALM 148

For godly sorrow worketh repentance to salvation not to be repented of: but the sorrow of the world worketh death.
2 CORINTHIANS 7:10

Grief and sorrow over sin is good so far as it leads to repentance. Understanding the weightiness of sin and how abhorrent it is to God is essential as you strive to banish it from your life. But sorrow over sin that leads to undue guilt is not healthy. As a redeemed child of God, holding on to the guilt of sin is essentially not to accept Christ's work on the cross for you. When you sin, grieve over it, repent, and then accept God's grace and forgiveness.

REFLECTIONS ON TODAY'S BIBLE READING

TOP 3 PRIORITIES:
- ☐ ....
- ☐ ....
- ☐ ....

SCHEDULE/TO-DO LIST:
- ☐ ....
- ☐ ....
- ☐ ....
- ☐ ....

8 glasses a day: ☐☐☐☐☐☐☐☐

REMEMBER

October

S	M	T	W	T	F	S
1	2	3	4	5	6	7
8	9	10	11	12	13	14
15	16	17	18	19	20	21
22	23	24	25	26	27	28
29	30	31				

Wednesday
SEPTEMBER 20

Today's Bible Reading:

Let every thing that hath breath praise the LORD. Praise ye the LORD.
PSALM 150:6

Psalm 150 is a glorious picture of how all of God's creation should be and how it will be one day. One day everything that has breath will praise the Lord. In the meantime, our praise of Him should fill our lives and spill over into the lives of others. He is entirely worthy of all our praise. He is worthy simply because of who He is—the great God above all gods. But He is also worthy because of the wonderful things He has done for us. Praise Him now and continue to praise Him until all the earth and the entire universe joins in.

TOP 3 PRIORITIES:

- [ ] ....
- [ ] ....
- [ ] ....

SCHEDULE/TO-DO LIST:

- [ ] ....
- [ ] ....
- [ ] ....
- [ ] ....

REFLECTIONS ON TODAY'S BIBLE READING

8 glasses a day: ▢ ▢ ▢ ▢ ▢ ▢ ▢ ▢

REMEMBER

September

S	M	T	W	T	F	S
					1	2
3	4	5	6	7	8	9
10	11	12	13	14	15	16
17	18	19	20	21	22	23
24	25	26	27	28	29	30

Today's Bible Reading:

ISAIAH 29–30; 2 CORINTHIANS 9; PROVERBS 1:1-9

And therefore will the LORD wait, that he may be gracious unto you, and therefore will he be exalted, that he may have mercy upon you: for the LORD is a God of judgment: blessed are all they that wait for him.
ISAIAH 30:18

Just as a loving parent will wait for a wayward child to behave, so too will God wait patiently to be gracious to you. He will not get fed up with you. You won't be able to try His patience beyond what He can handle. He desires that you walk with Him and keep His commandments. He will never give up on those who are His.

REFLECTIONS ON TODAY'S BIBLE READING

8 glasses a day:

TOP 3 PRIORITIES:

☐ ....
☐ ....
☐ ....

SCHEDULE/TO-DO LIST:

☐ ....
☐ ....
☐ ....
☐ ....

REMEMBER

October

S	M	T	W	T	F	S
1	2	3	4	5	6	7
8	9	10	11	12	13	14
15	16	17	18	19	20	21
22	23	24	25	26	27	28
29	30	31				

Friday
SEPTEMBER 22

Today's Bible Reading:

ISAIAH 31–33; 2 CORINTHIANS 10; PROVERBS 1:10–22

(For the weapons of our warfare are not carnal, but mighty through God to the pulling down of strong holds;) casting down imaginations, and every high thing that exalteth itself against the knowledge of God, and bringing into captivity every thought to the obedience of Christ.
2 CORINTHIANS 10:4–5

So often our greatest struggles are against intangible things like our thought life or wayward desires. Fortunately, God has provided us weapons with divine power, capable of fighting the most insidious of enemies. Ask that God might help you take every thought captive in obedience to Christ–imagine how different (and more productive) your thought life would be! God is powerful enough even to conquer your most private thoughts of insecurity, pride, lust, or fear.

TOP 3 PRIORITIES:

- ☐ ....
- ☐ ....
- ☐ ....

SCHEDULE/TO-DO LIST:

- ☐ ....
- ☐ ....
- ☐ ....
- ☐ ....

REFLECTIONS ON TODAY'S BIBLE READING

8 glasses a day: ☐ ☐ ☐ ☐ ☐ ☐ ☐ ☐

September

S	M	T	W	T	F	S
					1	2
3	4	5	6	7	8	9
10	11	12	13	14	15	16
17	18	19	20	21	22	23
24	25	26	27	28	29	30

REMEMBER

First Day of Autumn

Today's Bible Reading:

ISAIAH 34–36; 2 CORINTHIANS 11; PROVERBS 1:23–26

If I must needs glory, I will glory of the things which concern mine infirmities. . . .
And through a window in a basket was I let down by the wall, and escaped his hands.
2 CORINTHIANS 11:30, 33

Paul was not in the least concerned about keeping up personal appearances. In fact, if he were to boast, he would boast in the very things that most of us would desire to keep hidden. Embarrassing accounts of how he, the mighty apostle of God, had to be saved from situations in the most humble of ways were merely fodder for his message about God's power. Don't be afraid to tell the stories that make you "look bad" but that showcase the goodness and power of God.

REFLECTIONS ON TODAY'S BIBLE READING

8 glasses a day:

TOP 3 PRIORITIES:

SCHEDULE/TO-DO LIST:

REMEMBER

October

S	M	T	W	T	F	S
1	2	3	4	5	6	7
8	9	10	11	12	13	14
15	16	17	18	19	20	21
22	23	24	25	26	27	28
29	30	31				

Today's Bible Reading:

ISAIAH 37–38; 2 CORINTHIANS 12:1–10; PROVERBS 1:27–33

Whom hast thou reproached and blasphemed? and against whom hast thou exalted thy voice, and lifted up thine eyes on high? even against the Holy One of Israel.
ISAIAH 37:23

Those who reproach and revile God's people are really reproaching God Himself. Situations in which you are berated for being a Christian can make you feel very vulnerable and alone. But remember in those circumstances that God is standing right there beside you, bearing the revilement with you. Though you may feel like the target, it is really the Holy One of Israel that those people are pitting themselves against. It may be easy to scorn another human, but taunting the Maker of heaven and earth is never a good idea.

TOP 3 PRIORITIES:

- ☐ ....
- ☐ ....
- ☐ ....

SCHEDULE/TO-DO LIST:

- ☐ ....
- ☐ ....
- ☐ ....
- ☐ ....

REFLECTIONS ON TODAY'S BIBLE READING

8 glasses a day: ⬜ ⬜ ⬜ ⬜ ⬜ ⬜ ⬜ ⬜

September

S	M	T	W	T	F	S
					1	2
3	4	5	6	7	8	9
10	11	12	13	14	15	16
17	18	19	20	21	22	23
24	25	26	27	28	29	30

REMEMBER

Today's Bible Reading:

ISAIAH 39–40; 2 CORINTHIANS 12:11-13:14; PROVERBS 2:1-15

*He shall feed his flock like a shepherd: he shall gather the lambs with his arm,
and carry them in his bosom, and shall gently lead those that are with young.*
ISAIAH 40:11

There is a beautiful juxtaposition in Isaiah 40:10–11 that speaks clearly of God's character. Verse 10 depicts a strong warrior king who comes to rule the earth with a strong arm. Verse 11 completely changes imagery and speaks of a caring shepherd who carries the lambs in His arms and gently leads His sheep. We serve a God who is so powerful that He conquered death and evil but so good and loving that He gently leads and cares for us. In His mighty arms can be found true protection and blissful rest.

REFLECTIONS ON TODAY'S BIBLE READING

TOP 3 PRIORITIES:

☐ ....
☐ ....
☐ ....

SCHEDULE/TO-DO LIST:

☐ ....
☐ ....
☐ ....
☐ ....

8 glasses a day: ☐ ☐ ☐ ☐ ☐ ☐ ☐ ☐

REMEMBER

October

S	M	T	W	T	F	S
1	2	3	4	5	6	7
8	9	10	11	12	13	14
15	16	17	18	19	20	21
22	23	24	25	26	27	28
29	30	31				

Tuesday
SEPTEMBER 26

Today's Bible Reading:

ISAIAH 41–42; GALATIANS 1; PROVERBS 2:16–22

For I the LORD thy God will hold thy right hand,
saying unto thee, Fear not; I will help thee.
ISAIAH 41:13

God has chosen you. He set you aside as one of His children before the foundation of the world. There is nothing to fear when you grasp that your whole life was planned far in advance by a loving Father. And in those times when fear is too strong to hold at bay, He holds you by the hand to reassure and strengthen you. Listen as He says to you, "Fear not; I will help you."

TOP 3 PRIORITIES:

- ☐ ....
- ☐ ....
- ☐ ....

SCHEDULE/TO-DO LIST:

- ☐ ....
- ☐ ....
- ☐ ....
- ☐ ....

REFLECTIONS ON TODAY'S BIBLE READING

8 glasses a day: ▢ ▢ ▢ ▢ ▢ ▢ ▢ ▢

REMEMBER

September

S	M	T	W	T	F	S
					1	2
3	4	5	6	7	8	9
10	11	12	13	14	15	16
17	18	19	20	21	22	23
24	25	26	27	28	29	30

Today's Bible Reading:

ISAIAH 43:1–44:20; GALATIANS 2; PROVERBS 3:1–12

Since thou wast precious in my sight, thou hast been honourable, and I have loved thee: therefore will I give men for thee, and people for thy life.
ISAIAH 43:4

Do you truly believe that you are precious in God's eyes? Do you believe that He loves you as fully as He says? Do you believe that He would go to the ends of the earth in order to bring you back? With the fallacy of love that we've all experienced in this world, it's sometimes easier not to believe that we can be perfectly and fully loved. And yet, your heavenly Father, who considers you precious, will prove His love for you as He ceaselessly seeks you to draw you to Himself.

REFLECTIONS ON TODAY'S BIBLE READING

8 glasses a day:

TOP 3 PRIORITIES:

- [ ] ....
- [ ] ....
- [ ] ....

SCHEDULE/TO-DO LIST:

- [ ] ....
- [ ] ....
- [ ] ....
- [ ] ....

REMEMBER

October

S	M	T	W	T	F	S
1	2	3	4	5	6	7
8	9	10	11	12	13	14
15	16	17	18	19	20	21
22	23	24	25	26	27	28
29	30	31				

Thursday
SEPTEMBER 28

Today's Bible Reading:

ISAIAH 44:21–46:13; GALATIANS 3:1–18; PROVERBS 3:13–26

*The Lord by wisdom hath founded the earth; by understanding
hath he established the heavens. By his knowledge the depths
are broken up, and the clouds drop down the dew.*
PROVERBS 3:19–20

The book of Proverbs has lots to say about wisdom–its value, how we should search for it, and how a wise person behaves. Why is wisdom so important? Because it is an attribute of God. In wisdom, God created the earth and established the universe. Attaining wisdom will make us more like God. To be more like God is truly of more value than any gold or jewels.

TOP 3 PRIORITIES:

SCHEDULE/TO-DO LIST:

REFLECTIONS ON TODAY'S BIBLE READING

8 glasses a day:

September

S	M	T	W	T	F	S
					1	2
3	4	5	6	7	8	9
10	11	12	13	14	15	16
17	18	19	20	21	22	23
24	25	26	27	28	29	30

REMEMBER

Today's Bible Reading:

ISAIAH 47:1–49:13; GALATIANS 3:19-29; PROVERBS 3:27-35

*Stand now with thine enchantments, and with the multitude
of thy sorceries, wherein thou hast laboured from thy youth;
if so be thou shalt be able to profit, if so be thou mayest prevail.*
ISAIAH 47:12

The idols that we so foolishly cling to are no match for God. We work so hard to develop and protect our idols. We hold on to them as something precious. But there is no chance that any of those things could prevail against God. All our idols and foolish sins will be cast down before the throne of Christ, and we will have no answer as to why we exchanged the unmatchable glory of God for a filthy and worthless idol.

REFLECTIONS ON TODAY'S BIBLE READING

8 glasses a day: ☐ ☐ ☐ ☐ ☐ ☐ ☐ ☐

TOP 3 PRIORITIES:

☐ ....
☐ ....
☐ ....

SCHEDULE/TO-DO LIST:

☐ ....
☐ ....
☐ ....
☐ ....

REMEMBER

October

S	M	T	W	T	F	S
1	2	3	4	5	6	7
8	9	10	11	12	13	14
15	16	17	18	19	20	21
22	23	24	25	26	27	28
29	30	31				

Today's Bible Reading:

ISAIAH 49:14–51:23; GALATIANS 4:1–11; PROVERBS 4:1–19

*I, even I, am he that comforteth you: who art thou, that thou shouldest
be afraid of a man that shall die, and of the son of man which shall be
made as grass; and forgettest the LORD thy maker, that hath stretched
forth the heavens, and laid the foundations of the earth.*
ISAIAH 51:12–13

Why do we fear the power and opinions of man? We get so caught up with people pleasing and appearances that we forget the one whom we should actually fear–the one who has the power to destroy or sustain, to curse or bless. Humans are inherently mortal. God is everlasting. Whose side would you rather be on?

TOP 3 PRIORITIES:

☐ ....
☐ ....
☐ ....

SCHEDULE/TO-DO LIST:

☐ ....
☐ ....
☐ ....
☐ ....

REFLECTIONS ON TODAY'S BIBLE READING

8 glasses a day: ☐ ☐ ☐ ☐ ☐ ☐ ☐ ☐

REMEMBER

September

S	M	T	W	T	F	S
					1	2
3	4	5	6	7	8	9
10	11	12	13	14	15	16
17	18	19	20	21	22	23
24	25	26	27	28	29	30

Today's Bible Reading:

ISAIAH 52–54; GALATIANS 4:12–31; PROVERBS 4:20–27

Keep thy heart with all diligence; for out of it are the issues of life.
PROVERBS 4:23

Be diligent to guard your heart. Don't fill it with worthless lusts and empty entertainment. Be more concerned about your own heart than anyone else's. Hate your sins more than the sins of your friends or family. How easily we fall into busying ourselves with accusing others while our own hearts are harboring sin. Be diligent over your own heart–the life that will overflow from a well-kept heart will in turn bring others to Christ.

REFLECTIONS ON TODAY'S BIBLE READING

8 glasses a day:

TOP 3 PRIORITIES:
- ☐ ....
- ☐ ....
- ☐ ....

SCHEDULE/TO-DO LIST:
- ☐ ....
- ☐ ....
- ☐ ....
- ☐

REMEMBER

October

S	M	T	W	T	F	S
1	2	3	4	5	6	7
8	9	10	11	12	13	14
15	16	17	18	19	20	21
22	23	24	25	26	27	28
29	30	31				

Today's Bible Reading:

ISAIAH 55–57; GALATIANS 5; PROVERBS 5:1–14

Stand fast therefore in the liberty wherewith Christ hath made us free, and be not entangled again with the yoke of bondage.
GALATIANS 5:1

Stand firm in the freedom that you have in Christ. In what areas of your life do you tend to slip into legalism or moralism? You cannot possibly earn your salvation. Christ's work alone is what grants you righteousness and salvation. If your equation for salvation is Christ plus anything else (good works, keeping the Ten Commandments, etc.), then you have lost your stand in Christ's freedom and have slipped into a false gospel. Our standing before God is based on a past action of Christ on the cross. Our obedience to God is an outworking of our gratefulness to Him for our salvation.

TOP 3 PRIORITIES:

- ☐ ....
- ☐ ....
- ☐ ....

SCHEDULE/TO-DO LIST:

- ☐ ....
- ☐ ....
- ☐ ....
- ☐ ....

REFLECTIONS ON TODAY'S BIBLE READING

8 glasses a day: ☐ ☐ ☐ ☐ ☐ ☐ ☐ ☐

October

S	M	T	W	T	F	S
1	2	3	4	5	6	7
8	9	10	11	12	13	14
15	16	17	18	19	20	21
22	23	24	25	26	27	28
29	30	31				

REMEMBER

Today's Bible Reading:

ISAIAH 58–59; GALATIANS 6; PROVERBS 5:15–23

Then shalt thou call, and the LORD shall answer;
thou shalt cry, and he shall say, Here I am.
ISAIAH 58:9

God promises to bless, heal, and answer us and to grant us righteousness when we feed the hungry, bring the homeless into our homes, and clothe the naked. God's love and care for the needy is impossible to miss while reading through the Bible. His heart is fully turned toward those who have no voice of their own. If this is where His heart is, isn't it where your heart should be as well?

REFLECTIONS ON TODAY'S BIBLE READING

8 glasses a day:

TOP 3 PRIORITIES:

- ☐ ....
- ☐ ....
- ☐ ....

SCHEDULE/TO-DO LIST:

- ☐ ....
- ☐ ....
- ☐ ....
- ☐ ....

REMEMBER

November

S	M	T	W	T	F	S
			1	2	3	4
5	6	7	8	9	10	11
12	13	14	15	16	17	18
19	20	21	22	23	24	25
26	27	28	29	30		

Today's Bible Reading:

ISAIAH 60–62; EPHESIANS 1; PROVERBS 6:1–5

According as he hath chosen us in him before the foundation of the world, that we should be holy and without blame before him in love: having predestinated us unto the adoption of children by Jesus Christ to himself, according to the good pleasure of his will.
EPHESIANS 1:4–5

God chose you as His child before the foundations of the world were set. He has ordained that you be holy and without blame before Him. He planned far ahead of your physical birth that you would be adopted as one of His children and fully invited into His family. He did all this simply because it pleased Him to do so. There is no ulterior motive or manipulation. A love this full and this pure is virtually impossible for us to comprehend but something for us to be grateful for every single day.

TOP 3 PRIORITIES:

- ☐ ....
- ☐ ....
- ☐ ....

SCHEDULE/TO-DO LIST:

- ☐ ....
- ☐ ....
- ☐ ....
- ☐ ....

REFLECTIONS ON TODAY'S BIBLE READING

8 glasses a day: ☐ ☐ ☐ ☐ ☐ ☐ ☐ ☐

REMEMBER

October

S	M	T	W	T	F	S
1	2	3	4	5	6	7
8	9	10	11	12	13	14
15	16	17	18	19	20	21
22	23	24	25	26	27	28
29	30	31				

Today's Bible Reading:

ISAIAH 63:1–65:16; EPHESIANS 2; PROVERBS 6:6–19

*That in the ages to come he might shew the exceeding riches of
his grace in his kindness toward us through Christ Jesus.*
EPHESIANS 2:7

At the start of Ephesians 2 is a list of the things that God has done for you–loved you, made you alive, saved you, raised you up, and seated you with Christ. Why would He do all these things for you? Does He want something in return? The astounding and humbling answer comes in verse 7–He did all these things so that He might show you His grace and His kindness toward you. His desire is to shower you with love and grace. How undeserving we are to belong to a God who is so selflessly gracious to us.

REFLECTIONS ON TODAY'S BIBLE READING

8 glasses a day:

REMEMBER

TOP 3 PRIORITIES:

- [ ]
- [ ]
- [ ]

SCHEDULE/TO-DO LIST:

- [ ]
- [ ]
- [ ]
- [ ]

November

S	M	T	W	T	F	S
			1	2	3	4
5	6	7	8	9	10	11
12	13	14	15	16	17	18
19	20	21	22	23	24	25
26	27	28	29	30		

Friday
OCTOBER 6

Today's Bible Reading:

ISAIAH 65:17–66:24; EPHESIANS 3:1–4:16; PROVERBS 6:20–26

*And to know the love of Christ, which passeth knowledge,
that ye might be filled with all the fulness of God.*
EPHESIANS 3:19

Paul prayed that the Ephesians would know the love of Christ that surpasses knowledge. He wanted them to know the unknowable. Christ's love for us is so vast that our finite minds cannot grasp it. But to know even the smallest drop of this unknowable love would be life changing. Ask God to begin to help you comprehend His incomprehensible love.

TOP 3 PRIORITIES:

☐ ....
☐ ....
☐ ....

SCHEDULE/TO-DO LIST:

☐ ....
☐ ....
☐ ....
☐ ....

REFLECTIONS ON TODAY'S BIBLE READING

8 glasses a day: ☐ ☐ ☐ ☐ ☐ ☐ ☐ ☐

REMEMBER

October

S	M	T	W	T	F	S
1	2	3	4	5	6	7
8	9	10	11	12	13	14
15	16	17	18	19	20	21
22	23	24	25	26	27	28
29	30	31				

Today's Bible Reading:

JEREMIAH 1–2; EPHESIANS 4:17–32; PROVERBS 6:27–35

Before I formed thee in the belly I knew thee; and before thou camest forth out of the womb I sanctified thee, and I ordained thee a prophet unto the nations.
JEREMIAH 1:5

God knew the entire plan He had for Jeremiah's life before he was even born. He knew him better than anyone would know him before he was even conceived. He was completely sovereign over his life. He is completely sovereign over yours as well. The same care with which He formed Jeremiah in the womb He used to form you. Take courage. God is fully aware of the circumstances in your life–He knew about them before they had even happened. You don't have to fill Him in or catch Him up–He is the perfect one to go to with your fears and petitions.

REFLECTIONS ON TODAY'S BIBLE READING

8 glasses a day:

TOP 3 PRIORITIES:

- ☐ ....
- ☐ ....
- ☐ ....

SCHEDULE/TO-DO LIST:

- ☐ ....
- ☐ ....
- ☐ ....
- ☐

REMEMBER

November

S	M	T	W	T	F	S
			1	2	3	4
5	6	7	8	9	10	11
12	13	14	15	16	17	18
19	20	21	22	23	24	25
26	27	28	29	30		

Today's Bible Reading:

JEREMIAH 3:1–4:22; EPHESIANS 5; PROVERBS 7:1–5

And have no fellowship with the unfruitful
works of darkness, but rather reprove them.
EPHESIANS 5:11

Don't even let yourself toy with the works of darkness. They are entirely unfruitful, worthless, and destructive. Instead of ignoring or trying to hide the sin in your life, expose it. Sin is strongest in the darkness; being exposed to the light will cause it to shrivel and weaken. Talk to other trustworthy Christians who can help you throw off the load of sin so that you can spend your time and effort pursuing works of righteousness.

TOP 3 PRIORITIES:

- ☐ ....
- ☐ ....
- ☐ ....

SCHEDULE/TO-DO LIST:

- ☐ ....
- ☐ ....
- ☐ ....
- ☐ ....

REFLECTIONS ON TODAY'S BIBLE READING

8 glasses a day: ☐ ☐ ☐ ☐ ☐ ☐ ☐ ☐

October

S	M	T	W	T	F	S
1	2	3	4	5	6	7
8	9	10	11	12	13	14
15	16	17	18	19	20	21
22	23	24	25	26	27	28
29	30	31				

REMEMBER

Columbus Day

Today's Bible Reading:

JEREMIAH 4:23–5:31; EPHESIANS 6; PROVERBS 7:6–27

For we wrestle not against flesh and blood, but against
principalities, against powers, against the rulers of the darkness
of this world, against spiritual wickedness in high places.
EPHESIANS 6:12

How often do you consider the spiritual warfare that is raging at this very moment in the world? While it would be unfruitful to fixate on these thoughts, it is important to keep in mind the gravity of the battle at hand. Use prayer as a weapon against the powers and rulers of the darkness in this world. Work to spread God's light to conquer the darkness.

REFLECTIONS ON TODAY'S BIBLE READING

8 glasses a day:

TOP 3 PRIORITIES:

☐ ....
☐ ....
☐ ....

SCHEDULE/TO-DO LIST:

☐ ....
☐ ....
☐ ....
☐ ....

REMEMBER

November

S	M	T	W	T	F	S
			1	2	3	4
5	6	7	8	9	10	11
12	13	14	15	16	17	18
19	20	21	22	23	24	25
26	27	28	29	30		

Tuesday
OCTOBER 10

Today's Bible Reading:

JEREMIAH 6:1–7:26; PHILIPPIANS 1:1–26; PROVERBS 8:1–11

*Being confident of this very thing, that he which hath begun
a good work in you will perform it until the day of Jesus Christ.*
PHILIPPIANS 1:6

God is a promise keeper. He has proven Himself as such throughout history. Because of this, you can trust Him fully to fulfill His promise that He will perfect the good work He has started in you. This means that no sin, guilt, or apathy can keep Him from working in your life. Thoughts of your own worthlessness have no room or authority in your heart and mind. God will make perfect His work that He started in you–you can count on it.

TOP 3 PRIORITIES:

- ☐ ....
- ☐ ....
- ☐ ....

SCHEDULE/TO-DO LIST:

- ☐ ....
- ☐ ....
- ☐ ....
- ☐ ....

REFLECTIONS ON TODAY'S BIBLE READING

8 glasses a day: ☐ ☐ ☐ ☐ ☐ ☐ ☐ ☐

REMEMBER

October

S	M	T	W	T	F	S
1	2	3	4	5	6	7
8	9	10	11	12	13	14
15	16	17	18	19	20	21
22	23	24	25	26	27	28
29	30	31				

Today's Bible Reading:

JEREMIAH 7:27–9:16; PHILIPPIANS 1:27–2:18; PROVERBS 8:12–21

Do all things without murmurings and disputings: that ye may be blameless and harmless, the sons of God, without rebuke, in the midst of a crooked and perverse nation, among whom ye shine as lights in the world.
PHILIPPIANS 2:14–15

You have daily opportunities to shine God's light into this crooked and perverse world. Something as simple as doing everything without grumbling or complaining makes it apparent to the watching world that there is something different about you. Conversely, to fit right into the world with its grumblings and disputes does absolutely nothing for the cause of Christ. Seek ways to be a light. Let the world know through the way you live that you are a child of God.

REFLECTIONS ON TODAY'S BIBLE READING

TOP 3 PRIORITIES:

- ☐ ....
- ☐ ....
- ☐ ....

SCHEDULE/TO-DO LIST:

- ☐ ....
- ☐ ....
- ☐ ....
- ☐

8 glasses a day: ▭ ▭ ▭ ▭ ▭ ▭ ▭ ▭

REMEMBER

November

S	M	T	W	T	F	S
			1	2	3	4
5	6	7	8	9	10	11
12	13	14	15	16	17	18
19	20	21	22	23	24	25
26	27	28	29	30		

Today's Bible Reading:

JEREMIAH 9:17–11:17; PHILIPPIANS 2:19–30; PROVERBS 8:22–36

Thus saith the LORD, Let not the wise man glory in his wisdom, neither let the mighty man glory in his might, let not the rich man glory in his riches: but let him that glorieth glory in this, that he understandeth and knoweth me.
JEREMIAH 9:23–24

In what do you find your worth? In your strength? Athletic ability? Looks? Social status? Good works? Knowledge? Though all these things can be gifts from God, the only thing in which you should truly glory is knowing the Lord. When thinking about the blessings in your life, does knowing God typically make it on the list? It is a privilege beyond anything else we can experience on this earth. Work to be defined more by how well you know your Savior than by anything else.

TOP 3 PRIORITIES:

- ☐ ....
- ☐ ....
- ☐ ....

SCHEDULE/TO-DO LIST:

- ☐ ....
- ☐ ....
- ☐ ....
- ☐ ....

REFLECTIONS ON TODAY'S BIBLE READING

8 glasses a day: ☐ ☐ ☐ ☐ ☐ ☐ ☐ ☐

October

S	M	T	W	T	F	S
1	2	3	4	5	6	7
8	9	10	11	12	13	14
15	16	17	18	19	20	21
22	23	24	25	26	27	28
29	30	31				

REMEMBER

Today's Bible Reading:

JEREMIAH 11:18–13:27; PHILIPPIANS 3; PROVERBS 9:1-6

*And be found in him, not having mine own righteousness,
which is of the law, but that which is through the faith of
Christ, the righteousness which is of God by faith.*
PHILIPPIANS 3:9

The "famous" followers of Christ are not perfect people. Rather, they are people who are especially aware of their imperfections and who, because of their flaws, learn to rely more on Christ. They know that even when they stumble, they are covered by Christ's righteousness.

REFLECTIONS ON TODAY'S BIBLE READING

TOP 3 PRIORITIES:

- ☐ ....
- ☐ ....
- ☐ ....

SCHEDULE/TO-DO LIST:

- ☐ ....
- ☐ ....
- ☐ ....
- ☐

8 glasses a day: ☐ ☐ ☐ ☐ ☐ ☐ ☐ ☐

REMEMBER

November

S	M	T	W	T	F	S
			1	2	3	4
5	6	7	8	9	10	11
12	13	14	15	16	17	18
19	20	21	22	23	24	25
26	27	28	29	30		

Today's Bible Reading:

JEREMIAH 14–15; PHILIPPIANS 4; PROVERBS 9:7–18

*Be careful for nothing; but in every thing by prayer and supplication
with thanksgiving let your requests be made known unto God.*
PHILIPPIANS 4:6

Philippians 4:6 is not just a pleasant suggestion or a quaint platitude. It is a command—do not be anxious. Bring your prayers and supplications to God. Paul could give this command because he was absolutely certain that worrying was of no benefit. He was also absolutely sure that no anxiety-producing situation was too big or difficult for God to handle. To be anxious is to question that God is doing the right thing in your life. There is, therefore, zero reason to be anxious because He is undoubtedly in control and doing the right thing. So, instead of worrying, carry your burdens to Him and drop them at His feet.

TOP 3 PRIORITIES:

- ☐ ....
- ☐ ....
- ☐ ....

SCHEDULE/TO-DO LIST:

- ☐ ....
- ☐ ....
- ☐ ....
- ☐ ....

REFLECTIONS ON TODAY'S BIBLE READING

8 glasses a day: ☐ ☐ ☐ ☐ ☐ ☐ ☐ ☐

REMEMBER

October

S	M	T	W	T	F	S
1	2	3	4	5	6	7
8	9	10	11	12	13	14
15	16	17	18	19	20	21
22	23	24	25	26	27	28
29	30	31				

Today's Bible Reading:

JEREMIAH 16–17; COLOSSIANS 1:1–23; PROVERBS 10:1–5

For this cause we also, since the day we heard it, do not cease to pray for you, and to desire that ye might be filled with the knowledge of his will in all wisdom and spiritual understanding; that ye might walk worthy of the Lord unto all pleasing, being fruitful in every good work, and increasing in the knowledge of God.
COLOSSIANS 1:9–10

Paul did not cease to pray for the Colossians that they would be filled with knowledge and wisdom and that they would "walk worthy of the Lord" in good works. Is there anything that you care about enough to never cease to pray for it? Maybe start with this prayer in Colossians 1.

REFLECTIONS ON TODAY'S BIBLE READING

8 glasses a day:

TOP 3 PRIORITIES:

SCHEDULE/TO-DO LIST:

REMEMBER

November

S	M	T	W	T	F	S
			1	2	3	4
5	6	7	8	9	10	11
12	13	14	15	16	17	18
19	20	21	22	23	24	25
26	27	28	29	30		

Today's Bible Reading:

JEREMIAH 18:1–20:6; COLOSSIANS 1:24–2:15; PROVERBS 10:6–14

Blotting out the handwriting of ordinances that was against us, which was contrary to us, and took it out of the way, nailing it to his cross; and having spoiled principalities and powers, he made a shew of them openly, triumphing over them in it.
COLOSSIANS 2:14–15

Christ made a public spectacle of the devil on the cross. The devil must have thought that he had finally triumphed over God as he saw Christ hanging on the cross. Little did he know that in that moment was his greatest loss. The curtain that had separated God from His people was torn in two, the dead were raised, and the very earth quaked under the weight of the victory of Christ. On that cross, any hold that the devil had over us was destroyed as the decree that documented our debt was nailed to the cross and erased by Christ's blood. In Christ's death and resurrection was His and our victory.

TOP 3 PRIORITIES:

☐ ....
☐ ....
☐ ....

SCHEDULE/TO-DO LIST:

☐ ....
☐ ....
☐ ....
☐ ....

REFLECTIONS ON TODAY'S BIBLE READING

8 glasses a day: ☐ ☐ ☐ ☐ ☐ ☐ ☐ ☐

REMEMBER

October

S	M	T	W	T	F	S
1	2	3	4	5	6	7
8	9	10	11	12	13	14
15	16	17	18	19	20	21
22	23	24	25	26	27	28
29	30	31				

Today's Bible Reading:

JEREMIAH 20:7–22:19; COLOSSIANS 2:16–3:4; PROVERBS 10:15–26

*He judged the cause of the poor and needy; then it was well
with him: was not this to know me? saith the LORD.*
JEREMIAH 22:16

What is it to know God? God said that King Josiah knew Him because he pled the cause of the poor and needy. We could probably think of far more glamorous ways to know God. And yet, this is what God Himself says it means to know Him. Could His heart for those in need be any more clear? And could His call for you to minister to the poor and needy be any more obvious?

REFLECTIONS ON TODAY'S BIBLE READING

8 glasses a day:

REMEMBER

TOP 3 PRIORITIES:

☐ ....
☐ ....
☐ ....

SCHEDULE/TO-DO LIST:

☐ ....
☐ ....
☐ ....
☐ ....

November

S	M	T	W	T	F	S
			1	2	3	4
5	6	7	8	9	10	11
12	13	14	15	16	17	18
19	20	21	22	23	24	25
26	27	28	29	30		

Today's Bible Reading:

JEREMIAH 22:20–23:40; COLOSSIANS 3:5–4:1; PROVERBS 10:27–32

*And let the peace of God rule in your hearts, to the which
also ye are called in one body; and be ye thankful.*
COLOSSIANS 3:15

"Let the peace of God rule in your hearts." You are not called to "make" the peace of God rule in your heart or even to "ask for" it. Rather, you only need to let it rule. God's peace already dwells in your heart. Stop trying to anxiously figure out your life, and instead, let His peace rule your every thought and action. Don't allow any room for doubt or fear to usurp the throne in your heart.

TOP 3 PRIORITIES:

- ☐ ....
- ☐ ....
- ☐ ....

SCHEDULE/TO-DO LIST:

- ☐ ....
- ☐ ....
- ☐ ....
- ☐ ....

October

S	M	T	W	T	F	S
1	2	3	4	5	6	7
8	9	10	11	12	13	14
15	16	17	18	19	20	21
22	23	24	25	26	27	28
29	30	31				

REFLECTIONS ON TODAY'S BIBLE READING

8 glasses a day: ☐ ☐ ☐ ☐ ☐ ☐ ☐ ☐

REMEMBER

Today's Bible Reading:

JEREMIAH 24–25; COLOSSIANS 4:2–18; PROVERBS 11:1–11

And I will give them an heart to know me, that I am the LORD: and they shall be my people, and I will be their God: for they shall return unto me with their whole heart.
JEREMIAH 24:7

God gives you a heart to know Him. On your own you would be helpless in seeking out God. But He desires that you know Him, and He does not hide from you. He has given you all that you need to know Him. The Lord controls the hearts of everyone on this earth and can turn them wherever He chooses. If your heart is His, it always will be.

REFLECTIONS ON TODAY'S BIBLE READING

TOP 3 PRIORITIES:

SCHEDULE/TO-DO LIST:

8 glasses a day:

REMEMBER

November

S	M	T	W	T	F	S
			1	2	3	4
5	6	7	8	9	10	11
12	13	14	15	16	17	18
19	20	21	22	23	24	25
26	27	28	29	30		

Friday
OCTOBER 20

Today's Bible Reading:

JEREMIAH 26–27; 1 THESSALONIANS 1:1–2:8; PROVERBS 11:12–21

*A talebearer revealeth secrets: but he that
is of a faithful spirit concealeth the matter.*
PROVERBS 11:13

How many grudges, arguments, and lost relationships could have been avoided by concealing a matter? Gossip is often used to allay our own insecurities. If we can just get someone else to look bad, we assume that we'll look so much better. There are much more productive ways of dealing with insecurities. Dwell on how much you, as an image bearer, are loved by your Creator. And dwell even more on how much everyone around you is also highly valuable simply for bearing the image of their Father. Be a secret keeper and not a talebearer.

TOP 3 PRIORITIES:

- ☐ ....
- ☐ ....
- ☐ ....

SCHEDULE/TO-DO LIST:

- ☐ ....
- ☐ ....
- ☐ ....
- ☐ ....

REFLECTIONS ON TODAY'S BIBLE READING

8 glasses a day: ☐ ☐ ☐ ☐ ☐ ☐ ☐ ☐

October

S	M	T	W	T	F	S
1	2	3	4	5	6	7
8	9	10	11	12	13	14
15	16	17	18	19	20	21
22	23	24	25	26	27	28
29	30	31				

REMEMBER

Today's Bible Reading:

JEREMIAH 28–29; 1 THESSALONIANS 2:9–3:13; PROVERBS 11:22–26

And the Lord make you to increase and abound in love one toward another, and toward all men, even as we do toward you: to the end he may stablish your hearts unblameable in holiness before God, even our Father, at the coming of our Lord Jesus Christ with all his saints.
1 THESSALONIANS 3:12–13

Paul prayed that the Thessalonians' love would increase for each other and for all people. Why? So that God would establish their hearts as blameless and holy at the coming of Christ. Love for one another is so central to the message of the Gospel. This is not a surface love that allows others to do whatever they want as long as it makes them happy, even if it's ultimately detrimental. Rather, it's a love that encourages and spurs each other on to live a blameless and holy life. How often do you think about the people you love standing in judgment before a holy God? Would that perspective change the way you love them here on earth?

REFLECTIONS ON TODAY'S BIBLE READING

TOP 3 PRIORITIES:

SCHEDULE/TO-DO LIST:

8 glasses a day:

REMEMBER

November

S	M	T	W	T	F	S
			1	2	3	4
5	6	7	8	9	10	11
12	13	14	15	16	17	18
19	20	21	22	23	24	25
26	27	28	29	30		

Today's Bible Reading:

JEREMIAH 30:1–31:22; 1 THESSALONIANS 4:1–5:11; PROVERBS 11:27–31

The Lord hath appeared of old unto me, saying, Yea, I have loved thee with an everlasting love: therefore with lovingkindness have I drawn thee.
JEREMIAH 31:3

Even when God reprimands and punishes His children, He still loves them. In fact, it's because He loves His children that He rebukes them. But no matter what trials He may bring you through, His love is everlasting and therefore will not cease or fail you. With loving-kindness He will draw you in, and one day you will see the clearest evidence of His love threading all the way through your life, both in the trials and in the joys.

TOP 3 PRIORITIES:

- ☐ ....
- ☐ ....
- ☐ ....

SCHEDULE/TO-DO LIST:

- ☐ ....
- ☐ ....
- ☐ ....
- ☐ ....

October

S	M	T	W	T	F	S
1	2	3	4	5	6	7
8	9	10	11	12	13	14
15	16	17	18	19	20	21
22	23	24	25	26	27	28
29	30	31				

REFLECTIONS ON TODAY'S BIBLE READING

8 glasses a day: ☐ ☐ ☐ ☐ ☐ ☐ ☐ ☐

REMEMBER

Today's Bible Reading:

JEREMIAH 31:23–32:35; 1 THESSALONIANS 5:12–28; PROVERBS 12:1–14

Faithful is he that calleth you, who also will do it.
1 THESSALONIANS 5:24

We all know the feeling of being let down, of watching promises be broken, of seeing expectations shattered. In this life we can expect to be disappointed and hurt. This is why it is so important that we have a God who will never fail us. He is perfectly and unwaveringly faithful. What He has promised to do He will do. No exceptions. It's in the chaos and uncertainty of this world that we begin to more fully appreciate the steadfastness of God.

REFLECTIONS ON TODAY'S BIBLE READING

8 glasses a day:

TOP 3 PRIORITIES:

- [ ] ....
- [ ] ....
- [ ] ....

SCHEDULE/TO-DO LIST:

- [ ] ....
- [ ] ....
- [ ] ....
- [ ]

REMEMBER

November

S	M	T	W	T	F	S
			1	2	3	4
5	6	7	8	9	10	11
12	13	14	15	16	17	18
19	20	21	22	23	24	25
26	27	28	29	30		

Today's Bible Reading:

JEREMIAH 32:36–34:7; 2 THESSALONIANS 1–2; PROVERBS 12:15–20

*Call unto me, and I will answer thee, and show thee great
and mighty things, which thou knowest not.*
JEREMIAH 33:3

God promises that if you call on Him, He will answer you. This in itself is a remarkable promise that the God of the universe will always answer you when you call on Him. But He doesn't just promise to give a quick answer and then move on before you take up too much of His time. On the contrary, He will invest in you, guide and teach you, and show you great and mighty things. The amount of time and energy that God chooses to put into such insignificant creatures as ourselves is truly breathtaking.

TOP 3 PRIORITIES:

☐ ....
☐ ....
☐ ....

SCHEDULE/TO-DO LIST:

☐ ....
☐ ....
☐ ....
☐ ....

REFLECTIONS ON TODAY'S BIBLE READING

8 glasses a day: ☐ ☐ ☐ ☐ ☐ ☐ ☐ ☐

October

S	M	T	W	T	F	S
1	2	3	4	5	6	7
8	9	10	11	12	13	14
15	16	17	18	19	20	21
22	23	24	25	26	27	28
29	30	31				

REMEMBER

Today's Bible Reading:

JEREMIAH 34:8–36:10; 2 THESSALONIANS 3; PROVERBS 12:21–28

But ye, brethren, be not weary in well doing.
2 Thessalonians 3:13

Do not grow weary in doing good. Doing good should not just be something on the side. It should be a lifestyle, something that defines who you are. The power of a kind word, a listening ear, or time taken out of your day for someone else should not be underestimated. Be hospitable. Reach out to the lonely and needy. Listen to the grieving. Serve as Christ served while He walked among us.

REFLECTIONS ON TODAY'S BIBLE READING

8 glasses a day:

TOP 3 PRIORITIES:

- [ ]
- [ ]
- [ ]

SCHEDULE/TO-DO LIST:

- [ ]
- [ ]
- [ ]
- [ ]

REMEMBER

November

S	M	T	W	T	F	S
			1	2	3	4
5	6	7	8	9	10	11
12	13	14	15	16	17	18
19	20	21	22	23	24	25
26	27	28	29	30		

Today's Bible Reading:

JEREMIAH 36:11–38:13; 1 TIMOTHY 1:1–17; PROVERBS 13:1–4

He that keepeth his mouth keepeth his life: but he that openeth wide his lips shall have destruction.
PROVERBS 13:3

It's no mistake that in several places in the Bible, emphasis is put on the dangers of what you say. Would you have less regrets in life had you faithfully kept your mouth as Solomon advises in Proverbs? Life is the outcome for those who are wise and uplifting with their words. But destruction waits for those who use their words carelessly.

TOP 3 PRIORITIES:

☐ ....
☐ ....
☐ ....

SCHEDULE/TO-DO LIST:

☐ ....
☐ ....
☐ ....
☐ ....

REFLECTIONS ON TODAY'S BIBLE READING

8 glasses a day: ☐ ☐ ☐ ☐ ☐ ☐ ☐ ☐

October

S	M	T	W	T	F	S
1	2	3	4	5	6	7
8	9	10	11	12	13	14
15	16	17	18	19	20	21
22	23	24	25	26	27	28
29	30	31				

REMEMBER

Today's Bible Reading:

JEREMIAH 38:14–40:6; 1 TIMOTHY 1:18–3:13; PROVERBS 13:5–13

There is that maketh himself rich, yet hath nothing:
there is that maketh himself poor, yet hath great riches.
PROVERBS 13:7

Where does your wealth lie? Are you making yourself rich on things that amount to nothing? Or are you in possession of greater riches than this world could ever offer? The treasure that will last is your relationship with God and your investment in other people for the kingdom. These riches are those that are stored up in heaven. Everything else cannot come with you. Invest in the riches that will last into eternity.

REFLECTIONS ON TODAY'S BIBLE READING

TOP 3 PRIORITIES:

- ☐ ....
- ☐ ....
- ☐ ....

SCHEDULE/TO-DO LIST:

- ☐ ....
- ☐ ....
- ☐ ....
- ☐

8 glasses a day: ☐ ☐ ☐ ☐ ☐ ☐ ☐ ☐

REMEMBER

November

S	M	T	W	T	F	S
			1	2	3	4
5	6	7	8	9	10	11
12	13	14	15	16	17	18
19	20	21	22	23	24	25
26	27	28	29	30		

Today's Bible Reading:

JEREMIAH 40:7–42:22; 1 TIMOTHY 3:14–4:10; PROVERBS 13:14–21

For bodily exercise profiteth little: but godliness is profitable unto all things,
having promise of the life that now is, and of that which is to come.
1 TIMOTHY 4:8

Physical exercise is healthy and good but is only profitable in this lifetime. Spiritual exercise is profitable not only in this lifetime but in the one to come. Put the same effort into spiritual fitness as an Olympian would into physical fitness. Set aside time each morning for "training." Meditate on God's Word throughout the day. Recite God's Word to yourself as you fall asleep.

TOP 3 PRIORITIES:

- ☐ ....
- ☐ ....
- ☐ ....

SCHEDULE/TO-DO LIST:

- ☐ ....
- ☐ ....
- ☐ ....
- ☐ ....

REFLECTIONS ON TODAY'S BIBLE READING

8 glasses a day: ☐ ☐ ☐ ☐ ☐ ☐ ☐ ☐

REMEMBER

October

S	M	T	W	T	F	S
1	2	3	4	5	6	7
8	9	10	11	12	13	14
15	16	17	18	19	20	21
22	23	24	25	26	27	28
29	30	31				

Today's Bible Reading:

JEREMIAH 43–44; 1 TIMOTHY 4:11–5:16; PROVERBS 13:22–25

But she that liveth in pleasure is dead while she liveth.
1 Timothy 5:6

Are you giving in to a sin that is killing you even while you live? God has promised you abundant life; don't throw that away for something that will only deaden your soul. Though we like to think that sin is a private matter, it almost inevitably affects more than just ourselves. Don't poison yourself and slowly suffocate the spirits of those around you for something worthless. Ask the Giver of life to take away your desire for sin and in its place give you an all-consuming desire for Him.

REFLECTIONS ON TODAY'S BIBLE READING

8 glasses a day:

TOP 3 PRIORITIES:

- [ ] ....
- [ ] ....
- [ ] ....

SCHEDULE/TO-DO LIST:

- [ ] ....
- [ ] ....
- [ ] ....
- [ ] ....

REMEMBER

November

S	M	T	W	T	F	S
			1	2	3	4
5	6	7	8	9	10	11
12	13	14	15	16	17	18
19	20	21	22	23	24	25
26	27	28	29	30		

Today's Bible Reading:

JEREMIAH 45–47; 1 TIMOTHY 5:17–6:21; PROVERBS 14:1–6

*But godliness with contentment is great gain. For we brought
nothing into this world, and it is certain we can carry nothing out.
And having food and raiment let us be therewith content.*
1 TIMOTHY 6:6–8

Paul's perspective on contentment is an excellent one. Why would we desire for more than we have when we are fully aware that just as we brought nothing into this world, we can certainly take nothing out of it. Our simple sustenance and clothing is all that we really need. The rest of what we have is a blessing and a gift from God. Be grateful for what God has given you, but hold on to your worldly possessions with a loose hand for the seed of discontent quickly grows into bitterness.

TOP 3 PRIORITIES:

- [ ] ....
- [ ] ....
- [ ] ....

SCHEDULE/TO-DO LIST:

- [ ] ....
- [ ] ....
- [ ] ....
- [ ] ....

REFLECTIONS ON TODAY'S BIBLE READING

8 glasses a day: ⬜ ⬜ ⬜ ⬜ ⬜ ⬜ ⬜ ⬜

October

S	M	T	W	T	F	S
1	2	3	4	5	6	7
8	9	10	11	12	13	14
15	16	17	18	19	20	21
22	23	24	25	26	27	28
29	30	31				

REMEMBER

Halloween

Today's Bible Reading:

JEREMIAH 48:1–49:6; 2 TIMOTHY 1; PROVERBS 14:7–22

*But is now made manifest by the appearing of our Saviour
Jesus Christ, who hath abolished death, and hath brought
life and immortality to light through the gospel.*
2 TIMOTHY 1:10

Christ abolished death, having completely decimated it when He rose from the dead. Covered in His blood shed for you, death cannot touch you either. This means that you are immortal until the day that God has long ago appointed for you to go home to Him. And even then, death is nothing to fear, merely a necessary doorway into life everlasting. A passage through which Christ will walk with you as He has already walked before.

REFLECTIONS ON TODAY'S BIBLE READING

8 glasses a day:

TOP 3 PRIORITIES:

- ☐ ....
- ☐ ....
- ☐ ....

SCHEDULE/TO-DO LIST:

- ☐ ....
- ☐ ....
- ☐ ....
- ☐ ....

REMEMBER

November

S	M	T	W	T	F	S
			1	2	3	4
5	6	7	8	9	10	11
12	13	14	15	16	17	18
19	20	21	22	23	24	25
26	27	28	29	30		

Today's Bible Reading:

JEREMIAH 49:7–50:16; 2 TIMOTHY 2; PROVERBS 14:23–27

If we believe not, yet he abideth faithful: he cannot deny himself.
2 Timothy 2:13

Thank God that our lack of faith and obedience doesn't affect Him. Even when we are unfaithful and stumble badly, God remains entirely faithful and secure. Our sins do not mar Him since they are now and evermore carried in the scars of Jesus. For our sins Christ was sacrificed. By His wounds we are forgiven. Because God cannot deny Himself, this sacrifice was necessary. But because God is merciful beyond anything we deserve, He gave His Son in our place.

TOP 3 PRIORITIES:

- ☐ ....
- ☐ ....
- ☐ ....

SCHEDULE/TO-DO LIST:

- ☐ ....
- ☐ ....
- ☐ ....
- ☐ ....

REFLECTIONS ON TODAY'S BIBLE READING

8 glasses a day: ☐ ☐ ☐ ☐ ☐ ☐ ☐ ☐

November

S	M	T	W	T	F	S
			1	2	3	4
5	6	7	8	9	10	11
12	13	14	15	16	17	18
19	20	21	22	23	24	25
26	27	28	29	30		

REMEMBER

Today's Bible Reading:

JEREMIAH 50:17–51:14; 2 TIMOTHY 3; PROVERBS 14:28–35

Their Redeemer is strong; the LORD of hosts is his name:
he shall throughly plead their cause, that he may give rest
to the land, and disquiet the inhabitants of Babylon.
JEREMIAH 50:34

"[Your] Redeemer is strong; the LORD of hosts is his name." There is no shortcoming on your part that He can't fill. There is no fear that He can't conquer. There is no wound that He can't heal. There is no grief that He can't assuage. There is no mourning that He can't turn into dancing. This is your God. He pleads your cause. Rest in Him.

REFLECTIONS ON TODAY'S BIBLE READING

8 glasses a day:

TOP 3 PRIORITIES:

SCHEDULE/TO-DO LIST:

REMEMBER

December

S	M	T	W	T	F	S
					1	2
3	4	5	6	7	8	9
10	11	12	13	14	15	16
17	18	19	20	21	22	23
24	25	26	27	28	29	30
31						

Today's Bible Reading:

JEREMIAH 51:15-64; 2 TIMOTHY 4; PROVERBS 15:1-9

Notwithstanding the Lord stood with me, and strengthened me; that by me the preaching might be fully known, and that all the Gentiles might hear: and I was delivered out of the mouth of the lion.
2 TIMOTHY 4:17

Paul recounted one of many times that the Lord stood by him. Christ stands by His people even though no one stood by Him in His hour of need. The abandonment and loneliness He felt on the cross is a grief and a pain that we can never imagine–nor will we ever have to since He bore it for us. We will never be forsaken, because He was. We will never be alone, because He was. We will never bear the just wrath of God, because He did. You can be confident that Christ will always stand by you because He does so based on no merit of your own.

TOP 3 PRIORITIES:

- ☐ ....
- ☐ ....
- ☐ ....

SCHEDULE/TO-DO LIST:

- ☐ ....
- ☐ ....
- ☐ ....
- ☐ ....

REFLECTIONS ON TODAY'S BIBLE READING

8 glasses a day: ☐ ☐ ☐ ☐ ☐ ☐ ☐ ☐

REMEMBER

November

S	M	T	W	T	F	S
			1	2	3	4
5	6	7	8	9	10	11
12	13	14	15	16	17	18
19	20	21	22	23	24	25
26	27	28	29	30		

Today's Bible Reading:

JEREMIAH 52–LAMENTATIONS 1; TITUS 1:1–9; PROVERBS 15:10–17

In hope of eternal life, which God, that cannot lie,
promised before the world began.
TITUS 1:2

God cannot lie. This means that the promises and truths He speaks in His Word are fully reliable and trustworthy. He has promised eternal life to those who are His children. Therefore, as a child of God, you have a true and sure hope in eternal life with Him. This life and all its grief and sorrow is not even a drop in the ocean compared to the life of perfect joy and blessing that you have waiting for you.

REFLECTIONS ON TODAY'S BIBLE READING

8 glasses a day:

TOP 3 PRIORITIES:

SCHEDULE/TO-DO LIST:

REMEMBER

December

S	M	T	W	T	F	S
					1	2
3	4	5	6	7	8	9
10	11	12	13	14	15	16
17	18	19	20	21	22	23
24	25	26	27	28	29	30
31						

Sunday
NOVEMBER 5

Daylight Savings Time ends

Today's Bible Reading:

LAMENTATIONS 2:1–3:38; TITUS 1:10–2:15; PROVERBS 15:18–26

It is of the Lord's mercies that we are not consumed, because his compassions fail not. They are new every morning: great is thy faithfulness. The Lord is my portion, saith my soul; therefore will I hope in him.
LAMENTATIONS 3:22–24

This beautifully uplifting passage in Lamentations 3 is often taken out of context. It's easy to think that this sentiment was spoken by someone whose life was going well, who woke up every morning excited for a new day. But these precious verses are all the more beautiful because they were written from the pit of despair. This faith in God's daily compassion was held to in a dark place. These words were spoken by someone who clung to God's mercies as the only hope of life. No matter the darkness, God's light will find its way to you.

TOP 3 PRIORITIES:

- [ ] ....
- [ ] ....
- [ ] ....

SCHEDULE/TO-DO LIST:

- [ ] ....
- [ ] ....
- [ ] ....
- [ ] ....

REFLECTIONS ON TODAY'S BIBLE READING

8 glasses a day:

REMEMBER

November

S	M	T	W	T	F	S
			1	2	3	4
5	6	7	8	9	10	11
12	13	14	15	16	17	18
19	20	21	22	23	24	25
26	27	28	29	30		

Today's Bible Reading:

LAMENTATIONS 3:39–5:22; TITUS 3; PROVERBS 15:27–33

The heart of the righteous studieth to answer:
but the mouth of the wicked poureth out evil things.
PROVERBS 15:28

"Think before you speak" may seem like a tired adage, but it's a valuable one nonetheless. A righteous person studies his answer before making a reply. A wicked person pours forth evil and worthless things with no thought or care. Whose speech do your words resemble more–the wicked, careless person or the righteous, mindful person?

REFLECTIONS ON TODAY'S BIBLE READING

8 glasses a day:

TOP 3 PRIORITIES:

☐ ....
☐ ....
☐ ....

SCHEDULE/TO-DO LIST:

☐ ....
☐ ....
☐ ....
☐ ....

REMEMBER

December

S	M	T	W	T	F	S
					1	2
3	4	5	6	7	8	9
10	11	12	13	14	15	16
17	18	19	20	21	22	23
24	25	26	27	28	29	30
31						

Election Day

Today's Bible Reading:

EZEKIEL 1:1–3:21; PHILEMON; PROVERBS 16:1–9

A man's heart deviseth his way:
*but the L*ORD *directeth his steps.*
PROVERBS 16:9

No matter what plans you devise in your own heart regarding how your life should go, God is the one who ultimately guides your steps. He may (and often does) take you down a totally different path than you had planned. The story of Onesimus in the book of Philemon is just one example of this. Onesimus left Philemon as a runaway slave and was commended by Paul to return to Philemon as a fellow brother in Christ. It is doubtful that this was at all the plan that Onesimus had for his life when he ran away. But the story God crafted for him was more glorious than anything he could have devised.

TOP 3 PRIORITIES:

- [ ] ....
- [ ] ....
- [ ] ....

SCHEDULE/TO-DO LIST:

- [ ] ....
- [ ] ....
- [ ] ....
- [ ] ....

REFLECTIONS ON TODAY'S BIBLE READING

8 glasses a day: ☐ ☐ ☐ ☐ ☐ ☐ ☐ ☐

REMEMBER

November

S	M	T	W	T	F	S
			1	2	3	4
5	6	7	8	9	10	11
12	13	14	15	16	17	18
19	20	21	22	23	24	25
26	27	28	29	30		

Today's Bible Reading:

EZEKIEL 3:22–5:17; HEBREWS 1:1–2:4; PROVERBS 16:10–21

How shall we escape, if we neglect so great salvation; which at the first began to be spoken by the Lord, and was confirmed unto us by them that heard him; God also bearing them witness, both with signs and wonders, and with divers miracles, and gifts of the Holy Ghost, according to his own will?
HEBREWS 2:3–4

We cannot deny the Gospel. We cannot overlook the work of God that is so evident in the lives of the people whom He touches. We cannot reject the work of the Holy Spirit as He turns hearts of stone into hearts that fervently seek the Lord. We cannot escape the condemnation that comes to those who disavow their Creator who put His fingerprints so clearly over all creation. Only through accepting and embracing the work of Christ can you be truly free. Spread this essential news to all around you.

REFLECTIONS ON TODAY'S BIBLE READING

TOP 3 PRIORITIES:

SCHEDULE/TO-DO LIST:

8 glasses a day:

REMEMBER

December

S	M	T	W	T	F	S
					1	2
3	4	5	6	7	8	9
10	11	12	13	14	15	16
17	18	19	20	21	22	23
24	25	26	27	28	29	30
31						

Today's Bible Reading:

EZEKIEL 6–7; HEBREWS 2:5–18; PROVERBS 16:22–33

Forasmuch then as the children are partakers of flesh and blood, he also himself likewise took part of the same; that through death he might destroy him that had the power of death, that is, the devil; and deliver them who through fear of death were all their lifetime subject to bondage.
HEBREWS 2:14–15

Death has no power in your life. The conqueror of death now rules in your heart, leaving no room for fear. The effects of death are temporary and fleeting and quickly give way to a more glorious reality. Christ has turned the devil's greatest weapon into His most beautiful gift, for through death is the doorway to a much better life.

TOP 3 PRIORITIES:

- ☐ ....
- ☐ ....
- ☐ ....

SCHEDULE/TO-DO LIST:

- ☐ ....
- ☐ ....
- ☐ ....
- ☐ ....

REFLECTIONS ON TODAY'S BIBLE READING

8 glasses a day: ☐ ☐ ☐ ☐ ☐ ☐ ☐ ☐

November

S	M	T	W	T	F	S
			1	2	3	4
5	6	7	8	9	10	11
12	13	14	15	16	17	18
19	20	21	22	23	24	25
26	27	28	29	30		

REMEMBER

Today's Bible Reading:

EZEKIEL 8–10; HEBREWS 3:1–4:3; PROVERBS 17:1–5

*Whoso mocketh the poor reproacheth his Maker: and he
that is glad at calamities shall not be unpunished.*
PROVERBS 17:5

It is undeniably evident all throughout scripture that God defends and loves the poor and needy. As a God who is defined by love and justice, it's no wonder that He pays special attention to those who through injustice receive little love. Those who mistreat or mock the poor are really just mocking their Maker, which is an enormously bad idea. Those who speak up for and defend the poor become more like their Maker in that very act.

REFLECTIONS ON TODAY'S BIBLE READING

8 glasses a day:

TOP 3 PRIORITIES:

SCHEDULE/TO-DO LIST:

REMEMBER

December

S	M	T	W	T	F	S
					1	2
3	4	5	6	7	8	9
10	11	12	13	14	15	16
17	18	19	20	21	22	23
24	25	26	27	28	29	30
31						

Today's Bible Reading:

EZEKIEL 11–12; HEBREWS 4:4–5:10; PROVERBS 17:6–12

Let us therefore come boldly unto the throne of grace, that we may obtain mercy, and find grace to help in time of need.
HEBREWS 4:16

We are to come boldly to the throne of grace. Why? So that we might receive grace and mercy. If we need grace and mercy, then it means we are far from perfect. In our imperfection, what right do we have to enter into the throne room of a holy God? And yet, God calls us to come–and to come boldly no less. Clearly, this is not an us-centered boldness based on what we have done and how clean our man-made robes are. Rather, it is a God-centered boldness based on what He has done and how clean the blood-washed, heavenly robes are that we have been given.

TOP 3 PRIORITIES:

- [ ] ....
- [ ] ....
- [ ] ....

SCHEDULE/TO-DO LIST:

- [ ] ....
- [ ] ....
- [ ] ....
- [ ] ....

REFLECTIONS ON TODAY'S BIBLE READING

8 glasses a day: ☐ ☐ ☐ ☐ ☐ ☐ ☐ ☐

REMEMBER

November

S	M	T	W	T	F	S
			1	2	3	4
5	6	7	8	9	10	11
12	13	14	15	16	17	18
19	20	21	22	23	24	25
26	27	28	29	30		

Today's Bible Reading:

EZEKIEL 13–14; HEBREWS 5:11–6:20; PROVERBS 17:13–22

*Which hope we have as an anchor of the soul, both sure
and stedfast, and which entereth into that within the veil.*
HEBREWS 6:19

If a ship is moored by a trustworthy anchor, it can only go a certain distance from that anchor. It may be tossed around by the wind and pummeled with waves, but the anchor will not let it break free and get pushed out into the ocean. So too, the hope that we have in God will never allow us to drift out to sea. We may be tossed and battered by life's waves but only within the confines of the anchor's reach. God has anchored our soul to Himself through Christ's work on the cross. No matter how big the waves get, we have a hope in something sure.

REFLECTIONS ON TODAY'S BIBLE READING

8 glasses a day:

TOP 3 PRIORITIES:

- ☐ ....
- ☐ ....
- ☐ ....

SCHEDULE/TO-DO LIST:

- ☐ ....
- ☐ ....
- ☐ ....
- ☐ ....

REMEMBER

December

S	M	T	W	T	F	S
					1	2
3	4	5	6	7	8	9
10	11	12	13	14	15	16
17	18	19	20	21	22	23
24	25	26	27	28	29	30
31						

Today's Bible Reading:

EZEKIEL 15:1–16:43; HEBREWS 7; PROVERBS 17:23–28

But this man, because he continueth ever, hath an unchangeable priesthood. Wherefore he is able also to save them to the uttermost that come unto God by him, seeing he ever liveth to make intercession for them.
HEBREWS 7:24–25

Christ intercedes for you. Have you ever really pondered that? As you would lift up in prayer a family member or friend that you care deeply about, so too Christ, your truest friend, intercedes for you to the Father. You could not ask for a better advocate. He has been where you have been and has seen and felt the weight of this world. That the Son of God would know how your suffering feels is astonishing. He is deeply connected to your human needs and desires. Having been your sacrificial Lamb, He is now and forever will be your High Priest.

TOP 3 PRIORITIES:

☐ ....
☐ ....
☐ ....

SCHEDULE/TO-DO LIST:

☐ ....
☐ ....
☐ ....
☐ ....

REFLECTIONS ON TODAY'S BIBLE READING

8 glasses a day: ▯ ▯ ▯ ▯ ▯ ▯ ▯ ▯

November

S	M	T	W	T	F	S
			1	2	3	4
5	6	7	8	9	10	11
12	13	14	15	16	17	18
19	20	21	22	23	24	25
26	27	28	29	30		

REMEMBER

Today's Bible Reading:

EZEKIEL 16:44–17:24; HEBREWS 8:1–9:10; PROVERBS 18:1–7

Behold, this was the iniquity of thy sister Sodom, pride, fulness of bread, and abundance of idleness was in her and in her daughters, neither did she strengthen the hand of the poor and needy.
EZEKIEL 16:49

We often comfortably compare ourselves with Sodom, knowing that we are far more holy than the people living there who were truly evil and debased. And yet, what are the sins cited against Sodom? Pride, careless prosperity, idleness, and an inattention to the poor and needy. . .all of a sudden this seems a little uncomfortable. Is your life free of these sins? Just like the people of Sodom, we are wretched sinners whom God has every right to do away with. But He chose to redeem us and make us one of His family instead. Praise be to Him!

REFLECTIONS ON TODAY'S BIBLE READING

TOP 3 PRIORITIES:

☐ ....
☐ ....
☐ ....

SCHEDULE/TO-DO LIST:

☐ ....
☐ ....
☐ ....
☐

8 glasses a day: ☐ ☐ ☐ ☐ ☐ ☐ ☐ ☐

REMEMBER

December

S	M	T	W	T	F	S
					1	2
3	4	5	6	7	8	9
10	11	12	13	14	15	16
17	18	19	20	21	22	23
24	25	26	27	28	29	30
31						

Wednesday
NOVEMBER 15

Today's Bible Reading:

EZEKIEL 18–19; HEBREWS 9:11–28; PROVERBS 18:8–17

*Yet ye say, The way of the LORD is not equal. Hear now, O house
of Israel; Is not my way equal? are not your ways unequal?*
EZEKIEL 18:25

We have all heard the accusation that God is not fair. In fact, maybe you've thought that at times in your life. But how do we have any right to say that God's ways are not fair? To begin with, we can't even come close to comprehending the plans that God has for us. Also, we have done nothing for God compared to the matchless gifts and grace that He has given us. With all our fickleness, lack of gratefulness, and idolatry, we are the ones who are not fair.

TOP 3 PRIORITIES:

REFLECTIONS ON TODAY'S BIBLE READING

SCHEDULE/TO-DO LIST:

8 glasses a day:

November

S	M	T	W	T	F	S
			1	2	3	4
5	6	7	8	9	10	11
12	13	14	15	16	17	18
19	20	21	22	23	24	25
26	27	28	29	30		

REMEMBER

Today's Bible Reading:

EZEKIEL 20; HEBREWS 10:1–25; PROVERBS 18:18–24

*But this man, after he had offered one sacrifice
for sins for ever, sat down on the right hand of God.*
HEBREWS 10:12

Christ sat down at the right hand of God. The action of sitting down signified that His work was completed. It was finished. Unlike the other priests who would have to continually offer sacrifices, Christ's sacrifice was so powerful it put an end to the need for any further sacrifices. His work is finished, which means that your sins are already paid for. There is nothing that you have done that will fall outside the boundaries of His atoning sacrifice.

REFLECTIONS ON TODAY'S BIBLE READING

8 glasses a day:

TOP 3 PRIORITIES:

SCHEDULE/TO-DO LIST:

REMEMBER

December

S	M	T	W	T	F	S
					1	2
3	4	5	6	7	8	9
10	11	12	13	14	15	16
17	18	19	20	21	22	23
24	25	26	27	28	29	30
31						

Today's Bible Reading:

EZEKIEL 21–22; HEBREWS 10:26–39; PROVERBS 19:1–8

It is a fearful thing to fall into the hands of the living God.
HEBREWS 10:31

God's love fully encompasses who He is. But to only consider that He is a loving God is to truncate your knowledge of Him, to diminish His glory, and ultimately to lack a full understanding of His love. God is also a God who can be moved to wrath. He is a God to be feared in all His unattainable holiness. He can either create or destroy with a simple word. Knowing the power and fearfulness of God only makes the truth that He loves and cares for you more glorious.

TOP 3 PRIORITIES:

- ☐ ....
- ☐ ....
- ☐ ....

SCHEDULE/TO-DO LIST:

- ☐ ....
- ☐ ....
- ☐ ....
- ☐ ....

REFLECTIONS ON TODAY'S BIBLE READING

8 glasses a day: ☐ ☐ ☐ ☐ ☐ ☐ ☐ ☐

November

S	M	T	W	T	F	S
			1	2	3	4
5	6	7	8	9	10	11
12	13	14	15	16	17	18
19	20	21	22	23	24	25
26	27	28	29	30		

REMEMBER

Today's Bible Reading:

EZEKIEL 23; HEBREWS 11:1–31; PROVERBS 19:9–14

*For they that say such things declare plainly that they seek a country. . . .
But now they desire a better country, that is, an heavenly: wherefore God is
not ashamed to be called their God: for he hath prepared for them a city.*
HEBREWS 11:14, 16

Would those who interact with you on a daily basis recognize that you seek a homeland that is not of this world? Does your anticipation of your true home seep into your words and actions so much that it inspires others to seek this kingdom as well? What are you doing to seek out this heavenly land of which you are a citizen? Just as refugees on this earth often surround themselves with the comforts and reminders of their country of origin, so too, remind yourself often of where you are going.

REFLECTIONS ON TODAY'S BIBLE READING

8 glasses a day:

TOP 3 PRIORITIES:

SCHEDULE/TO-DO LIST:

REMEMBER

December

S	M	T	W	T	F	S
					1	2
3	4	5	6	7	8	9
10	11	12	13	14	15	16
17	18	19	20	21	22	23
24	25	26	27	28	29	30
31						

Today's Bible Reading:

EZEKIEL 24–26; HEBREWS 11:32–40; PROVERBS 19:15–21

(Of whom the world was not worthy.)
HEBREWS 11:38

In Hebrews 11 is a small parenthetical phrase that just may be the most powerful words ever put into parentheses–"Of whom the world was not worthy." This comfort-driven world is not worthy of people who will gladly be killed, beaten, and exiled so that they might follow their Savior. This selfish world is not worthy of people who value their lives so lightly that they would give them up for the sake of another. This compromising world is not worthy of people who refuse to budge an inch on the truth of the Gospel even when this steadfastness will cost them in this life. This world is not worthy of them. . .but they are worthy of their homes in heaven where every day they will dine with the Savior they so faithfully followed.

TOP 3 PRIORITIES:

- [ ] ....
- [ ] ....
- [ ] ....

SCHEDULE/TO-DO LIST:

- [ ] ....
- [ ] ....
- [ ] ....
- [ ] ....

REFLECTIONS ON TODAY'S BIBLE READING

8 glasses a day: ▢ ▢ ▢ ▢ ▢ ▢ ▢ ▢

REMEMBER

November

S	M	T	W	T	F	S
			1	2	3	4
5	6	7	8	9	10	11
12	13	14	15	16	17	18
19	20	21	22	23	24	25
26	27	28	29	30		

Today's Bible Reading:

EZEKIEL 27–28; HEBREWS 12:1–13; PROVERBS 19:22–29

*But if ye be without chastisement, whereof all are
partakers, then are ye bastards, and not sons.*
HEBREWS 12:8

Chastisement and discipline from God are not things that we generally look forward to. And yet, to not be disciplined is far worse. God will inevitably reprimand His children—it is how He lovingly makes us more like Himself. If you have not been corrected by Him, the sobering truth is that you may not truly be a child of His. Though it may seem a bit frightening, ask for God to make you more like Himself no matter what it takes—for it is far better to be one of His children than an outsider to His family.

REFLECTIONS ON TODAY'S BIBLE READING

8 glasses a day:

TOP 3 PRIORITIES:

SCHEDULE/TO-DO LIST:

REMEMBER

December

S	M	T	W	T	F	S
					1	2
3	4	5	6	7	8	9
10	11	12	13	14	15	16
17	18	19	20	21	22	23
24	25	26	27	28	29	30
31						

Today's Bible Reading:

EZEKIEL 29–30; HEBREWS 12:14–29; PROVERBS 20:1–18

Most men will proclaim every one his own goodness:
but a faithful man who can find?
PROVERBS 20:6

Be careful to avoid being the kind of person who proclaims your own goodness but in whom none of this proclaimed goodness can be found. Rather, be the kind of person who doesn't speak much of yourself but, through your actions and character, proves yourself a faithful person. Be more concerned about building others up. Humbly let your praise come from God or others.

TOP 3 PRIORITIES:

- ☐ ....
- ☐ ....
- ☐ ....

SCHEDULE/TO-DO LIST:

- ☐ ....
- ☐ ....
- ☐ ....
- ☐ ....

REFLECTIONS ON TODAY'S BIBLE READING

8 glasses a day: ☐ ☐ ☐ ☐ ☐ ☐ ☐ ☐

REMEMBER

November

S	M	T	W	T	F	S
			1	2	3	4
5	6	7	8	9	10	11
12	13	14	15	16	17	18
19	20	21	22	23	24	25
26	27	28	29	30		

Today's Bible Reading:

EZEKIEL 31–32; HEBREWS 13; PROVERBS 20:19–24

Wherefore Jesus also, that he might sanctify the people with his own blood, suffered without the gate. Let us go forth therefore unto him without the camp, bearing his reproach.
HEBREWS 13:12–13

Are you willing to bear the reproach of Jesus and go with Him outside the camp? Christians often find that they are not welcome in the upper reaches of society or the inner circles of secular culture. And yet, should we be surprised when we serve a Savior who suffered outside the gate? An outcast life with Him is far better than a thousand lives of earthly comfort without Him. No suffering can compare with the joy that He offers.

REFLECTIONS ON TODAY'S BIBLE READING

8 glasses a day:

TOP 3 PRIORITIES:

SCHEDULE/TO-DO LIST:

REMEMBER

December

S	M	T	W	T	F	S
					1	2
3	4	5	6	7	8	9
10	11	12	13	14	15	16
17	18	19	20	21	22	23
24	25	26	27	28	29	30
31						

Today's Bible Reading:

EZEKIEL 33:1–34:10; JAMES 1; PROVERBS 20:25–30

Pure religion and undefiled before God and the Father is this,
To visit the fatherless and widows in their affliction,
and to keep himself unspotted from the world.
JAMES 1:27

What would you say is pure and undefiled religion? James says that pure religion is visiting the fatherless and widows in their distress and keeping yourself unstained from the world. This is likely not the first answer that we would come up with. And yet, it is what God calls us to. If you aren't caring for those in need, is your heart where it should be? Are you serving God as you ought to serve Him?

TOP 3 PRIORITIES:

- [ ] ....
- [ ] ....
- [ ] ....

SCHEDULE/TO-DO LIST:

- [ ] ....
- [ ] ....
- [ ] ....
- [ ] ....

REFLECTIONS ON TODAY'S BIBLE READING

8 glasses a day: ☐ ☐ ☐ ☐ ☐ ☐ ☐ ☐

November

S	M	T	W	T	F	S
			1	2	3	4
5	6	7	8	9	10	11
12	13	14	15	16	17	18
19	20	21	22	23	24	25
26	27	28	29	30		

REMEMBER

Today's Bible Reading:

EZEKIEL 34:11–36:15; JAMES 2; PROVERBS 21:1–8

Even so faith, if it hath not works, is dead, being alone.
JAMES 2:17

While good works by no means secure your salvation, they are an excellent barometer regarding your faith. A faith that is not played out in and invigorated by works is a faith that may not be genuine. The God in whom you have faith is a God who daily reaches out to and sustains His people, orchestrating every aspect of their lives. He is a God who is constantly working for our good. If your faith in this God is not similarly accented by working for others, then maybe you do not know your God as you should. Our good works are one of the most obvious ways that we can imitate Christ on this earth and reach others for Him. Let us not be people with a skeletal faith.

REFLECTIONS ON TODAY'S BIBLE READING

8 glasses a day:

TOP 3 PRIORITIES:

- ☐ ....
- ☐ ....
- ☐ ....

SCHEDULE/TO-DO LIST:

- ☐ ....
- ☐ ....
- ☐ ....
- ☐ ....

REMEMBER

December

S	M	T	W	T	F	S
					1	2
3	4	5	6	7	8	9
10	11	12	13	14	15	16
17	18	19	20	21	22	23
24	25	26	27	28	29	30
31						

Saturday
NOVEMBER 25

Today's Bible Reading:

EZEKIEL 36:16–37:28; JAMES 3; PROVERBS 21:9–18

And shall put my spirit in you, and ye shall live, and I shall place you in your own land: then shall ye know that I the Lord have spoken it, and performed it, saith the Lord.
EZEKIEL 37:14

Ezekiel is mostly a very desolate book. God does not treat sin lightly–the punishment for ignoring the law of God is real. The intensity of the book makes the passages about God's redemption stand out all the more vividly. Even when your life feels desolate, God's Spirit remains alive and active within you. He does not abandon His people in the desert. He will bring you into a new and vibrant land. It's the experiences of being drawn out of the desert that cause us to look back and recognize that it is the Lord at work in us.

TOP 3 PRIORITIES:

- [ ] ....
- [ ] ....
- [ ] ....

SCHEDULE/TO-DO LIST:

- [ ] ....
- [ ] ....
- [ ] ....
- [ ] ....

REFLECTIONS ON TODAY'S BIBLE READING

8 glasses a day: ▢ ▢ ▢ ▢ ▢ ▢ ▢ ▢

November

S	M	T	W	T	F	S
			1	2	3	4
5	6	7	8	9	10	11
12	13	14	15	16	17	18
19	20	21	22	23	24	25
26	27	28	29	30		

REMEMBER

Today's Bible Reading:

EZEKIEL 38–39; JAMES 4:1–5:6; PROVERBS 21:19–24

Ye ask, and receive not, because ye ask amiss,
that ye may consume it upon your lusts.
JAMES 4:3

How often do we ask for something simply for our own comfort or pleasure without regard to how it will fit into God's kingdom plan or how it will affect others? We are masters at molding our idea of God's will to fit perfectly into our preconstructed plan for our lives. Would your prayers sound different if your greatest desire was to be of use to God's kingdom? Would your prayers sound different if your first thought was toward others rather than yourself?

REFLECTIONS ON TODAY'S BIBLE READING

8 glasses a day:

TOP 3 PRIORITIES:

☐ ....
☐ ....
☐ ....

SCHEDULE/TO-DO LIST:

☐ ....
☐ ....
☐ ....
☐ ....

REMEMBER

December

S	M	T	W	T	F	S
					1	2
3	4	5	6	7	8	9
10	11	12	13	14	15	16
17	18	19	20	21	22	23
24	25	26	27	28	29	30
31						

Today's Bible Reading:

EZEKIEL 40; JAMES 5:7–20; PROVERBS 21:25–31

Be ye also patient; stablish your hearts:
for the coming of the Lord draweth nigh.
JAMES 5:8

You are to establish your heart to prepare for the coming of Christ. Just as a tree needs water and nutrients for its roots to grow, so you also must feed your heart with the sustenance from God's Word so that your spiritual roots will burrow down into a deeper relationship with Him. Bask in the light of His presence that you may be filled up with His joy.

TOP 3 PRIORITIES:

- ☐ ....
- ☐ ....
- ☐ ....

SCHEDULE/TO-DO LIST:

- ☐ ....
- ☐ ....
- ☐ ....
- ☐ ....

REFLECTIONS ON TODAY'S BIBLE READING

8 glasses a day: ☐ ☐ ☐ ☐ ☐ ☐ ☐ ☐

November

S	M	T	W	T	F	S
				1	2	3	4
5	6	7	8	9	10	11
12	13	14	15	16	17	18
19	20	21	22	23	24	25
26	27	28	29	30		

REMEMBER

Today's Bible Reading:

EZEKIEL 41:1–43:12; 1 PETER 1:1–12; PROVERBS 22:1–9

To an inheritance incorruptible, and undefiled, and that fadeth not away, reserved in heaven for you, who are kept by the power of God through faith unto salvation ready to be revealed in the last time.
1 PETER 1:4–5

The kind of inheritance that we should be working for in this life is the one that is being stored up in heaven for us as an incorruptible, undefiled, and everlasting reward. This inheritance has nothing to do with money, ease of life, or status. Our heavenly inheritance is based on what our Father has already done for us and consists of riches beyond our imaginings. Our inheritance is sure because God Himself keeps us by His power and will grant us this inheritance based on no merit of our own.

REFLECTIONS ON TODAY'S BIBLE READING

8 glasses a day:

TOP 3 PRIORITIES:

SCHEDULE/TO-DO LIST:

REMEMBER

December

S	M	T	W	T	F	S
					1	2
3	4	5	6	7	8	9
10	11	12	13	14	15	16
17	18	19	20	21	22	23
24	25	26	27	28	29	30
31						

Today's Bible Reading:

EZEKIEL 43:13–44:31; 1 PETER 1:13–2:3; PROVERBS 22:10–23

But as he which hath called you is holy, so be ye holy in all manner
of conversation; because it is written, Be ye holy; for I am holy.
1 PETER 1:15–16

You are called to be holy just as God is holy. This is a high and daunting calling. You will certainly fall short of it aside from the atoning work of Christ. But sometimes we use an avoidance of legalism as an excuse to not even try to be holy. While we certainly can't muster holiness on our own, this is no excuse not to strive for it in this life. The purity of our lives is one way that God shows Himself to those around us. The brokenness of our lives is how God reminds us of our need for Him. Both our striving for holiness and our admittance of our weakness are important factors in God's work in our lives.

TOP 3 PRIORITIES:

- ☐ ....
- ☐ ....
- ☐ ....

SCHEDULE/TO-DO LIST:

- ☐ ....
- ☐ ....
- ☐ ....
- ☐ ....

REFLECTIONS ON TODAY'S BIBLE READING

8 glasses a day: ☐ ☐ ☐ ☐ ☐ ☐ ☐ ☐

REMEMBER

November

S	M	T	W	T	F	S
			1	2	3	4
5	6	7	8	9	10	11
12	13	14	15	16	17	18
19	20	21	22	23	24	25
26	27	28	29	30		

Today's Bible Reading:

EZEKIEL 45-46; 1 PETER 2:4-17; PROVERBS 22:24-29

Honour all men. Love the brotherhood.
Fear God. Honour the king.
1 PETER 2:17

First Peter 2:17 is a good and simple summation of how we ought to live our lives. Honor all people as image bearers of God, and in so doing, seek to serve them and bring them to Christ. Love your fellow Christians in a self-sacrificial way as Christ has taught us to do by His example. Fear God as the just and holy God who has every right to punish us for our sin but who has mercifully chosen to redeem us instead. Honor those placed in authority over you, and live as an upright and obedient citizen of this temporary home as much as you can while still obeying the law of God as your utmost authority.

REFLECTIONS ON TODAY'S BIBLE READING

8 glasses a day:

REMEMBER

TOP 3 PRIORITIES:

☐ ....
☐ ....
☐ ....

SCHEDULE/TO-DO LIST:

☐ ....
☐ ....
☐ ....
☐

December

S	M	T	W	T	F	S
					1	2
3	4	5	6	7	8	9
10	11	12	13	14	15	16
17	18	19	20	21	22	23
24	25	26	27	28	29	30
31						

Friday
DECEMBER 1

Today's Bible Reading:

EZEKIEL 47–48; 1 PETER 2:18–3:7; PROVERBS 23:1–9

*It was round about eighteen thousand measures: and the
name of the city from that day shall be, The LORD is there.*
EZEKIEL 48:35

The city spoken of in Ezekiel was named "The Lord is there." May our lives and homes be worthy of such a name as well. When others look in on your family or your personal life, will they recognize that God dwells with you? Does your life speak of the presence and redeeming work of God?

TOP 3 PRIORITIES:

- ☐ ....
- ☐ ....
- ☐ ....

SCHEDULE/TO-DO LIST:

- ☐ ....
- ☐ ....
- ☐ ....
- ☐ ....

REFLECTIONS ON TODAY'S BIBLE READING

8 glasses a day: ☐ ☐ ☐ ☐ ☐ ☐ ☐ ☐

December

S	M	T	W	T	F	S
					1	2
3	4	5	6	7	8	9
10	11	12	13	14	15	16
17	18	19	20	21	22	23
24	25	26	27	28	29	30
31						

REMEMBER

Today's Bible Reading:

DANIEL 1:1–2:23; 1 PETER 3:8–4:19; PROVERBS 23:10–16

Then was the secret revealed unto Daniel in a night vision. Then Daniel blessed the God of heaven.
DANIEL 2:19

Daniel's first reaction to his answered prayer was to praise God. How often do you forget to praise God after He's answered a prayer? How often do you end up attributing the answer to your own intelligence or ability? We should live in an attitude of praise and gratefulness to God as He is constantly answering our prayers and granting us mercies that we didn't even think to pray for. He deserves the credit. Every good thing in our lives is ultimately a gift from Him.

REFLECTIONS ON TODAY'S BIBLE READING

8 glasses a day:

TOP 3 PRIORITIES:

- [ ] ....
- [ ] ....
- [ ] ....

SCHEDULE/TO-DO LIST:

- [ ] ....
- [ ] ....
- [ ] ....
- [ ] ....

REMEMBER

January

S	M	T	W	T	F	S
	1	2	3	4	5	6
7	8	9	10	11	12	13
14	15	16	17	18	19	20
21	22	23	24	25	26	27
28	29	30	31			

Today's Bible Reading:

DANIEL 2:24–3:30; 1 PETER 5; PROVERBS 23:17–25

*He answered and said, Lo, I see four men loose, walking in the midst of the fire,
and they have no hurt; and the form of the fourth is like the Son of God.*
DANIEL 3:25

The story of Shadrach, Meshach, and Abednego in the fiery furnace is a beautiful illustration of how Christ walks with us through trials. He does not abandon those who have been faithful to proclaim Him. Though we can't always see it, we are never alone. Oh, that God would open our eyes so that we could see that one "like the Son of God" walks by our side when we're in the midst of the fire.

TOP 3 PRIORITIES:

- ☐ ....
- ☐ ....
- ☐ ....

SCHEDULE/TO-DO LIST:

- ☐ ....
- ☐ ....
- ☐ ....
- ☐ ....

REFLECTIONS ON TODAY'S BIBLE READING

8 glasses a day: ☐ ☐ ☐ ☐ ☐ ☐ ☐ ☐

December

S	M	T	W	T	F	S
					1	2
3	4	5	6	7	8	9
10	11	12	13	14	15	16
17	18	19	20	21	22	23
24	25	26	27	28	29	30
31						

REMEMBER

Today's Bible Reading:

DANIEL 4; 2 PETER 1; PROVERBS 23:26–35

And at the end of the days I Nebuchadnezzar lifted up mine eyes unto heaven, and mine understanding returned unto me, and I blessed the most High, and I praised and honoured him that liveth for ever, whose dominion is an everlasting dominion, and his kingdom is from generation to generation.
DANIEL 4:34

As captives in Babylon, God's people must have felt that God had abandoned them or that He had somehow messed up His plan. They likely thought that maybe God wasn't sovereign after all. But they probably never would have imagined that God would use this very difficult circumstance to bring a pagan king into relationship with Himself. We can never possibly know what it is that God plans to do through the hard circumstances that He puts us in. We must tirelessly trust in His sovereignty and grace and believe that He does have a better plan than ours.

REFLECTIONS ON TODAY'S BIBLE READING

8 glasses a day:

TOP 3 PRIORITIES:

SCHEDULE/TO-DO LIST:

REMEMBER

January

S	M	T	W	T	F	S
	1	2	3	4	5	6
7	8	9	10	11	12	13
14	15	16	17	18	19	20
21	22	23	24	25	26	27
28	29	30	31			

Today's Bible Reading:

DANIEL 5; 2 PETER 2; PROVERBS 24:1-18

These are wells without water, clouds that are carried with a tempest; to whom the mist of darkness is reserved for ever.
2 PETER 2:17

False teaching and the warping of God's truth to fit our own lifestyles is a serious offense to God and something that He does not take lightly. He is gracious enough to hate and punish false teaching because to let us adhere to lies would ultimately destroy us. Be careful to test the teaching that you receive against the perfect Word of God. If it doesn't match up, side every time with the Word of God.

TOP 3 PRIORITIES:

- ☐ ....
- ☐ ....
- ☐ ....

SCHEDULE/TO-DO LIST:

- ☐ ....
- ☐ ....
- ☐ ....
- ☐ ....

REFLECTIONS ON TODAY'S BIBLE READING

8 glasses a day: ☐ ☐ ☐ ☐ ☐ ☐ ☐ ☐

December

S	M	T	W	T	F	S
					1	2
3	4	5	6	7	8	9
10	11	12	13	14	15	16
17	18	19	20	21	22	23
24	25	26	27	28	29	30
31						

REMEMBER

Today's Bible Reading:

DANIEL 6:1–7:14; 2 PETER 3; PROVERBS 24:19–27

*Then said these men, We shall not find any occasion against this Daniel,
except we find it against him concerning the law of his God.*
DANIEL 6:5

Daniel's enemies were fully aware that they could bring no accusation against him unless they could somehow use his unwavering faithfulness to God against him. What a testimony that is! Daniel was upright and pure in all his morals and obedience to the good laws of the land. He had no secret sin that could be used against him. He had not slightly bent or ignored any laws that could be brought to light as a witness against him. Could you say the same about yourself? Perhaps even more poignantly, his relationship with God was so well known that his enemies knew that he would never bend in regard to his faithfulness to God. Could you say the same about yourself?

REFLECTIONS ON TODAY'S BIBLE READING

TOP 3 PRIORITIES:

SCHEDULE/TO-DO LIST:

8 glasses a day:

REMEMBER

January

S	M	T	W	T	F	S
	1	2	3	4	5	6
7	8	9	10	11	12	13
14	15	16	17	18	19	20
21	22	23	24	25	26	27
28	29	30	31			

Hanukkah begins at Sundown

Today's Bible Reading:

DANIEL 7:15-8:27; 1 JOHN 1:1-2:17; PROVERBS 24:28-34

If we say that we have no sin, we deceive ourselves, and the truth is not in us. If we confess our sins, he is faithful and just to forgive us our sins, and to cleanse us from all unrighteousness.
1 John 1:8–9

There is no reason not to confess your sins to God. If you don't confess your sins and instead deny that they exist, then they become witnesses against you that God's truth does not dwell in you. For His truth will inevitably reveal to us how we fail to keep His law. But if you confess your sins, they are guaranteed to be forgiven so that you can live with a clear conscience before God. With this in mind, why would you not daily confess your sins to your faithful Father?

TOP 3 PRIORITIES:

- [ ] ....
- [ ] ....
- [ ] ....

SCHEDULE/TO-DO LIST:

- [ ] ....
- [ ] ....
- [ ] ....
- [ ] ....

REFLECTIONS ON TODAY'S BIBLE READING

8 glasses a day:

REMEMBER

December

S	M	T	W	T	F	S
					1	2
3	4	5	6	7	8	9
10	11	12	13	14	15	16
17	18	19	20	21	22	23
24	25	26	27	28	29	30
31						

Today's Bible Reading:

DANIEL 9-10; 1 JOHN 2:18-29; PROVERBS 25:1-12

Therefore hath the LORD watched upon the evil, and brought it upon us: for the LORD our God is righteous in all his works which he doeth: for we obeyed not his voice.
DANIEL 9:14

Because God is righteous and faithful, He must punish sin. If He chose to let an indiscretion slide here or there or simply pretended that He didn't see a sin, He could not be trusted. An unfaithful or fickle god is not one that you would want to put your trust in. It's His very wrath and justice that make Him trustworthy. Because of God's holiness, sin needs to be punished—you ought to be eternally grateful that the punishment fell on Christ instead of you. It was inevitable that the blow would fall, but God is incomprehensibly gracious, having taken the blow onto Himself rather than put it on those who truly deserved it.

REFLECTIONS ON TODAY'S BIBLE READING

TOP 3 PRIORITIES:

- [ ] ....
- [ ] ....
- [ ] ....

SCHEDULE/TO-DO LIST:

- [ ] ....
- [ ] ....
- [ ] ....
- [ ] ....

8 glasses a day:

REMEMBER

January

S	M	T	W	T	F	S
		1	2	3	4	5	6
7	8	9	10	11	12	13
14	15	16	17	18	19	20
21	22	23	24	25	26	27
28	29	30	31			

Today's Bible Reading:

DANIEL 11–12; 1 JOHN 3:1–12; PROVERBS 25:13–17

*Behold, what manner of love the Father hath bestowed upon us,
that we should be called the sons of God: therefore the
world knoweth us not, because it knew him not.*
1 JOHN 3:1

You can almost sense the wonder in John's words about the gift of being called a child of God. We should have the same wonder, as well, that the Creator of all things would bestow on us the honor and privilege of being one of His children. He redeemed and justified us so that we would be spared the punishment of sin. But the truly remarkable thing is that He didn't stop there. He went so far as to adopt us. In this adoption He identifies with us and puts the stamp on us that we belong forever to Him. This manner of love is one that is impossible to comprehend.

TOP 3 PRIORITIES:

- [ ] ....
- [ ] ....
- [ ] ....

SCHEDULE/TO-DO LIST:

- [ ] ....
- [ ] ....
- [ ] ....
- [ ] ....

REFLECTIONS ON TODAY'S BIBLE READING

8 glasses a day:

REMEMBER

December

S	M	T	W	T	F	S
					1	2
3	4	5	6	7	8	9
10	11	12	13	14	15	16
17	18	19	20	21	22	23
24	25	26	27	28	29	30
31						

Today's Bible Reading:

HOSEA 1–3; 1 JOHN 3:13–4:16; PROVERBS 25:18–28

And I will betroth thee unto me for ever; yea, I will betroth thee unto me in righteousness, and in judgment, and in lovingkindness, and in mercies. I will even betroth thee unto me in faithfulness: and thou shalt know the LORD.
HOSEA 2:19–20

In Hosea is depicted a painfully beautiful story that is analogous to God's relationship with us. God has betrothed Himself to us and will therefore continue to seek us out no matter how many times we spit in the face of His faithfulness. We may run from Him. We may muddy His reputation by the worthless and soul-destroying sins that we continue to pursue as though they are more precious to us than our relationship to Him. Even in the face of this heartbreaking betrayal, He lovingly draws us back to Himself. To say that we don't deserve this kind of love is a huge understatement.

REFLECTIONS ON TODAY'S BIBLE READING

TOP 3 PRIORITIES:

- ☐ ....
- ☐ ....
- ☐ ....

SCHEDULE/TO-DO LIST:

- ☐ ....
- ☐ ....
- ☐ ....
- ☐ ....

8 glasses a day: ☐ ☐ ☐ ☐ ☐ ☐ ☐ ☐

REMEMBER

January

S	M	T	W	T	F	S
	1	2	3	4	5	6
7	8	9	10	11	12	13
14	15	16	17	18	19	20
21	22	23	24	25	26	27
28	29	30	31			

Monday
DECEMBER 11

Today's Bible Reading:

HOSEA 4–6; 1 JOHN 4:17–5:21; PROVERBS 26:1–16

For whatsoever is born of God overcometh the world: and this is the victory that overcometh the world, even our faith. Who is he that overcometh the world, but he that believeth that Jesus is the Son of God?
1 JOHN 5:4–5

Because of our faith in Christ, we have overcome the world. This means that, being hidden in His wings, nothing on this earth can touch us. There is no power or darkness that could come close to pulling us away from Christ or darkening the light of His presence in our hearts. Christ defeated the powers of this fallen world. Since He lives in us, we have become conquerors as well. Live in light of your victory over the sins and enticements of this world.

TOP 3 PRIORITIES:

- ☐ ....
- ☐ ....
- ☐ ....

SCHEDULE/TO-DO LIST:

- ☐ ....
- ☐ ....
- ☐ ....
- ☐ ....

REFLECTIONS ON TODAY'S BIBLE READING

8 glasses a day: ☐ ☐ ☐ ☐ ☐ ☐ ☐ ☐

December

S	M	T	W	T	F	S
					1	2
3	4	5	6	7	8	9
10	11	12	13	14	15	16
17	18	19	20	21	22	23
24	25	26	27	28	29	30
31						

REMEMBER

Today's Bible Reading:

HOSEA 7–10; 2 JOHN; PROVERBS 26:17–21

As a mad man who casteth firebrands, arrows, and death, so is the man that deceiveth his neighbour, and saith, Am not I in sport?
PROVERBS 26:18–19

The book of Proverbs is fascinating in how accurately it identifies human character. Not much has changed in the way we behave in the centuries since it was written. Do you see yourself in any of the descriptions? For instance, one of Solomon's warnings is against people who are rude and hurtful to someone and then cover themselves by saying, "I was only joking." Solomon compared a person that does this to a mad man who casts death. This kind of deception and carelessness is not something to be taken lightly.

REFLECTIONS ON TODAY'S BIBLE READING

8 glasses a day:

TOP 3 PRIORITIES:

- ☐ ....
- ☐ ....
- ☐ ....

SCHEDULE/TO-DO LIST:

- ☐ ....
- ☐ ....
- ☐ ....
- ☐ ....

REMEMBER

January

S	M	T	W	T	F	S
		1	2	3	4	5	6
7	8	9	10	11	12	13
14	15	16	17	18	19	20
21	22	23	24	25	26	27
28	29	30	31			

Today's Bible Reading:

HOSEA 11–14; 3 JOHN; PROVERBS 26:22–27:9

Beloved, follow not that which is evil, but that which is good. He that doeth good is of God: but he that doeth evil hath not seen God.
3 JOHN 1:11

Follow and imitate what is good. When you do good, you are like God because God is good and only does what is good for His people. Surround yourself with people who are already doing good and working hard for God's kingdom and then imitate these people. By imitating others who are already walking in a way worthy of their God, you are really imitating Christ. The more Christlike you become, the more abhorrent evil will be and the more wholeheartedly you will strive to do good.

TOP 3 PRIORITIES:

- ☐ ....
- ☐ ....
- ☐ ....

SCHEDULE/TO-DO LIST:

- ☐ ....
- ☐ ....
- ☐ ....
- ☐ ....

REFLECTIONS ON TODAY'S BIBLE READING

8 glasses a day: ☐ ☐ ☐ ☐ ☐ ☐ ☐ ☐

December

S	M	T	W	T	F	S
					1	2
3	4	5	6	7	8	9
10	11	12	13	14	15	16
17	18	19	20	21	22	23
24	25	26	27	28	29	30
31						

REMEMBER

Today's Bible Reading:

JOEL 1:1–2:17; JUDE; PROVERBS 27:10–17

Now unto him that is able to keep you from falling, and to present you faultless before the presence of his glory with exceeding joy, to the only wise God our Saviour, be glory and majesty, dominion and power, both now and ever. Amen.
JUDE 1:24–25

God is able to keep you from falling and to present you faultless before God in glory. This certainly sounds nice, but do you really believe it? Have you let this truth seep into your thoughts about yourself? Under God's care you will not fall. Nothing you can do will mar the perfection of Jesus' robes that you are covered in. Not only will you be blameless at the final judgment, but you will actually be able to stand before the most holy and just God with joy–that is how confident you will be in the work that Christ has accomplished for you. Live in that freedom and confidence here and now.

REFLECTIONS ON TODAY'S BIBLE READING

TOP 3 PRIORITIES:

- [ ] ....
- [ ] ....
- [ ] ....

SCHEDULE/TO-DO LIST:

- [ ] ....
- [ ] ....
- [ ] ....
- [ ] ....

8 glasses a day:

REMEMBER

January

S	M	T	W	T	F	S
	1	2	3	4	5	6
7	8	9	10	11	12	13
14	15	16	17	18	19	20
21	22	23	24	25	26	27
28	29	30	31			

Friday
DECEMBER 15

Today's Bible Reading:

JOEL 2:18–3:21; REVELATION 1:1–2:11; PROVERBS 27:18–27

I am Alpha and Omega, the beginning and the ending, saith the Lord,
which is, and which was, and which is to come, the Almighty.
REVELATION 1:8

God is the Alpha and the Omega. He is the beginning and the ending of the entire stretch of history. He is the prologue and epilogue to all eternity. He has always and will always exist. Can you imagine anyone better in whom to put your trust? No matter who may disappoint or desert you in this life, your God is present beside you and will remain so throughout eternity. You will never know a day in which your heavenly Father is not caring for you.

TOP 3 PRIORITIES:

- ☐ ....
- ☐ ....
- ☐ ....

SCHEDULE/TO-DO LIST:

- ☐ ....
- ☐ ....
- ☐ ....
- ☐ ....

REFLECTIONS ON TODAY'S BIBLE READING

8 glasses a day: ☐ ☐ ☐ ☐ ☐ ☐ ☐ ☐

December

S	M	T	W	T	F	S
					1	2
3	4	5	6	7	8	9
10	11	12	13	14	15	16
17	18	19	20	21	22	23
24	25	26	27	28	29	30
31						

REMEMBER

Today's Bible Reading:

AMOS 1:1–4:5; REVELATION 2:12–29; PROVERBS 28:1–8

I know thy works, and where thou dwellest, even where Satan's seat is: and thou holdest fast my name, and hast not denied my faith, even in those days wherein Antipas was my faithful martyr, who was slain among you, where Satan dwelleth.
REVELATION 2:13

The Spirit commended the church of Pergamum for holding fast to God's name even though they dwelled where Satan's throne was. Though He goes on to point out some things that the church was not doing well, it remains a beautiful testimony that this faithful church was shining Christ's light into the darkest of places. They stood strong at the very gates of hell. They proclaimed Christ as victor over all the earth, even the parts where Satan's power seemed overwhelming.

REFLECTIONS ON TODAY'S BIBLE READING

TOP 3 PRIORITIES:

- [ ] ....
- [ ] ....
- [ ] ....

SCHEDULE/TO-DO LIST:

- [ ] ....
- [ ] ....
- [ ] ....
- [ ]

8 glasses a day:

REMEMBER

January

S	M	T	W	T	F	S
	1	2	3	4	5	6
7	8	9	10	11	12	13
14	15	16	17	18	19	20
21	22	23	24	25	26	27
28	29	30	31			

Today's Bible Reading:

AMOS 4:6–6:14; REVELATION 3; PROVERBS 28:9–16

Because thou sayest, I am rich, and increased with goods, and have need of nothing; and knowest not that thou art wretched, and miserable, and poor, and blind, and naked.
REVELATION 3:17

Take an inventory of your true, everlasting riches versus your false, fleeting riches. Sometimes earthly wealth lulls us into thinking that we are safe and secure. But apart from the riches that only come through a personal relationship with Christ, we are wretched, miserable, poor, blind, and naked. Seek the true riches that Christ offers you.

TOP 3 PRIORITIES:

- [ ] ....
- [ ] ....
- [ ] ....

SCHEDULE/TO-DO LIST:

- [ ] ....
- [ ] ....
- [ ] ....
- [ ] ....

REFLECTIONS ON TODAY'S BIBLE READING

8 glasses a day:

REMEMBER

December

S	M	T	W	T	F	S
					1	2
3	4	5	6	7	8	9
10	11	12	13	14	15	16
17	18	19	20	21	22	23
24	25	26	27	28	29	30
31						

Today's Bible Reading:

AMOS 7–9; REVELATION 4:1–5:5; PROVERBS 28:17–24

And the four beasts had each of them six wings about him; and they were full of eyes within: and they rest not day and night, saying, Holy, holy, holy, LORD God Almighty, which was, and is, and is to come.
Revelation 4:8

The four living creatures in heaven constantly proclaim, "Holy, holy, holy, LORD God Almighty, which was, and is, and is to come." They do not rest from their praise of their Maker. Though God has put us on this earth for a different purpose than to proclaim His holiness without ceasing, it is still of value to consider how often you praise God. Even if you aren't constantly speaking of His greatness, your life can still proclaim His perfect work in you. And one day we will join in this endless praise, because to encounter the Lord in all His holiness is to inevitably be inspired to praise Him.

REFLECTIONS ON TODAY'S BIBLE READING

TOP 3 PRIORITIES:

- [ ] ....
- [ ] ....
- [ ] ....

SCHEDULE/TO-DO LIST:

- [ ] ....
- [ ] ....
- [ ] ....
- [ ] ....

8 glasses a day: ☐ ☐ ☐ ☐ ☐ ☐ ☐ ☐

REMEMBER

January

S	M	T	W	T	F	S
	1	2	3	4	5	6
7	8	9	10	11	12	13
14	15	16	17	18	19	20
21	22	23	24	25	26	27
28	29	30	31			

Today's Bible Reading:

OBADIAH–JONAH; REVELATION 5:6–14; PROVERBS 28:25–28

And I beheld, and, lo, in the midst of the throne and of the four beasts, and in the midst of the elders, stood a Lamb as it had been slain, having seven horns and seven eyes, which are the seven Spirits of God sent forth into all the earth.
REVELATION 5:6

In his vision, John stood weeping because he saw no one who could open the scroll. But then one of the elders assured him that the Lion of Judah had the authority to open the scroll. We look with anticipation to see this Lion, but what does John see by the throne? A slain Lamb. What beautiful imagery that this conquering Lion is displayed in all His power and glory as a sacrificed Lamb. In His completely counterintuitive and glorious plan, God sent His most powerful weapon, a humble sacrifice, to conquer the world, death, and all the powers of darkness.

TOP 3 PRIORITIES:

- ☐ ....
- ☐ ....
- ☐ ....

SCHEDULE/TO-DO LIST:

- ☐ ....
- ☐ ....
- ☐ ....
- ☐ ....

REFLECTIONS ON TODAY'S BIBLE READING

8 glasses a day: ☐ ☐ ☐ ☐ ☐ ☐ ☐ ☐

December

S	M	T	W	T	F	S
					1	2
3	4	5	6	7	8	9
10	11	12	13	14	15	16
17	18	19	20	21	22	23
24	25	26	27	28	29	30
31						

REMEMBER

Today's Bible Reading:

MICAH 1:1–4:5; REVELATION 6:1–7:8; PROVERBS 29:1–8

But they shall sit every man under his vine and under his fig tree; and none shall make them afraid: for the mouth of the LORD of hosts hath spoken it.
MICAH 4:4

What a beautiful picture Micah prophecies that every person will sit peacefully under their tree with absolutely nothing to make them afraid. Imagine a world in which nothing could make you afraid. This is the world that we get to look forward to in eternity. And even during this life, there is nothing that can make us afraid if we truly grasp the status that we have before God. The Lord of hosts has spoken that you are one of His forever-kept children. With this perspective, fear has no place in your heart or mind.

REFLECTIONS ON TODAY'S BIBLE READING

8 glasses a day:

TOP 3 PRIORITIES:

SCHEDULE/TO-DO LIST:

REMEMBER

January

S	M	T	W	T	F	S
	1	2	3	4	5	6
7	8	9	10	11	12	13
14	15	16	17	18	19	20
21	22	23	24	25	26	27
28	29	30	31			

Today's Bible Reading:

MICAH 4:6–7:20; REVELATION 7:9–8:13; PROVERBS 29:9–14

He hath shewed thee, O man, what is good; and what doth the Lord require of thee, but to do justly, and to love mercy, and to walk humbly with thy God?
Micah 6:8

Verses 6 and 7 of Micah 6 lay out increasingly costly scenarios of ways to pay for our sins. The last one Micah suggested almost incredulously, as it would be too much to bear–"shall I give my firstborn for my transgression?" And yet, this is exactly what the Lord has done for you. Since He did not desire to ask such a heart-wrenching sacrifice of you, He did it instead. Micah went on to lay out what God requires of us. It is not sacrifices of ten thousand bulls or the surrender of our firstborn. We are simply to do justly, love mercy, and walk humbly with Him–He's done the rest for us.

TOP 3 PRIORITIES:

- ☐ ....
- ☐ ....
- ☐ ....

SCHEDULE/TO-DO LIST:

- ☐ ....
- ☐ ....
- ☐ ....
- ☐ ....

REFLECTIONS ON TODAY'S BIBLE READING

8 glasses a day: ☐ ☐ ☐ ☐ ☐ ☐ ☐ ☐

December

S	M	T	W	T	F	S
					1	2
3	4	5	6	7	8	9
10	11	12	13	14	15	16
17	18	19	20	21	22	23
24	25	26	27	28	29	30
31						

REMEMBER

First Day of Winter

Today's Bible Reading:

NAHUM; REVELATION 9–10; PROVERBS 29:15–23

Who can stand before his indignation? and who can abide in the fierceness of his anger? his fury is poured out like fire, and the rocks are thrown down by him. The Lord is good, a strong hold in the day of trouble; and he knoweth them that trust in him.

NAHUM 1:6–7

The book of Nahum starts out aggressively depicting God's power and wrath against offending nations. It gives us a good picture of why we ought to fear God. And then verse 6 abruptly switches gears to talk about the goodness of the Lord and how He is a stronghold in the day of trouble. How reassuring in the face of His wrath to be reminded that He knows and cares for those who trust in Him. In the midst of whirling chaos, He is ever your stronghold.

REFLECTIONS ON TODAY'S BIBLE READING

TOP 3 PRIORITIES:

- ☐ ....
- ☐ ....
- ☐ ....

SCHEDULE/TO-DO LIST:

- ☐ ....
- ☐ ....
- ☐ ....
- ☐ ....

8 glasses a day: ▢ ▢ ▢ ▢ ▢ ▢ ▢ ▢

REMEMBER

January

S	M	T	W	T	F	S
	1	2	3	4	5	6
7	8	9	10	11	12	13
14	15	16	17	18	19	20
21	22	23	24	25	26	27
28	29	30	31			

Today's Bible Reading:

HABAKKUK; REVELATION 11; PROVERBS 29:24–27

Although the fig tree shall not blossom, neither shall fruit be in the vines; the labour of the olive shall fail, and the fields shall yield no meat; the flock shall be cut off from the fold, and there shall be no herd in the stalls: yet I will rejoice in the LORD, I will joy in the God of my salvation.
HABAKKUK 3:17–18

Habakkuk was a man of true resilience. Was this because he was especially powerful or well-off or had a good network of support? No, it was because no matter what the circumstance, he had made the choice to rejoice in the Lord. His was a God-based prosperity, not a circumstance-based prosperity. For this reason, no negative earthly circumstance could touch him because no amount of failed crops or empty stalls would change his opinion of his God. His joy lay in his Savior, not his stuff.

TOP 3 PRIORITIES:

- [ ]
- [ ]
- [ ]

SCHEDULE/TO-DO LIST:

- [ ]
- [ ]
- [ ]
- [ ]

REFLECTIONS ON TODAY'S BIBLE READING

8 glasses a day: ▢ ▢ ▢ ▢ ▢ ▢ ▢ ▢

December

S	M	T	W	T	F	S
					1	2
3	4	5	6	7	8	9
10	11	12	13	14	15	16
17	18	19	20	21	22	23
24	25	26	27	28	29	30
31						

REMEMBER

Sunday
DECEMBER 24

Christmas Eve

Today's Bible Reading:

ZEPHANIAH; REVELATION 12; PROVERBS 30:1-6

The LORD thy God in the midst of thee is mighty; he will save, he will rejoice over thee with joy; he will rest in his love, he will joy over thee with singing.
ZEPHANIAH 3:17

The Lord rejoices over you with singing. Can you believe that? Can you imagine that a God who created the universe, constantly sustains it, and listens to the prayers of billions of people every day rejoices over you? Insecurities, self-abasing self-talk, and low self-image have no place in the mind of someone who is rejoiced over by God. People will let you down and make you feel small and worthless, but when this happens, never forget that God continues to rejoice over you with joy and singing. Doesn't His opinion count for so much more than the opinion of anyone else?

REFLECTIONS ON TODAY'S BIBLE READING

8 glasses a day: ☐ ☐ ☐ ☐ ☐ ☐ ☐ ☐

TOP 3 PRIORITIES:

- ☐ ....
- ☐ ....
- ☐ ....

SCHEDULE/TO-DO LIST:

- ☐ ....
- ☐ ....
- ☐ ....
- ☐ ....

REMEMBER

January

S	M	T	W	T	F	S
	1	2	3	4	5	6
7	8	9	10	11	12	13
14	15	16	17	18	19	20
21	22	23	24	25	26	27
28	29	30	31			

Today's Bible Reading:

HAGGAI; REVELATION 13:1–14:13; PROVERBS 30:7–16

*Two things have I required of thee; deny me them not before
I die: remove far from me vanity and lies: give me neither
poverty nor riches; feed me with food convenient for me.*
PROVERBS 30:7–8

May God be so gracious that He gives us just the right amount of material wealth and comfort so that we continue to rely on and bless Him. May He be gracious enough to grant us contentment no matter what the circumstance. May our lives not be defined by vanity or treachery to get ahead in life, but rather, may they be lives of satisfaction in God alone without regard to material circumstances.

TOP 3 PRIORITIES:

- [ ]
- [ ]
- [ ]

SCHEDULE/TO-DO LIST:

- [ ]
- [ ]
- [ ]
- [ ]

REFLECTIONS ON TODAY'S BIBLE READING

8 glasses a day:

REMEMBER

December

S	M	T	W	T	F	S
					1	2
3	4	5	6	7	8	9
10	11	12	13	14	15	16
17	18	19	20	21	22	23
24	25	26	27	28	29	30
31						

Today's Bible Reading:

ZECHARIAH 1–4; REVELATION 14:14–16:3; PROVERBS 30:17–20

*For who hath despised the day of small things? for they shall rejoice,
and shall see the plummet in the hand of Zerubbabel with those seven;
they are the eyes of the LORD, which run to and fro through the whole earth.*
ZECHARIAH 4:10

Do not despise small beginnings. Do you ever have visions of what you want to be or do for God's kingdom? Then when you take stock of your current life, what you're doing seems so insignificant it's almost worthless? God uses small beginnings to make big movements in His kingdom. Who knows how He will use your faithful steps today? Take courage that nothing is wasted in God's economy.

REFLECTIONS ON TODAY'S BIBLE READING

TOP 3 PRIORITIES:

- ☐ ....
- ☐ ....
- ☐ ....

SCHEDULE/TO-DO LIST:

- ☐ ....
- ☐ ....
- ☐ ....
- ☐ ....

8 glasses a day: ▢ ▢ ▢ ▢ ▢ ▢ ▢ ▢

REMEMBER

January

S	M	T	W	T	F	S
		1	2	3	4	5	6
7	8	9	10	11	12	13
14	15	16	17	18	19	20
21	22	23	24	25	26	27
28	29	30	31			

Today's Bible Reading:

ZECHARIAH 5–8; REVELATION 16:4–21; PROVERBS 30:21–28

There be four things which are little upon the earth, but they are exceeding wise: the ants are a people not strong, yet they prepare their meat in the summer; the conies are but a feeble folk, yet make they their houses in the rocks; the locusts have no king, yet go they forth all of them by bands; the spider taketh hold with her hands, and is in kings' palaces.

PROVERBS 30:24–28

God's fingerprints are all over His creation. His character can be found in His creativity. Since He is the author of all living things, it makes sense that even the smallest of creatures can speak of His wisdom. Learn from the beautiful creation that He has given us to enjoy.

TOP 3 PRIORITIES:

- ☐ ....
- ☐ ....
- ☐ ....

SCHEDULE/TO-DO LIST:

- ☐ ....
- ☐ ....
- ☐ ....
- ☐ ....

REFLECTIONS ON TODAY'S BIBLE READING

8 glasses a day: ☐ ☐ ☐ ☐ ☐ ☐ ☐ ☐

December

S	M	T	W	T	F	S
					1	2
3	4	5	6	7	8	9
10	11	12	13	14	15	16
17	18	19	20	21	22	23
24	25	26	27	28	29	30
31						

REMEMBER

Today's Bible Reading:

ZECHARIAH 9–11; REVELATION 17:1–18:8; PROVERBS 30:29–33

These shall make war with the Lamb, and the Lamb shall overcome them: for he is Lord of lords, and King of kings: and they that are with him are called, and chosen, and faithful.
REVELATION 17:14

Today's reading in Revelation speaks of two things that are inevitable. First, the devil and his armies will wage war against the Lamb. We should not be surprised when we see the attempts of the darkness to overshadow Christ's light. But the second inevitable thing is that the Lamb shall overcome the powers of darkness. Always keep in mind that no matter how hotly the battles are raging, the end is sure.

REFLECTIONS ON TODAY'S BIBLE READING

8 glasses a day:

TOP 3 PRIORITIES:

- ☐ ....
- ☐ ....
- ☐ ....

SCHEDULE/TO-DO LIST:

- ☐ ....
- ☐ ....
- ☐ ....
- ☐ ....

REMEMBER

January

S	M	T	W	T	F	S
		1	2	3	4	5	6
7	8	9	10	11	12	13
14	15	16	17	18	19	20
21	22	23	24	25	26	27
28	29	30	31			

Friday
DECEMBER 29

Today's Bible Reading:

ZECHARIAH 12–14; REVELATION 18:9–24; PROVERBS 31:1–9

Open thy mouth for the dumb in the cause of all such as are appointed to destruction. Open thy mouth, judge righteously, and plead the cause of the poor and needy.
PROVERBS 31:8–9

We are to be a voice for those who don't have one. We are to be the arms of Christ here on earth to reach out to those who are headed for destruction. We are to speak up against injustice. We are to judge righteously (without regard to social status, economic status, age, race, or gender) just as our heavenly Father does. We are to plead the cause of the poor and needy so that they do not get trampled on. How are you doing with all these things?

TOP 3 PRIORITIES:

- ☐ ....
- ☐ ....
- ☐ ....

SCHEDULE/TO-DO LIST:

- ☐ ....
- ☐ ....
- ☐ ....
- ☐ ....

REFLECTIONS ON TODAY'S BIBLE READING

8 glasses a day: ☐ ☐ ☐ ☐ ☐ ☐ ☐ ☐

December

S	M	T	W	T	F	S
					1	2
3	4	5	6	7	8	9
10	11	12	13	14	15	16
17	18	19	20	21	22	23
24	25	26	27	28	29	30
31						

REMEMBER

Today's Bible Reading:

MALACHI 1–2; REVELATION 19–20; PROVERBS 31:10–17

And he was clothed with a vesture dipped in blood: and his name is called The Word of God. And the armies which were in heaven followed him upon white horses, clothed in fine linen, white and clean.
REVELATION 19:13–14

The robe of Christ was marred by the stain of blood as He rode forth into battle. Those who followed after Him, the heavenly armies, were clothed in perfectly clean and white linen. No spot of blood stained their robes. Your robe is perfectly white because He who stands next to you wears a robe that speaks of the bloody sacrifice that earned you your freedom. His blood stains are your salvation and power. Follow Him into battle boldly, knowing that nothing can mar the white linen He has given you.

REFLECTIONS ON TODAY'S BIBLE READING

TOP 3 PRIORITIES:

- ☐ ....
- ☐ ....
- ☐ ....

SCHEDULE/TO-DO LIST:

- ☐ ....
- ☐ ....
- ☐ ....
- ☐ ....

8 glasses a day: ☐ ☐ ☐ ☐ ☐ ☐ ☐ ☐

REMEMBER

January

S	M	T	W	T	F	S
	1	2	3	4	5	6
7	8	9	10	11	12	13
14	15	16	17	18	19	20
21	22	23	24	25	26	27
28	29	30	31			

Today's Bible Reading:

MALACHI 3–4; REVELATION 21–22; PROVERBS 31:18–31

*And God shall wipe away all tears from their eyes; and there shall
be no more death, neither sorrow, nor crying, neither shall there
be any more pain: for the former things are passed away.*
REVELATION 21:4

God will wipe away every tear from your eye with the very hands that are scarred by the nails that were driven in the cross for your sins. Death will be vanquished for all eternity and slowly forgotten as we live in blissful praise of our God, who conquered it for us. There will be no place for crying, sorrow, or pain as all things will finally be made right again. Could there be a more hopeful vision to hold on to in this life? Your struggles, pain, and tears are ephemeral and like a vapor that will be quickly forgotten in the all-encompassing light of God's glory. *Come, Lord Jesus, and make this future our present reality.*

TOP 3 PRIORITIES:

- ☐ ....
- ☐ ....
- ☐ ....

SCHEDULE/TO-DO LIST:

- ☐ ....
- ☐ ....
- ☐ ....
- ☐ ....

REFLECTIONS ON TODAY'S BIBLE READING

8 glasses a day: ☐ ☐ ☐ ☐ ☐ ☐ ☐ ☐

December

S	M	T	W	T	F	S
					1	2
3	4	5	6	7	8	9
10	11	12	13	14	15	16
17	18	19	20	21	22	23
24	25	26	27	28	29	30
31						

REMEMBER

CONTACTS

Name:

Address:

Phone: Cell:

Email:

Name:

Address:

Phone: Cell:

Email:

Name:

Address:

Phone: Cell:

Email:

Name:

Address:

Phone: Cell:

Email:

CONTACTS

Name:

Address:

Phone: Cell:

Email:

Name:

Address:

Phone: Cell:

Email:

Name:

Address:

Phone: Cell:

Email:

Name:

Address:

Phone: Cell:

Email:

CONTACTS

Name:

Address:

Phone: Cell:

Email:

Name:

Address:

Phone: Cell:

Email:

Name:

Address:

Phone: Cell:

Email:

Name:

Address:

Phone: Cell:

Email:

READ THROUGH THE BIBLE IN A YEAR PLAN

1-Jan	Gen. 1–2	Matt. 1	Ps. 1
2-Jan	Gen. 3–4	Matt. 2	Ps. 2
3-Jan	Gen. 5–7	Matt. 3	Ps. 3
4-Jan	Gen. 8–10	Matt. 4	Ps. 4
5-Jan	Gen. 11–13	Matt. 5:1–20	Ps. 5
6-Jan	Gen. 14–16	Matt. 5:21–48	Ps. 6
7-Jan	Gen. 17–18	Matt. 6:1–18	Ps. 7
8-Jan	Gen. 19–20	Matt. 6:19–34	Ps. 8
9-Jan	Gen. 21–23	Matt. 7:1–11	Ps. 9:1–8
10-Jan	Gen. 24	Matt. 7:12–29	Ps. 9:9–20
11-Jan	Gen. 25–26	Matt. 8:1–17	Ps. 10:1–11
12-Jan	Gen. 27:1–28:9	Matt. 8:18–34	Ps. 10:12–18
13-Jan	Gen. 28:10–29:35	Matt. 9	Ps. 11
14-Jan	Gen. 30:1–31:21	Matt. 10:1–15	Ps. 12
15-Jan	Gen. 31:22–32:21	Matt. 10:16–36	Ps. 13
16-Jan	Gen. 32:22–34:31	Matt. 10:37–11:6	Ps. 14
17-Jan	Gen. 35–36	Matt. 11:7–24	Ps. 15
18-Jan	Gen. 37–38	Matt. 11:25–30	Ps. 16
19-Jan	Gen. 39–40	Matt. 12:1–29	Ps. 17
20-Jan	Gen. 41	Matt. 12:30–50	Ps. 18:1–15
21-Jan	Gen. 42–43	Matt. 13:1–9	Ps. 18:16–29
22-Jan	Gen. 44–45	Matt. 13:10–23	Ps. 18:30–50
23-Jan	Gen. 46:1–47:26	Matt. 13:24–43	Ps. 19
24-Jan	Gen. 47:27–49:28	Matt. 13:44–58	Ps. 20
25-Jan	Gen. 49:29–Exod. 1:22	Matt. 14	Ps. 21
26-Jan	Exod. 2–3	Matt. 15:1–28	Ps. 22:1–21
27-Jan	Exod. 4:1–5:21	Matt. 15:29–16:12	Ps. 22:22–31
28-Jan	Exod. 5:22–7:24	Matt. 16:13–28	Ps. 23
29-Jan	Exod. 7:25–9:35	Matt. 17:1–9	Ps. 24
30-Jan	Exod. 10–11	Matt. 17:10–27	Ps. 25
31-Jan	Exod. 12	Matt. 18:1–20	Ps. 26
1-Feb	Exod. 13–14	Matt. 18:21–35	Ps. 27
2-Feb	Exod. 15–16	Matt. 19:1–15	Ps. 28
3-Feb	Exod. 17–19	Matt. 19:16–30	Ps. 29
4-Feb	Exod. 20–21	Matt. 20:1–19	Ps. 30
5-Feb	Exod. 22–23	Matt. 20:20–34	Ps. 31:1–8
6-Feb	Exod. 24–25	Matt. 21:1–27	Ps. 31:9–18
7-Feb	Exod. 26–27	Matt. 21:28–46	Ps. 31:19–24
8-Feb	Exod. 28	Matt. 22	Ps. 32
9-Feb	Exod. 29	Matt. 23:1–36	Ps. 33:1–12
10-Feb	Exod. 30–31	Matt. 23:37–24:28	Ps. 33:13–22
11-Feb	Exod. 32–33	Matt. 24:29–51	Ps. 34:1–7
12-Feb	Exod. 34:1–35:29	Matt. 25:1–13	Ps. 34:8–22
13-Feb	Exod. 35:30–37:29	Matt. 25:14–30	Ps. 35:1–8
14-Feb	Exod. 38–39	Matt. 25:31–46	Ps. 35:9–17
15-Feb	Exod. 40	Matt. 26:1–35	Ps. 35:18–28
16-Feb	Lev. 1–3	Matt. 26:36–68	Ps. 36:1–6
17-Feb	Lev. 4:1–5:13	Matt. 26:69–27:26	Ps. 36:7–12
18-Feb	Lev. 5:14–7:21	Matt. 27:27–50	Ps. 37:1–6
19-Feb	Lev. 7:22–8:36	Matt. 27:51–66	Ps. 37:7–26
20-Feb	Lev. 9–10	Matt. 28	Ps. 37:27–40
21-Feb	Lev. 11–12	Mark 1:1–28	Ps. 38
22-Feb	Lev. 13	Mark 1:29–39	Ps. 39
23-Feb	Lev. 14	Mark 1:40–2:12	Ps. 40:1–8
24-Feb	Lev. 15	Mark 2:13–3:35	Ps. 40:9–17
25-Feb	Lev. 16–17	Mark 4:1–20	Ps. 41:1–4
26-Feb	Lev. 18–19	Mark 4:21–41	Ps. 41:5–13
27-Feb	Lev. 20	Mark 5	Ps. 42–43

28-Feb	Lev. 21–22	Mark 6:1–13	Ps. 44
1-Mar	Lev. 23–24	Mark 6:14–29	Ps. 45:1–5
2-Mar	Lev. 25	Mark 6:30–56	Ps. 45:6–12
3-Mar	Lev. 26	Mark 7	Ps. 45:13–17
4-Mar	Lev. 27	Mark 8	Ps. 46
5-Mar	Num. 1–2	Mark 9:1–13	Ps. 47
6-Mar	Num. 3	Mark 9:14–50	Ps. 48:1–8
7-Mar	Num. 4	Mark 10:1–34	Ps. 48:9–14
8-Mar	Num. 5:1–6:21	Mark 10:35–52	Ps. 49:1–9
9-Mar	Num. 6:22–7:47	Mark 11	Ps. 49:10–20
10-Mar	Num. 7:48–8:4	Mark 12:1–27	Ps. 50:1–15
11-Mar	Num. 8:5–9:23	Mark 12:28–44	Ps. 50:16–23
12-Mar	Num. 10–11	Mark 13:1–8	Ps. 51:1–9
13-Mar	Num. 12–13	Mark 13:9–37	Ps. 51:10–19
14-Mar	Num. 14	Mark 14:1–31	Ps. 52
15-Mar	Num. 15	Mark 14:32–72	Ps. 53
16-Mar	Num. 16	Mark 15:1–32	Ps. 54
17-Mar	Num. 17–18	Mark 15:33–47	Ps. 55
18-Mar	Num. 19–20	Mark 16	Ps. 56:1–7
19-Mar	Num. 21:1–22:20	Luke 1:1–25	Ps. 56:8–13
20-Mar	Num. 22:21–23:30	Luke 1:26–56	Ps. 57
21-Mar	Num. 24–25	Luke 1:57–2:20	Ps. 58
22-Mar	Num. 26:1–27:11	Luke 2:21–38	Ps. 59:1–8
23-Mar	Num. 27:12–29:11	Luke 2:39–52	Ps. 59:9–17
24-Mar	Num. 29:12–30:16	Luke 3	Ps. 60:1–5
25-Mar	Num. 31	Luke 4	Ps. 60:6–12
26-Mar	Num. 32–33	Luke 5:1–16	Ps. 61
27-Mar	Num. 34–36	Luke 5:17–32	Ps. 62:1–6
28-Mar	Deut. 1:1–2:25	Luke 5:33–6:11	Ps. 62:7–12
29-Mar	Deut. 2:26–4:14	Luke 6:12–35	Ps. 63:1–5
30-Mar	Deut. 4:15–5:22	Luke 6:36–49	Ps. 63:6–11
31-Mar	Deut. 5:23–7:26	Luke 7:1–17	Ps. 64:1–5
1-Apr	Deut. 8–9	Luke 7:18–35	Ps. 64:6–10
2-Apr	Deut. 10–11	Luke 7:36–8:3	Ps. 65:1–8
3-Apr	Deut. 12–13	Luke 8:4–21	Ps. 65:9–13
4-Apr	Deut. 14:1–16:8	Luke 8:22–39	Ps. 66:1–7
5-Apr	Deut. 16:9–18:22	Luke 8:40–56	Ps. 66:8–15
6-Apr	Deut. 19:1–21:9	Luke 9:1–22	Ps. 66:16–20
7-Apr	Deut. 21:10–23:8	Luke 9:23–42	Ps. 67
8-Apr	Deut. 23:9–25:19	Luke 9:43–62	Ps. 68:1–6
9-Apr	Deut. 26:1–28:14	Luke 10:1–20	Ps. 68:7–14
10-Apr	Deut. 28:15–68	Luke 10:21–37	Ps. 68:15–19
11-Apr	Deut. 29–30	Luke 10:38–11:23	Ps. 68:20–27
12-Apr	Deut. 31:1–32:22	Luke 11:24–36	Ps. 68:28–35
13-Apr	Deut. 32:23–33:29	Luke 11:37–54	Ps. 69:1–9
14-Apr	Deut. 34–Josh. 2	Luke 12:1–15	Ps. 69:10–17
15-Apr	Josh. 3:1–5:12	Luke 12:16–40	Ps. 69:18–28
16-Apr	Josh. 5:13–7:26	Luke 12:41–48	Ps. 69:29–36
17-Apr	Josh. 8–9	Luke 12:49–59	Ps. 70
18-Apr	Josh. 10:1–11:15	Luke 13:1–21	Ps. 71:1–6
19-Apr	Josh. 11:16–13:33	Luke 13:22–35	Ps. 71:7–16
20-Apr	Josh. 14–16	Luke 14:1–15	Ps. 71:17–21
21-Apr	Josh. 17:1–19:16	Luke 14:16–35	Ps. 71:22–24
22-Apr	Josh. 19:17–21:42	Luke 15:1–10	Ps. 72:1–11
23-Apr	Josh. 21:43–22:34	Luke 15:11–32	Ps. 72:12–20
24-Apr	Josh. 23–24	Luke 16:1–18	Ps. 73:1–9
25-Apr	Judg. 1–2	Luke 16:19–17:10	Ps. 73:10–20
26-Apr	Judg. 3–4	Luke 17:11–37	Ps. 73:21–28
27-Apr	Judg. 5:1–6:24	Luke 18:1–17	Ps. 74:1–3
28-Apr	Judg. 6:25–7:25	Luke 18:18–43	Ps. 74:4–11
29-Apr	Judg. 8:1–9:23	Luke 19:1–28	Ps. 74:12–17

30-Apr	Judg. 9:24–10:18	Luke 19:29–48	Ps. 74:18–23
1-May	Judg. 11:1–12:7	Luke 20:1–26	Ps. 75:1–7
2-May	Judg. 12:8–14:20	Luke 20:27–47	Ps. 75:8–10
3-May	Judg. 15–16	Luke 21:1–19	Ps. 76:1–7
4-May	Judg. 17–18	Luke 21:20–22:6	Ps. 76:8–12
5-May	Judg. 19:1–20:23	Luke 22:7–30	Ps. 77:1–11
6-May	Judg. 20:24–21:25	Luke 22:31–54	Ps. 77:12–20
7-May	Ruth 1–2	Luke 22:55–23:25	Ps. 78:1–4
8-May	Ruth 3–4	Luke 23:26–24:12	Ps. 78:5–8
9-May	1 Sam. 1:1–2:21	Luke 24:13–53	Ps. 78:9–16
10-May	1 Sam. 2:22–4:22	John 1:1–28	Ps. 78:17–24
11-May	1 Sam. 5–7	John 1:29–51	Ps. 78:25–33
12-May	1 Sam. 8:1–9:26	John 2	Ps. 78:34–41
13-May	1 Sam. 9:27–11:15	John 3:1–22	Ps. 78:42–55
14-May	1 Sam. 12–13	John 3:23–4:10	Ps. 78:56–66
15-May	1 Sam. 14	John 4:11–38	Ps. 78:67–72
16-May	1 Sam. 15–16	John 4:39–54	Ps. 79:1–7
17-May	1 Sam. 17	John 5:1–24	Ps. 79:8–13
18-May	1 Sam. 18–19	John 5:25–47	Ps. 80:1–7
19-May	1 Sam. 20–21	John 6:1–21	Ps. 80:8–19
20-May	1 Sam. 22–23	John 6:22–42	Ps. 81:1–10
21-May	1 Sam. 24:1–25:31	John 6:43–71	Ps. 81:11–16
22-May	1 Sam. 25:32–27:12	John 7:1–24	Ps. 82
23-May	1 Sam. 28–29	John 7:25–8:11	Ps. 83
24-May	1 Sam. 30–31	John 8:12–47	Ps. 84:1–4
25-May	2 Sam. 1–2	John 8:48–9:12	Ps. 84:5–12
26-May	2 Sam. 3–4	John 9:13–34	Ps. 85:1–7
27-May	2 Sam. 5:1–7:17	John 9:35–10:10	Ps. 85:8–13
28-May	2 Sam. 7:18–10:19	John 10:11–30	Ps. 86:1–10
29-May	2 Sam. 11:1–12:25	John 10:31–11:16	Ps. 86:11–17
30-May	2 Sam. 12:26–13:39	John 11:17–54	Ps. 87
31-May	2 Sam. 14:1–15:12	John 11:55–12:19	Ps. 88:1–9
1-Jun	2 Sam. 15:13–16:23	John 12:20–43	Ps. 88:10–18
2-Jun	2 Sam. 17:1–18:18	John 12:44–13:20	Ps. 89:1–6
3-Jun	2 Sam. 18:19–19:39	John 13:21–38	Ps. 89:7–13
4-Jun	2 Sam. 19:40–21:22	John 14:1–17	Ps. 89:14–18
5-Jun	2 Sam. 22:1–23:7	John 14:18–15:27	Ps. 89:19–29
6-Jun	2 Sam. 23:8–24:25	John 16:1–22	Ps. 89:30–37
7-Jun	1 Kings 1	John 16:23–17:5	Ps. 89:38–52
8-Jun	1 Kings 2	John 17:6–26	Ps. 90:1–12
9-Jun	1 Kings 3–4	John 18:1–27	Ps. 90:13–17
10-Jun	1 Kings 5–6	John 18:28–19:5	Ps. 91:1–10
11-Jun	1 Kings 7	John 19:6–25a	Ps. 91:11–16
12-Jun	1 Kings 8:1–53	John 19:25b–42	Ps. 92:1–9
13-Jun	1 Kings 8:54–10:13	John 20:1–18	Ps. 92:10–15
14-Jun	1 Kings 10:14–11:43	John 20:19–31	Ps. 93
15-Jun	1 Kings 12:1–13:10	John 21	Ps. 94:1–11
16-Jun	1 Kings 13:11–14:31	Acts 1:1–11	Ps. 94:12–23
17-Jun	1 Kings 15:1–16:20	Acts 1:12–26	Ps. 95
18-Jun	1 Kings 16:21–18:19	Acts 2:1–21	Ps. 96:1–8
19-Jun	1 Kings 18:20–19:21	Acts 2:22–41	Ps. 96:9–13
20-Jun	1 Kings 20	Acts 2:42–3:26	Ps. 97:1–6
21-Jun	1 Kings 21:1–22:28	Acts 4:1–22	Ps. 97:7–12
22-Jun	1 Kings 22:29– 2 Kings 1:18	Acts 4:23–5:11	Ps. 98
23-Jun	2 Kings 2–3	Acts 5:12–28	Ps. 99
24-Jun	2 Kings 4	Acts 5:29–6:15	Ps. 100
25-Jun	2 Kings 5:1–6:23	Acts 7:1–16	Ps. 101
26-Jun	2 Kings 6:24–8:15	Acts 7:17–36	Ps. 102:1–7
27-Jun	2 Kings 8:16–9:37	Acts 7:37–53	Ps. 102:8–17
28-Jun	2 Kings 10–11	Acts 7:54–8:8	Ps. 102:18–28

29-Jun	2 Kings 12–13	Acts 8:9–40	Ps. 103:1–9
30-Jun	2 Kings 14–15	Acts 9:1–16	Ps. 103:10–14
1-Jul	2 Kings 16–17	Acts 9:17–31	Ps. 103:15–22
2-Jul	2 Kings 18:1–19:7	Acts 9:32–10:16	Ps. 104:1–9
3-Jul	2 Kings 19:8–20:21	Acts 10:17–33	Ps. 104:10–23
4-Jul	2 Kings 21:1–22:20	Acts 10:34–11:18	Ps. 104:24–30
5-Jul	2 Kings 23	Acts 11:19–12:17	Ps. 104:31–35
6-Jul	2 Kings 24–25	Acts 12:18–13:13	Ps. 105:1–7
7-Jul	1 Chron. 1–2	Acts 13:14–43	Ps. 105:8–15
8-Jul	1 Chron. 3:1–5:10	Acts 13:44–14:10	Ps. 105:16–28
9-Jul	1 Chron. 5:11–6:81	Acts 14:11–28	Ps. 105:29–36
10-Jul	1 Chron. 7:1–9:9	Acts 15:1–18	Ps. 105:37–45
11-Jul	1 Chron. 9:10–11:9	Acts 15:19–41	Ps. 106:1–12
12-Jul	1 Chron. 11:10–12:40	Acts 16:1–15	Ps. 106:13–27
13-Jul	1 Chron. 13–15	Acts 16:16–40	Ps. 106:28–33
14-Jul	1 Chron. 16–17	Acts 17:1–14	Ps. 106:34–43
15-Jul	1 Chron. 18–20	Acts 17:15–34	Ps. 106:44–48
16-Jul	1 Chron. 21–22	Acts 18:1–23	Ps. 107:1–9
17-Jul	1 Chron. 23–25	Acts 18:24–19:10	Ps. 107:10–16
18-Jul	1 Chron. 26–27	Acts 19:11–22	Ps. 107:17–32
19-Jul	1 Chron. 28–29	Acts 19:23–41	Ps. 107:33–38
20-Jul	2 Chron. 1–3	Acts 20:1–16	Ps. 107:39–43
21-Jul	2 Chron. 4:1–6:11	Acts 20:17–38	Ps. 108
22-Jul	2 Chron. 6:12–7:10	Acts 21:1–14	Ps. 109:1–20
23-Jul	2 Chron. 7:11–9:28	Acts 21:15–32	Ps. 109:21–31
24-Jul	2 Chron. 9:29–12:16	Acts 21:33–22:16	Ps. 110:1–3
25-Jul	2 Chron. 13–15	Acts 22:17–23:11	Ps. 110:4–7
26-Jul	2 Chron. 16–17	Acts 23:12–24:21	Ps. 111
27-Jul	2 Chron. 18–19	Acts 24:22–25:12	Ps. 112
28-Jul	2 Chron. 20–21	Acts 25:13–27	Ps. 113
29-Jul	2 Chron. 22–23	Acts 26	Ps. 114
30-Jul	2 Chron. 24:1–25:16	Acts 27:1–20	Ps. 115:1–10
31-Jul	2 Chron. 25:17–27:9	Acts 27:21–28:6	Ps. 115:11–18
1-Aug	2 Chron. 28:1–29:19	Acts 28:7–31	Ps. 116:1–5
2-Aug	2 Chron. 29:20–30:27	Rom. 1:1–17	Ps. 116:6–19
3-Aug	2 Chron. 31–32	Rom. 1:18–32	Ps. 117
4-Aug	2 Chron. 33:1–34:7	Rom. 2	Ps. 118:1–18
5-Aug	2 Chron. 34:8–35:19	Rom. 3:1–26	Ps. 118:19–23
6-Aug	2 Chron. 35:20–36:23	Rom. 3:27–4:25	Ps. 118:24–29
7-Aug	Ezra 1–3	Rom. 5	Ps. 119:1–8
8-Aug	Ezra 4–5	Rom. 6:1–7:6	Ps. 119:9–16
9-Aug	Ezra 6:1–7:26	Rom. 7:7–25	Ps. 119:17–32
10-Aug	Ezra 7:27–9:4	Rom. 8:1–27	Ps. 119:33–40
11-Aug	Ezra 9:5–10:44	Rom. 8:28–39	Ps. 119:41–64
12-Aug	Neh. 1:1–3:16	Rom. 9:1–18	Ps. 119:65–72
13-Aug	Neh. 3:17–5:13	Rom. 9:19–33	Ps. 119:73–80
14-Aug	Neh. 5:14–7:73	Rom. 10:1–13	Ps. 119:81–88
15-Aug	Neh. 8:1–9:5	Rom. 10:14–11:24	Ps. 119:89–104
16-Aug	Neh. 9:6–10:27	Rom. 11:25–12:8	Ps. 119:105–120
17-Aug	Neh. 10:28–12:26	Rom. 12:9–13:7	Ps. 119:121–128
18-Aug	Neh. 12:27–13:31	Rom. 13:8–14:12	Ps. 119:129–136
19-Aug	Esther 1:1–2:18	Rom. 14:13–15:13	Ps. 119:137–152
20-Aug	Esther 2:19–5:14	Rom. 15:14–21	Ps. 119:153–168
21-Aug	Esther. 6–8	Rom. 15:22–33	Ps. 119:169–176
22-Aug	Esther 9–10	Rom. 16	Pss. 120–122
23-Aug	Job 1–3	1 Cor. 1:1–25	Ps. 123
24-Aug	Job 4–6	1 Cor. 1:26–2:16	Pss. 124–125
25-Aug	Job 7–9	1 Cor. 3	Pss. 126–127
26-Aug	Job 10–13	1 Cor. 4:1–13	Pss. 128–129
27-Aug	Job 14–16	1 Cor. 4:14–5:13	Ps. 130
28-Aug	Job 17–20	1 Cor. 6	Ps. 131

29-Aug	Job 21–23	1 Cor. 7:1–16	Ps. 132
30-Aug	Job 24–27	1 Cor. 7:17–40	Pss. 133–134
31-Aug	Job 28–30	1 Cor. 8	Ps. 135
1-Sep	Job 31–33	1 Cor. 9:1–18	Ps. 136:1–9
2-Sep	Job 34–36	1 Cor. 9:19–10:13	Ps. 136:10–26
3-Sep	Job 37–39	1 Cor. 10:14–11:1	Ps. 137
4-Sep	Job 40–42	1 Cor. 11:2–34	Ps. 138
5-Sep	Eccles. 1:1–3:15	1 Cor. 12:1–26	Ps. 139:1–6
6-Sep	Eccles. 3:16–6:12	1 Cor. 12:27–13:13	Ps. 139:7–18
7-Sep	Eccles. 7:1–9:12	1 Cor. 14:1–22	Ps. 139:19–24
8-Sep	Eccles. 9:13–12:14	1 Cor. 14:23–15:11	Ps. 140:1–8
9-Sep	SS 1–4	1 Cor. 15:12–34	Ps. 140:9–13
10-Sep	SS 5–8	1 Cor. 15:35–58	Ps. 141
11-Sep	Isa. 1–2	1 Cor. 16	Ps. 142
12-Sep	Isa. 3–5	2 Cor. 1:1–11	Ps. 143:1–6
13-Sep	Isa. 6–8	2 Cor. 1:12–2:4	Ps. 143:7–12
14-Sep	Isa. 9–10	2 Cor. 2:5–17	Ps. 144
15-Sep	Isa. 11–13	2 Cor. 3	Ps. 145
16-Sep	Isa. 14–16	2 Cor. 4	Ps. 146
17-Sep	Isa. 17–19	2 Cor. 5	Ps. 147:1–11
18-Sep	Isa. 20–23	2 Cor. 6	Ps. 147:12–20
19-Sep	Isa. 24:1–26:19	2 Cor. 7	Ps. 148
20-Sep	Isa. 26:20–28:29	2 Cor. 8	Pss. 149–150
21-Sep	Isa. 29–30	2 Cor. 9	Prov. 1:1–9
22-Sep	Isa. 31–33	2 Cor. 10	Prov. 1:10–22
23-Sep	Isa. 34–36	2 Cor. 11	Prov. 1:23–26
24-Sep	Isa. 37–38	2 Cor. 12:1–10	Prov. 1:27–33
25-Sep	Isa. 39–40	2 Cor. 12:11–13:14	Prov. 2:1–15
26-Sep	Isa. 41–42	Gal. 1	Prov. 2:16–22
27-Sep	Isa. 43:1–44:20	Gal. 2	Prov. 3:1–12
28-Sep	Isa. 44:21–46:13	Gal. 3:1–18	Prov. 3:13–26
29-Sep	Isa. 47:1–49:13	Gal. 3:19–29	Prov. 3:27–35
30-Sep	Isa. 49:14–51:23	Gal. 4:1–11	Prov. 4:1–19
1-Oct	Isa. 52–54	Gal. 4:12–31	Prov. 4:20–27
2-Oct	Isa. 55–57	Gal. 5	Prov. 5:1–14
3-Oct	Isa. 58–59	Gal. 6	Prov. 5:15–23
4-Oct	Isa. 60–62	Eph. 1	Prov. 6:1–5
5-Oct	Isa. 63:1–65:16	Eph. 2	Prov. 6:6–19
6-Oct	Isa. 65:17–66:24	Eph. 3:1–4:16	Prov. 6:20–26
7-Oct	Jer. 1–2	Eph. 4:17–32	Prov. 6:27–35
8-Oct	Jer. 3:1–4:22	Eph. 5	Prov. 7:1–5
9-Oct	Jer. 4:23–5:31	Eph. 6	Prov. 7:6–27
10-Oct	Jer. 6:1–7:26	Phil. 1:1–26	Prov. 8:1–11
11-Oct	Jer. 7:26–9:16	Phil. 1:27–2:18	Prov. 8:12–21
12-Oct	Jer. 9:17–11:17	Phil 2:19–30	Prov. 8:22–36
13-Oct	Jer. 11:18–13:27	Phil. 3	Prov. 9:1–6
14-Oct	Jer. 14–15	Phil. 4	Prov. 9:7–18
15-Oct	Jer. 16–17	Col. 1:1–23	Prov. 10:1–5
16-Oct	Jer. 18:1–20:6	Col. 1:24–2:15	Prov. 10:6–14
17-Oct	Jer. 20:7–22:19	Col. 2:16–3:4	Prov. 10:15–26
18-Oct	Jer. 22:20–23:40	Col. 3:5–4:1	Prov. 10:27–32
19-Oct	Jer. 24–25	Col. 4:2–18	Prov. 11:1–11
20-Oct	Jer. 26–27	1 Thess. 1:1–2:8	Prov. 11:12–21
21-Oct	Jer. 28–29	1 Thess. 2:9–3:13	Prov. 11:22–26
22-Oct	Jer. 30:1–31:22	1 Thess. 4:1–5:11	Prov. 11:27–31
23-Oct	Jer. 31:23–32:35	1 Thess. 5:12–28	Prov. 12:1–14
24-Oct	Jer. 32:36–34:7	2 Thess. 1–2	Prov. 12:15–20
25-Oct	Jer. 34:8–36:10	2 Thess. 3	Prov. 12:21–28
26-Oct	Jer. 36:11–38:13	1 Tim. 1:1–17	Prov. 13:1–4
27-Oct	Jer. 38:14–40:6	1 Tim. 1:18–3:13	Prov. 13:5–13
28-Oct	Jer. 40:7–42:22	1 Tim. 3:14–4:10	Prov. 13:14–21
29-Oct	Jer. 43–44	1 Tim. 4:11–5:16	Prov. 13:22–25
30-Oct	Jer. 45–47	1 Tim. 5:17–6:21	Prov. 14:1–6

31-Oct	Jer. 48:1–49:6	2 Tim. 1	Prov. 14:7–22
1-Nov	Jer. 49:7–50:16	2 Tim. 2	Prov. 14:23–27
2-Nov	Jer. 50:17–51:14	2 Tim. 3	Prov. 14:28–35
3-Nov	Jer. 51:15–64	2 Tim. 4	Prov. 15:1–9
4-Nov	Jer. 52–Lam. 1	Titus 1:1–9	Prov. 15:10–17
5-Nov	Lam. 2:1–3:38	Titus 1:10–2:15	Prov. 15:18–26
6-Nov	Lam. 3:39–5:22	Titus 3	Prov. 15:27–33
7-Nov	Ezek. 1:1–3:21	Philemon	Prov. 16:1–9
8-Nov	Ezek. 3:22–5:17	Heb. 1:1–2:4	Prov. 16:10–21
9-Nov	Ezek. 6–7	Heb. 2:5–18	Prov. 16:22–33
10-Nov	Ezek. 8–10	Heb. 3:1–4:3	Prov. 17:1–5
11-Nov	Ezek. 11–12	Heb. 4:4–5:10	Prov. 17:6–12
12-Nov	Ezek. 13–14	Heb. 5:11–6:20	Prov. 17:13–22
13-Nov	Ezek. 15:1–16:43	Heb. 7:1–28	Prov. 17:23–28
14-Nov	Ezek. 16:44–17:24	Heb. 8:1–9:10	Prov. 18:1–7
15-Nov	Ezek. 18–19	Heb. 9:11–28	Prov. 18:8–17
16-Nov	Ezek. 20	Heb. 10:1–25	Prov. 18:18–24
17-Nov	Ezek. 21–22	Heb. 10:26–39	Prov. 19:1–8
18-Nov	Ezek. 23	Heb. 11:1–31	Prov. 19:9–14
19-Nov	Ezek. 24–26	Heb. 11:32–40	Prov. 19:15–21
20-Nov	Ezek. 27–28	Heb. 12:1–13	Prov. 19:22–29
21-Nov	Ezek. 29–30	Heb. 12:14–29	Prov. 20:1–18
22-Nov	Ezek. 31–32	Heb. 13	Prov. 20:19–24
23-Nov	Ezek. 33:1–34:10	James 1	Prov. 20:25–30
24-Nov	Ezek. 34:11–36:15	James 2	Prov. 21:1–8
25-Nov	Ezek. 36:16–37:28	James 3	Prov. 21:9–18
26-Nov	Ezek. 38–39	James 4:1–5:6	Prov. 21:19–24
27-Nov	Ezek. 40	James 5:7–20	Prov. 21:25–31
28-Nov	Ezek. 41:1–43:12	1 Pet. 1:1–12	Prov. 22:1–9
29-Nov	Ezek. 43:13–44:31	1 Pet. 1:13–2:3	Prov. 22:10–23
30-Nov	Ezek. 45–46	1 Pet. 2:4–17	Prov. 22:24–29
1-Dec	Ezek. 47–48	1 Pet. 2:18–3:7	Prov. 23:1–9
2-Dec	Dan. 1:1–2:23	1 Pet. 3:8–4:19	Prov. 23:10–16
3-Dec	Dan. 2:24–3:30	1 Pet. 5	Prov. 23:17–25
4-Dec	Dan. 4	2 Pet. 1	Prov. 23:26–35
5-Dec	Dan. 5	2 Pet. 2	Prov. 24:1–18
6-Dec	Dan. 6:1–7:14	2 Pet. 3	Prov. 24:19–27
7-Dec	Dan. 7:15–8:27	1 John 1:1–2:17	Prov. 24:28–34
8-Dec	Dan. 9–10	1 John 2:18–29	Prov. 25:1–12
9-Dec	Dan. 11–12	1 John 3:1–12	Prov. 25:13–17
10-Dec	Hos. 1–3	1 John 3:13–4:16	Prov. 25:18–28
11-Dec	Hos. 4–6	1 John 4:17–5:21	Prov. 26:1–16
12-Dec	Hos. 7–10	2 John	Prov. 26:17–21
13-Dec	Hos. 11–14	3 John	Prov. 26:22–27:9
14-Dec	Joel 1:1–2:17	Jude	Prov. 27:10–17
15-Dec	Joel 2:18–3:21	Rev. 1:1–2:11	Prov. 27:18–27
16-Dec	Amos 1:1–4:5	Rev. 2:12–29	Prov. 28:1–8
17-Dec	Amos 4:6–6:14	Rev. 3	Prov. 28:9–16
18-Dec	Amos 7–9	Rev. 4:1–5:5	Prov. 28:17–24
19-Dec	Obad.–Jonah	Rev. 5:6–14	Prov. 28:25–28
20-Dec	Mic. 1:1–4:5	Rev. 6:1–7:8	Prov. 29:1–8
21-Dec	Mic. 4:6–7:20	Rev. 7:9–8:13	Prov. 29:9–14
22-Dec	Nah. 1–3	Rev. 9–10	Prov. 29:15–23
23-Dec	Hab. 1–3	Rev. 11	Prov. 29:24–27
24-Dec	Zeph. 1–3	Rev. 12	Prov. 30:1–6
25-Dec	Hag. 1–2	Rev. 13:1–14:13	Prov. 30:7–16
26-Dec	Zech. 1–4	Rev. 14:14–16:3	Prov. 30:17–20
27-Dec	Zech. 5–8	Rev. 16:4–21	Prov. 30:21–28
28-Dec	Zech. 9–11	Rev. 17:1–18:8	Prov. 30:29–33
29-Dec	Zech. 12–14	Rev. 18:9–24	Prov. 31:1–9
30-Dec	Mal. 1–2	Rev. 19–20	Prov. 31:10–17
31-Dec	Mal. 3–4	Rev. 21–22	Prov. 31:18–31

WHAT GOD'S WORD SAYS ABOUT:

Acceptance
John 13:20; 14:16–17; 17:8
Acts 22:17–18
Romans 15:7
1 Corinthians 2:14
1 Timothy 1:15
Hebrews 12:6

Anxiety
Numbers 6:26
Psalm 20:7; 27:14; 28:7; 37:3–8;
    46:10; 55:22; 91:1–6; 94:19;
    107:30; 118:6; 119:143;
    121:4; 127:1–2; 131:1–3;
    139:23
Proverbs 1:33; 3:5–6; 12:25
Ecclesiastes 4:6
Isaiah 12:2; 32:18; 41:13; 43:1–2;
    49:14–16
Jeremiah 6:16; 17:7–8
Matthew 6:27–34; 10:29–31;
    11:28–30
Mark 4:18–19
Luke 10:41; 12:24–34
John 14:27; 16:33
Romans 8:35–39
Philippians 4:6–7
Colossians 3:15
2 Thessalonians 3:16
1 Timothy 6:6
1 Peter 2:6–7; 5:6–7

Blessings
Genesis 12:1–3
Numbers 6:24–26
Job 33:4
Psalm 16:5; 23:1–3; 63:5–6; 68:19;
    84:11; 115:12–15; 119:57–59;
    126:2
Isaiah 44:2–4
Ezekiel 34:26–27
Hosea 14:5–8
Luke 6:20–23, 27–28
John 1:16; 10:10
Acts 14:17
2 Corinthians 9:8–11
Ephesians 1:3
Hebrews 6:7–8
James 1:17
1 Peter 3:8–9

Comfort
Psalm 9:9; 18:2; 22:24; 23:4;
    27:14; 30:11; 37:23–24, 39;
    46:1–3; 55:22; 56:8, 13;
    71:20–21; 86:17; 119:49–50,
    52, 76; 121:1–5; 138:7
Isaiah 25:8; 26:3; 41:13; 43:1-2;
    49:13; 66:13
Lamentations 3:31–33
Nahum 1:7
Matthew 5:4; 10:29–31; 11:28;
    28:20
Luke 6:20–23

John 14:16, 26; 16:33
Romans 8:26–27
2 Corinthians 1:3–5; 2:7
Philippians 2:1–2
1 Thessalonians 4:16–18
2 Thessalonians 2:16–17
Revelation 21:4

Courage
Deuteronomy 31:6
Joshua 1:9
2 Kings 6:16–18
1 Chronicles 28:20
Psalm 18:28–31; 27:14; 31:24;
   37:3, 28; 91:1–6; 138:3
Proverbs 3:26; 14:26; 28:1
Isaiah 9:6; 40:29; 41:10; 43:1
Ezekiel 2:6
Luke 21:16–19
John 16:33
Acts 4:13; 23:11; 27:25
1 Corinthians 16:13
2 Corinthians 4:7–11
Ephesians 3:12; 6:10
Philippians 1:27–28; 4:12–13
2 Timothy 1:7
Hebrews 4:16; 10:19; 13:5–6
1 John 2:28; 3:21

Encouragement
Psalm 46:1–3; 118:14–15
Proverbs 12:25; 27:17
Isaiah 40:29; 41:10
Jeremiah 31:3
Zephaniah 3:17

Romans 8:31; 14:19; 15:4
2 Corinthians 1:6
Galatians 6:2
Ephesians 3:17–21; 5:18–20
1 Thessalonians 5:11
2 Thessalonians 2:15–17
2 Timothy 1:7
1 John 3:18; 5:4–5, 14–15

Eternal Life
Job 19:26–27
Psalm 16:10
Isaiah 26:19
Daniel 12:2
Matthew 8:11; 19:29
Luke 20:35–36
John 3:16; 5:24, 28–29; 6:27,
   39–40, 47, 54; 10:27–28;
   11:25–26; 12:25; 14:2–3; 17:3
Romans 2:6–7; 6:22–23; 8:11
1 Corinthians 2:9; 15:21, 42–44,
   51–54
2 Corinthians 5:1
Galatians 6:8
1 Thessalonians 4:16
1 Timothy 6:12
2 Timothy 1:10; 4:8
Titus 1:2; 3:7
James 1:12
1 Peter 1:3–5, 23; 5:4
1 John 2:17, 24–25; 4:9; 5:11–13, 20
Jude 21
Revelation 2:7, 26; 7:15–17; 21:4;
   22:3–5

Forgiveness

Numbers 14:18
Nehemiah 9:17
Daniel 9:9
Psalm 32:1–2; 51:1; 103:2–4, 10–12
Proverbs 17:9; 19:11; 20:22
Isaiah 44:22
Jeremiah 31:33–34
Ezekiel 33:14–16
Micah 7:18–19
Matthew 5:39–41, 44–45; 6:14–15;
    18:21–22, 32–35; 26:28
Mark 11:25–26
Luke 6:35–37; 7:47; 11:2–4;
    17:3–4; 23:34
Romans 12:20
2 Corinthians 2:5–8, 10–11
Ephesians 4:31–32
Colossians 2:13–14; 3:12–13
Hebrews 8:12; 10:15–18; 12:14–15
1 Peter 3:8–9
1 John 1:9

God Is in Control

1 Samuel 2:6–8
1 Chronicles 29:11–12
Psalm 33:4; 103:19; 121:7–8
Proverbs 16:9; 21:29
Isaiah 46:9–10; 55:10–11
Ezekiel 17:24
Daniel 4:35
Matthew 19:26
Romans 8:28

God's Love

Deuteronomy 4:31; 7:9, 12–13;
    10:15; 11:13–15
Psalm 5:12; 9:10; 17:7; 18:30;
    32:10; 37:4; 63:3; 86:15;
    91:14; 121:8; 136:1–2; 143:8;
    145:19–20; 146:8
Proverbs 8:17, 21; 15:9
Isaiah 54:10; 62:5
Jeremiah 31:3
Hosea 14:4
Jonah 4:2
Zephaniah 3:17
Matthew 28:20
Luke 12:6–7
John 3:16; 14:21; 15:9–11; 16:27;
    17:23, 26
Romans 5:5–8; 8:28, 38–39
1 Corinthians 2:9
Galatians 2:20
Ephesians 2:4–7; 3:17–19; 5:1–2
Philippians 4:19
2 Thessalonians 2:16–17
James 1:17–18
1 John 3:1; 4:9–10, 16, 19

Healing

Psalm 103:2–3; 107:19–20; 147:3
Isaiah 53:4–5; 57:18–21; 58:8;
    61:1–2; 63:9
Jeremiah 17:14; 30:17
Ezekiel 34:15–16
Malachi 4:2
Matthew 8:16–17; 9:35
James 5:13–15

Hope
Job 11:16–18
Psalm 31:24; 42:11; 62:5; 71:5;
    119:49, 81, 114, 166; 126:6;
    147:11
Proverbs 10:28; 13:12; 14:32
Isaiah 25:8–9
Jeremiah 17:7–8; 29:11
Lamentations 3:24–26
Acts 24:15
Romans 4:18; 5:1–5; 8:20, 22–25;
    12:12; 15:13
2 Corinthians 4:16–18
Galatians 5:5
Ephesians 1:18; 4:4
Philippians 1:18–20
Colossians 1:5, 27
1 Thessalonians 5:8
Titus 2:13
Hebrews 3:6; 6:11, 17–20; 11:1
1 Peter 1:3–4, 13, 21
1 John 3:2–3

Loneliness
Genesis 2:18; 28:15
Deuteronomy 4:7
2 Chronicles 16:9
Psalm 16:8–9; 25:16–18; 34:22;
    40:17; 68:6; 73:28; 94:14;
    125:1–2; 139:7–10; 143:3–6;
    145:18–19
Isaiah 43:4; 57:15; 58:9
Jeremiah 23:23–24
Lamentations 3:18–22
Matthew 28:20

John 1:14; 14:18
Romans 8:38–39
2 Corinthians 6:17–18
Colossians 2:10
1 Peter 3:12
1 John 4:15–16

Patience
Exodus 34:6
Psalm 25:3, 5; 27:14; 37:7–9; 40:1;
    103:8
Proverbs 14:29; 16:32
Ecclesiastes 7:8–9
Matthew 24:13
Romans 5:3–4; 12:12; 15:4
1 Corinthians 13:4
2 Corinthians 6:4–6
Galatians 6:9
Ephesians 4:2
Colossians 1:11; 3:12
1 Thessalonians 5:14
2 Thessalonians 3:5
1 Timothy 1:16
2 Timothy 2:24; 3:10–11
Hebrews 6:12, 15; 10:23, 36; 12:1
James 1:2–4; 5:7–8
1 Peter 2:19–20
2 Peter 3:9
Revelation 14:12

Peace
Numbers 6:24–26
Joshua 1:9
1 Kings 8:56
Psalm 4:8; 29:11; 34:14; 37:37;
    46:1–3; 85:8; 91:1–10; 119:165

Proverbs 16:7
Isaiah 9:6; 26:3; 32:17; 55:12;
    57:19
Matthew 5:9
Mark 5:34
Luke 7:50
John 14:27; 16:33
Romans 5:1; 8:5-6; 12:18; 14:17,
    19; 15:13
1 Corinthians 7:15; 14:33
2 Corinthians 13:11
Ephesians 2:13-18
Philippians 4:6-7
Colossians 3:15
1 Thessalonians 5:13
2 Thessalonians 3:16-17
Hebrews 12:14
James 3:18
1 Peter 3:10-11
1 John 4:4

Prayer
2 Chronicles 7:14
Job 22:27; 33:26
Psalm 4:1; 5:1-2; 6:9; 18:6; 28:2;
    32:6; 34:17; 40:1; 42:8; 54:2;
    55:17; 65:2; 91:15; 102:17;
    116:2; 145:18-19
Proverbs 15:8, 29
Isaiah 30:19; 58:9; 65:24
Jeremiah 29:11-13; 33:3
Lamentations 3:55-57
Zechariah 13:9
Matthew 6:6-13; 7:7-8, 11;
    18:19-20; 21:22

Mark 11:24
Luke 11:1-4, 9; 18:1-8
John 14:13-14; 15:7; 16:23-24
Acts 1:13-14
Romans 8:26-27; 12:12
Ephesians 1:15-16; 6:18
Philippians 4:6-7
Colossians 4:2
1 Thessalonians 5:16-18
1 Timothy 2:8
Hebrews 4:16
James 5:13-16
1 John 3:22; 5:14-15

Worry
Genesis 45:20
Deuteronomy 31:8
Psalm 6:3-4; 9:9-10; 32:7; 34:4;
    37:1-7; 46:1-3; 55:22; 91:15;
    94:19; 112:7
Proverbs 3:5-6; 12:25; 16:3;
    24:19-20
Isaiah 32:17
Jeremiah 17:7-8
Habakkuk 3:17-19
Matthew 6:25-34; 10:18-20
Luke 8:14-15; 10:41-42
John 14:1-3, 27
Romans 8:28
2 Corinthians 4:8-9
Philippians 4:6-7, 19
Hebrews 13:5-6
1 Peter 5:6-7
1 John 4:18